THE FIERY THRONE

The Prophets and
Old Testament Theology

WALTHER ZIMMERLI

Edited by K. C. Hanson

FORTRESS PRESS
MINNEAPOLIS

THE FIERY THRONE
Fortress Classics in Biblical Studies

Copyright © 2003 Augsburg Fortress. All rights reserved. Except for brief quotations in critical articles or reviews, no part of this book may be reproduced in any manner without prior written permission from the publisher. Write: Permissions, Augsburg Fortress, Box 1209, Minneapolis, MN 55440

Scripture is from the Revised Standard Version of the Bible, copyright © 1946, 1952, 1971 by the Division of Christian Education of the National Council of the Churches of Christ in the USA. Used by permission.

Cover image: *The Prophet Ezekiel* by Michelangelo (1475-1564). Detail of the Sistine Chapel ceiling, Vatican Palace. © Scala / Art Resource, N.Y. Used with permission.

Author photo: Reprinted from *Deutsche Alttestamentler in drei Jahrhunderten: mit 18 Abbildungen* by Rudolf Smend (Göttingen: Vandenhoeck & Ruprecht, 1989).

ISBN 0-8006-3620-1

The paper used in this publication meets the minimum requirements of American National Standard for Information Sciences — Permanence of Paper for Printed Library Materials, ANSI Z329.48-1984.

Manufactured in the U.S.A.

08   07   06   05   04   03   1   2   3   4   5   6   7   8   9   20

Contents

Abbreviations

DDD²	*Dictionary of Deities and Demons in the Bible,* 2d ed., edited by Karel van der Toorn et al., 1999
EB	Echter Bibel
EBib	*Études bibliques*
EvTh	*Evangelische Theologie*
FCBS	Fortress Classics in Biblical Studies
FOTL	Forms of the Old Testament Literature
FRLANT	Forschungen zur Religion und Literatur des Alten und Neuen Testaments
GBS	Guides to Biblical Scholarship
HAT	Handkommentar zum Alten Testament
HBT	*Horizons in Biblical Theology*
HSS	Harvard Semitic Studies
HTIBS	Historic Texts and Interpreters in Biblical Scholarship
IBC	Interpretation: A Biblical Commentary
ICC	International Critical Commentary
IDBS	*Interpreter's Dictionary of the Bible, Supplementary Volume,* edited by Keith Crim, 1976
Int	*Interpretation*
IRT	Issues in Religion and Theology
JBL	*Journal of Biblical Literature*
JSOT	*Journal for the Study of the Old Testament*
JSOTSup	JSOT Supplement Series
JSS	*Journal of Semitic Studies*
JTC	*Journal for Theology and the Church*
KAT	Kommentar zum Alten Testament
KBL	Ludwig Koehler and Walter Baumgartner, *Lexicon in Veteris Testamenti Libros*
KeH	Kurzgefasstes exegetisches Handbuch zum Alten Testament
KHAT	Kurzer Hand-Commentar zum Alten Testament
LAI	Library of Ancient Israel
LXX	Septuagint
MT	Masoretic text
NICOT	New International Commentary on the Old Testament
NKZ	*Neue kirchliche Zeitschrift*
OBT	Overtures to Biblical Theology
OTL	Old Testament Library
OTM	Oxford Theological Monographs
OtSt	Oudtestamentische Studiën
RHPR	*Revue d'histoire et de philosophie religieuses*

SAT	Die Schriften des Alten Testaments
SBL	Society of Biblical Literature
SBLDS	Society of Biblical Literature Dissertation Series
SBLSBS	SBL Sources for Biblical Studies
SBLSS	SBL Semeia Studies
SBLSymSer	SBL Symposium Series
SBT	Studies in Biblical Theology
SBTS	Sources for Biblical and Theological Study
SEÅ	*Svensk exegetisk årsbok*
SHBC	Smith and Helwys Bible Commentary
SHCANE	Studies in the History and Culture of the Ancient Near East
SNVAO	Skrifter utgitt av det Norske Videnskaps-Akademi i Oslo
STU	*Schweizerische Theologische Umschau*
SWBA	Social World of Biblical Antiquity
THE	Theologische Existenz Heute
ThBü	Theologische Bücherei
ThSt	Theologische Studien
TLZ	*Theologische Literaturzeitung*
TRE	*Theologische Realenzyklopädie,* edited by Gerhard Krause and Gerhard Müller, 1977–
TUMSR	Trinity University Monograph Series in Religion
TZ	*Theologische Zeitschrift*
UTB	Uni-Taschenbücher
VGTB	Van Gorcum's Theologische Bibliothek
VT	*Vetus Testamentum*
VTSup	VT Supplements
WBC	Word Biblical Commentary
WMANT	Wissenschaftliche Monographien zum Alten und Neuen Testament
WZMLU	*Wissenschaftliche Zeitschrift der Martin-Luther-Universität*
YOSR	Yale Oriental Series, Researches
ZAW	*Zeitschrift für die alttestamentliche Wissenschaft*
ZDPV	*Zeitschrift für die deutschen Palästina-Vereins*
ZTK	*Zeitschrift für Theologie und Kirche*

Editor's Foreword

COMBINING A LIFE OF SERVICE, ministry, teaching, administration, and research, the career of Walther Zimmerli was one of distinction at every turn. A renowned expert on the prophetic literature in the Hebrew Bible, he was also the leader of the Göttingen project on the Septuagint, a pastor, and an advisor of theological students.

Born in Schiers, Switzerland, in the canton of Graubünden, on 20 January 1907, he was the eighth of eleven children. His father, Jacob, was the director of the Evangelische Lehranstalt (Protestant Educational Institute), but died in 1918 when Walther was only eleven. His mother, Lily, was a major influence on him.

Zimmerli studied with some of the brightest lights in Old Testament research prior to World War II: in Zurich, Jakob Hausheer (linguist and translator of the Zurich Bibel); in Berlin, Ernst Sellin (exegete and archaeologist); in Göttingen, Mark Lidzbarski (Semitist), Albrecht Götze (Syriac), and Alfred Rahlfs (the renowned scholar of the Septuagint and Aramaic). He wrote his dissertation at Göttingen on the history and tradition of Beersheba in the Old Testament under Johannes Hempel (text critic and exegete).

As his practicum for his theological studies, he worked as an attendant at a care facility for epileptics in Zurich (1929–30). He then became an assistant for Old Testament at the University of Göttingen (1930–33), completing his doctorate in 1932. Returning to Switzerland, he held two pastorates—Aarburg (1933–35) and Zurich (1935–50)—while pursuing his teaching career. In 1935, he began teaching Old Testament, history of religion, and Oriental languages at the University of Zurich as *extraordinarius*, and in 1938 as *orindarius*, succeeding his former teacher, Hausheer. In 1940 he became the "house father" of the Reformed Theological Student House in Zurich as well, which he and his wife began. His also served as a chaplain in the Swiss army, beginning in 1940.

After the war, Zimmerli was a guest professor at the University of Berlin as well as the Kirchlichen Hochschule in East Berlin, in the summer semesters of 1947–50. Finally in 1950 he began his tenure as professor at the University of Göttingen, succeeding Gerhard von Rad. He was also invited to be a guest professor at Yale Divinity School in the spring of 1963. And that same year he was invited to deliver the James Sprunt Lectures at Union Theological Seminary in Richmond, Virginia, later published as *The Law and the Prophets* (1965). In 1975 he was given emeritus status at Göttingen.

In addition to his teaching, Zimmerli held numerous administrative posts at the University of Göttingen: twice he was Dekan of the faculty (1952–53 and 1960–61), as well as Prorektor (1963–64), Rektor (1964–66), and Conrektor (1966–67); and he was chair of the Conference of Rektors in Lower Saxony (1966–67). He was also Ephorus of the Göttingen Theological Seminary (1968–83). He became a member of the Göttingen Academy of Sciences in 1962, and then served as its president three times (1970–71, 1972–74, and 1976–78). He was the founding chair of the Conference of West German Academic Institutions (1973–74).

Zimmerli was a contemporary and colleague of other leading Old Testament scholars in Germany: Martin Noth, Gerhard von Rad, Claus Westermann, and Hans Walter Wolff. These were also his leading collaborators in the Biblischer Kommentar project, for which he wrote his famous Ezekiel commentary (later translated for the Hermeneia series). He was also close to colleagues in the U.S., such as John Bright and James Luther Mays, and in the United Kingdom, such as G. W. Anderson and Ronald E. Clements.

Zimmerli's leadership and expertise was recognized by his colleagues in a variety of ways. He succeeded Martin Noth as the German-language editor of *Vetus Testamentum* (1960–74), and he was elected president of the International Organization for the Study of the Old Testament in 1974. He received four honorary doctorates: from the universities of Edinburgh, Strasbourg, Zurich, and Göttingen. And he was named an honorary member of both the Society of Biblical Literature (U.S.) and the Society of Old Testament Studies (Great Britain). In 1972, he was awarded the prestigious Burkitt Medal for Biblical Studies by the British Academy, an award his Göttingen colleague, Joachim Jeremias, also received.

American colleagues dedicated a volume to his honor (*Festschrift*) in celebration of his seventieth birthday, *Canon and Theology: Essays in Old Testament Religion and Theology* (1977). His European colleagues celebrated that event with another Festschrift: *Beiträge zur alttestamentlichen Theologie* (1977).

Like other contributors to the Biblischer Kommentar series, Zimmerli was an expert in form criticism and tradition history. Nowhere is this more apparent than in his groundbreaking, two-volume commentary on Ezekiel (1969; ET 1979–83). In this masterwork, he demonstrated how Ezekiel's prophecies continued to be interpreted by others within the book. Brevard S. Childs says of this commentary, "It is certainly fair to say that he has succeeded in inaugurating a new phase in the study of the book by his numerous articles and massive commentary. . . . It is difficult to believe that critical scholarship will ever return to a pre-Zimmerli stage in evaluating the book" (*Introduction to the Old Testament as Scripture* [Philadelphia: Fortress Press, 1979] 359–60).

Along with his colleagues, he also shared a deep interest in the theological interpretation of the biblical text. While it permeates all his works, this theological interest came to fruition in his *Old Testament Theology in Outline* (2d German ed. 1975; ET 1978). There he makes it explicit that Yahweh's self-revelation is the foundation or beginning point for Old Testament theology. But for Zimmerli, passages such as Exod 20:2-3 and Deut 5:6-7 express more than Yahweh's self-revelation, they connect it to Yahweh's relationship to Israel. Particularly significant for Zimmerli's approach are his stress on Yahweh's revelation in history, the sense of hope in the Old Testament, the openness of the Old Testament to the future, and his call for ongoing dialogue between the synagogue and the church.

But as the final essay in this collection demonstrates, Zimmerli was also interested in "biblical theology." He sought to foster dialogue with New Testament scholars and systematic theologians on the role the Old Testament plays in Christian faith. The reading of the Old Testament in Christian liturgy must be acknowledged, understood, and appreciated rather than passed over. This, he argues, is important because both testaments witness to the same Lord. One should also note the importance of his work on Jürgen Moltmann's *Theology of Hope* (esp. 101–16).

After a long and fruitful life and career, Zimmerli died at the age of 76 in Oberdiessbach, in the canton of Bern, Switzerland, on 12 April 1983.

I have edited Zimmerli's essays in minor ways. Most importantly, I have added endnotes (marked by square brackets) as well as bibliographies in order to bring the reader up-to-date in the discussions. In many of Zimmerli's essays, he used number divisions only, so I have supplied some headings. I have also made occasional modifications in the RSV quotations by changing RSV's "Lord" to "Yahweh" and changing words such as "thou" to "you."

I would like to express my gratitude to the various translators who prepared these essays for their initial publications.

—K. C. Hanson

Acknowledgments

Chapter 1 was first published in *Tradition and Theology in the Old Testament,* edited by Douglas A. Knight (Philadelphia: Fortress Press, 1977) 69–100, and translated by Douglas A. Knight. A later German edition was published as "Die kritische Infragstellung der Tradition durch die Prophetie," in *Zu Tradition und Theologie im Alten Testament,* edited by Odil Hannes Steck, BTS 2 (Neukirchen-Vluyn: Neukirchener, 1978) 57–86.

Chapter 2 first appeared in English in *The Place Is Too Small for Us: The Israelite Prophets in Recent Scholarship,* edited by Robert P. Gordon, SBTS 5 (Winona Lake, Ind.: Eisenbrauns, 1995) 419–42, translated by Andreas Köstenberger. The German edition appeared as "Vom Prophetenwort zum Prophetenbuch," *TLZ* 104 (1979) 481–96.

Chapter 3 was first published as "The 'Land' in the Pre-Exilic and Early Post-Exilic Prophets," in *Understanding the Word: Essays in Honour of Bernhard W. Anderson,* edited by James T. Butler et al., JSOTSup 37 (Sheffield: JSOT Press, 1985) 247–62.

Chapter 4 was first published in *Israel's Prophetic Tradition: Essays in Honour of Peter R. Ackroyd,* edited by Richard Coggins et al. (Cambridge: Cambridge Univ. Press, 1982) 95–118.

Chapter 5 first appeared in English in *Interpretation* 23 (1969) 131–57, translated by Mrs. Lewis Wilkins and James D. Martin. The German edition appeared later in a collection of Zimmerli's articles as "Die Botschaft des Propheten Ezechiel," in *Studien zur alttestamentlichen Theologie und Prophetie: Gesammelte Aufsätze II,* ThBü 51 (Munich: Kaiser, 1974) 104–34.

Chapter 6 first appeared in English in *Journal for Theology and the Church* 4 (1967) 1–13, translated by James F. Ross. It was first published as "Das Gotteswort des Ezechiel," *ZTK* 48 (1951) 249–62, and was Zimmerli's inaugural lecture at the University of Göttingen on June 16, 1951. It is reprinted in Zimmerli, *Gottes Offenbarung: Gesammelte Aufsätze zum Alten Testament,* ThBü 19 (Munich: Kaiser, 1963) 133–47.

Chapter 7 was first published as "The Special Form- and Traditio-Historical Character of Ezekiel's Prophecy," *VT* 15 (1965) 515–27. Zimmerli originally read this as a paper at the meeting of the Society for Old Testament Study in Bangor, Wales, on 22 July 1964.

Chapter 8 was first published in *Horizons in Biblical Theology* 4.1 (1982) 95–130, translated by Ulrich Mauser. A later, slightly expanded German edition appeared as "Biblische Theologie," *BTZ* 1 (1984) 5–26.

The translators for chapters 3, 4, and 7 are not identified.

1

Prophetic Proclamation
and Reinterpretation

THE PROPHETIC "NO" TO ISRAEL'S TRADITIONS

In response to various attempts to anchor Amos's message within certain traditional institutional spheres,[1] Rudolf Smend selected as the title for an article "Amos's No."[2] With this keyword "No!" he has undoubtedly struck a characteristic note, not only of Amos, but also of the other great literary prophets of the pre-exilic period. Indeed, this "No" is found explicitly in the negative expressions by which Hosea names his children: "Not-my-people" (*lo' 'ammi*) for his youngest child (Hos 1:6) and "Not-pitied" (*lo' ruḥamah*) for his second child (Hos 1:9). Isaiah's utterances about "this people" (*ha'am hazzeh*; Isa 6:9-10; 8:11; and elsewhere), even though the explicit negative particle is lacking, approximate the Hoseanic *lo' 'ammi*.

This "No" negates ancient elements of tradition. It is Israel's heritage from antiquity to be the people of Yahweh. This tradition also contains confidence in Yahweh's love and mercy—precisely that which is countered in the name given Hosea's second child. The same "No" to an ancient religious tradition can be recognized in Mic 3:12 where the coming devastation of Zion and of the mountain of the temple is proclaimed,[3] as also in Ezekiel 15 where the picture of Israel as the noble vine, fetched from Egypt by Yahweh, is destroyed from within by treating it with insult as a useless vine branch. And how effectively they shatter the tradition of the loving relationship between Yahweh and his people when Hosea, after him Jeremiah, and most gruesome of all, Ezekiel, speak of Israel or Jerusalem with the picture of a whoring, faithless wife (or, in Ezekiel 23 concerning the two kingdoms, two such women at the outset in Egypt). In all of this, it is time-honored tradition, that which bore Israel's identity as the people of Yahweh, that is destroyed. One could close the cover on the pre-exilic prophets with the verdict: "Old Traditions—Non-Applicable!"

This impassioned and unmistakable "No," however, does not sufficiently describe all prophetic speech, not even just that of the great pre-exilic prophets—and in fact not even regarding only the question of their stance toward older Israelite traditions. Their "No" is the reverse side of an equally impassioned "Yes." We would be misunderstanding the prophets if we regarded them as revolutionary nihilists who rejected the entire heritage of pious Israel. Their polemic occurs, in the final analysis, on the basis of what they held in common with Israel's confessions and cultic traditions—although they could issue only a vehement "No" to what qualified as worship in their days.

We can begin with a very elementary matter that is obviously presupposed in all of their utterances and that links their speech fully with that of the people. When all of these prophets refer to God, they use the same name that is invoked in Israelite worship and that was handed down from generation to generation—the name Yahweh. It is not merely common religious language that could be immediately generalized worldwide. Rather, they are speaking about the One who is known by this proper name, the personal One who is designated unmistakably in this name, the One who under this name entered into Israel's history.

We would be in error to think that this is really only a self-evident matter and that no special significance is to be given this traditional element of the "Name" since it is only a casual cipher without specific content. To be sure, it is correct that this name is not used as a signifier, something that decodes the secret of God, with which the prophets also dealt.[4] It is not a predicative statement that reduces God to a concept and subjects him to certain categories of understanding. The name remains a proper name, with all the irrationality of a proper name that in the first instance designates the unmistakable identity of a person.

There is a specific rhetorical form that Ezekiel uses that shows precisely how this name is bound to an inner fullness, not to a void or to an easily interchangeable substance. This form of speech, which I have termed a "proof-saying" (*Erweiswort*),[5] was not coined by Ezekiel but was appropriated from older, preclassical prophets. We find it exclusively in connection with prophetic proclamation of impending divine activity. For example, a rhetorical unit proclaiming the coming "end" concludes in Ezek 7:4 with the following statement: "My eye will not spare you, nor will I have mercy; but I will cause your ways to come upon you, . . . and you will know that I am Yahweh." Thus it is Yahweh's imminent activity itself that is the locus and documentation for this very Yahweh. There is no predication in use here—not Yahweh as the powerful one, or as the exalted one, or as the wrathful one, who seeks to prove himself and to be known to Israel in his proof. Rather, all is expressed through the straightforward use of the proper name, the one recognizable in this activity is the one called by this name; through this very activity he will be identified and proven to be Yahweh.[6] "You will know that I am Yahweh."

The above discussion brings something else into focus as well. The name Yahweh has been characterized chiefly as a traditional element of the Israelite language of worship. Tradition is, by definition, oriented toward the past. The hand and the mouth carry on that which has been received, delivered over. In this element of prophetic speech, however, the transmitted material is related to that which is yet to come. In his coming activity Yahweh demonstrates who he is—namely, that he is Yahweh. The name Yahweh is thus completely opened up to the future.

In saying this, moreover, we have touched upon the essence of prophetic speech. In its primary and true pathos it is announcement of the imminent— and thus not chiefly retrospection, nor primarily penitential sermon.[7] This can be seen in Amos's report about his call. Yahweh took him away from his flock and commissioned him to preach against Israel and to announce the future judgment, for which the high priest in Bethel denounced him before the king: "By the sword Jeroboam will die, and Israel will be led into exile, away from his land" (Amos 7:11, 15). In like manner, Hosea is sent to proclaim, through the names of his children, that Yahweh will soon punish the blood-guilt in Jezreel, Jehu's murdering when he seized power (Hos 1:4-5), and that the "merciless" and the "not-my-people" will be manifest in history. Isaiah is dispatched with a message that will make the people obdurate and thus will effect the devastation of the land (Isa 6:8-11). Jeremiah sees in the second vision connected with his call (Jer 1:13-19) how disaster will spill over the land from the North like boiling water out of a pot held over fire. Thus his early message deals with the announcement of an unnamed foe from the North. In a strikingly formal speech of commission, Yahweh charges Ezekiel simply to proclaim: "Thus says the Lord Yahweh" (Ezek 2:4; 3:11)—regardless of whether the people will listen to it or ignore it. He is then ordered, however, to eat the scroll written on front and back with lamentations, groans, and woes (2:9-10), and in this we recognize the coming disaster that Ezekiel was to utter against Jerusalem.

The great pre-exilic prophets proclaim Yahweh as the One who comes— the same One who since antiquity has been invoked with this name. This "coming" of which they must speak, however, is the unexpected, that which runs counter to all familiar tradition. In Mic 3:11 we can observe how Micah's proclamation collides with what tradition said of Yahweh and what was cherished so by prophets opposing the classical pre-exilic prophets: "Its [Jerusalem's] prophets divine on payment [literally: for money]; they lean on Yahweh by saying: 'Is not Yahweh in our midst? No evil will come upon us.'"

Tradition says that Yahweh lives in the midst of the people. This is interpreted as Israel's great security against all danger. In contrast to this, Micah discerns the freedom of Yahweh in his coming. Yahweh cannot be domesticated by knowledge oriented toward the past, nor can he be attached, like some predictable element, to a pious view of existence. Rather, he shatters the fixed conception that Israel developed in her tradition, and in this, his new and terrifying coming, he proves himself to be Yahweh, the One invoked by the people as Yahweh.

Before we proceed with our examination of the extent to which the great pre-exilic prophets were influenced by traditional material, by memory of the past as it was transmitted in Israel's worship, we must be entirely clear about this central element of the prophetic proclamation. Whenever this prophecy does in fact take up traditional materials, it does not regard these as simple elements of tradition, as *traditum* in the neutral sense of material that can be conveyed from one person to another—like a plot of inherited land or other property that is handed down and then used by the new inheritor. Whatever the prophets appropriated from traditional language about the God of Israel, whatever they reiterated of this or fit into their own utterances—it is attached to the name of Yahweh. This latter, however, cannot in its true content be considered neutrally as *traditum*. It is the suggestive appellation of the One who, for all that is said about him, remains a personal subject and decides himself, in his freedom, what he will do when he comes. And as certainly as he once came to Israel, as tradition tells of him in Israel's worship and apart from this, he is never at the disposal of humans like earthly property.

To be sure, there are unmistakable future-oriented elements already present in the tradition at the disposal of the prophets. The way the great pre-exilic prophets appropriate these elements, however, shows how the Lord, who approaches his people freely and who is known by the name of Yahweh, weighs upon the prophets to make these elements into vehicles of new proclamation about this same Lord.

This can be elucidated with the help of a traditional element that from the outset corresponds structurally to prophetic discourse about the One who is approaching, yet which experiences a specific, innovative application at the hands of the prophets. I have in mind the discourse about "the Day of Yahweh." Amos 5:18-20, the earliest passage where we find this traditional element, verifies clearly that among the people to whom Amos was sent there was talk about the Day of Yahweh. We have had little success in finding a fully satisfactory answer to the question of the ultimate origin of this element. Gressmann thought he could discern in its background a mythical worldview that conceived of an alternation between evil and good time.[8] Mowinckel, on the other hand, pointed to the Israelite cult as the place of origin.[9] According to him, in the Israelite tradition of worship the great victory of Yahweh over the opposing forces was celebrated in every New Year festival. Thus the expectation of an approaching Day of Yahweh as a day of light and salvation would be the future projection of Yahweh's victory as recited and ritually enacted in the cultic practice of Israel. In contrast to this view, Gerhard von Rad thought that he could derive this image from the tradition of the holy war.[10] Thus this expectation of the day of salvation would be, in concentrated form, the future projection of old tradition stemming from the days of Yahweh's deliverance in battle.

However these lines are to be drawn, we are in any event obliged to see in the expectation of a Day of Yahweh, such as in the people's anticipation in Amos 5:18-20, the future projection of previously experienced salvation, which Israel remembered in its tradition.

Amos detaches the expression "the Day of Yahweh" from its association with the transmitted salvation tradition, and he preaches Yahweh as the One who in his freedom draws near to judge. The Day of Yahweh is not light but darkness. It is "as if a man runs from a lion, and a bear meets him. And he enters the house and rests his hand against the wall, and snake bites him."

All further utterances by other prophets about the Day of Yahweh have a similar meaning, except that we no longer find, as in the Amos text, a contrary expectation current among the people (Isa 2:12-22; Zephaniah 1–2; Ezekiel 7; 30:1-26; Joel; Malachi 3). In each case the reference to the Day of Yahweh is accentuated anew. What is appropriated is the traditional element about a day that is characterized entirely by Yahweh's presence. But the way in which Yahweh approaches breaks all traditional expectations; it is the nearness of the One who is free, the One who shows himself as the Lord, the One who cannot be restricted by past-oriented discourse.

It has just been stated that, unlike Amos, later prophets were not provoked to speak about the Day of Yahweh directly by the reassured expectation of the people. Rather, this concept was transmitted from one prophet to another, and this fact brings into view a problem of "tradition history" that has been scrutinized too little in the past. To the degree that, as their utterances about the Day of Yahweh show, the prophets oppose secure, traditional expectations of salvation and that they do this by announcing the sovereign freedom of Yahweh to destroy such expectations—to this degree we can see that there is also an inner-prophetic "process of tradition." Isaiah in his early preaching takes up elements from Amos's proclamation.[11] The connections between Hosea and Jeremiah have been isolated by K. Gross.[12] John Wolf Miller has worked on the question of the relationship between Jeremiah and Ezekiel,[13] and Dieter Baltzer has exposed ties from Ezekiel to Deutero-Isaiah, whereby the latter was not without influences from Proto-Isaiah as well.[14]

THE PROPHETS' CONCRETE USE AND TRANSFORMATION
OF HISTORICAL TRADITIONS

We need now to turn our attention to the question of how pre-exilic and later also exilic literary prophets treat the tradition of Israel as the people of Yahweh.

In his study on "The Form-Critical Problem of the Hexateuch," Gerhard von Rad found that the elements relevant for Israel's faith, the confessional underpinnings for their special relationship to Yahweh, were gathered together in the "short historical credo" that spoke of the Exodus, the wilderness wanderings, and the gift of the land.[15] The patriarchal history and the primeval history came later, independently of each other, as frontal extensions to the rest, while the narrative of the Sinai events, traditio-historically different in origin, is an insertion into this complex. Martin Noth distanced himself theologically from this by speaking of "themes" that are treated in Pentateuchal tradition.[16] He investigated five themes in the following order:

1. Guidance out of Egypt
2. Guidance into the Arable Land of Palestine
3. Promise to the Patriarchs
4. Guidance in the Wilderness
5. Revelation at Sinai

At this point we will need to ask how these elements, so important for the tradition of Israel, are appropriated, modified, or simply ignored in prophetic proclamation.

Amos

Amos makes no recognizable reference to the patriarchal tradition or to the Sinai tradition. The guidance out of Egypt is appraised positively in 2:10 and 3:1, although the authenticity of both passages is contested. In 9:7, however, a saying that surely stems from Amos, this same tradition is depreciated and set on a par with guidance of the Philistines out of Caphtor (Crete?) and the Arameans out of Kir. It is impossible to miss the polemic here against a false security derived from Israel's relation to Yahweh; it is a radical "No" to Israel's retreat into revered tradition. But Amos also knows and acknowledges the special connection between Yahweh and Israel (although he draws quite unexpected conclusions from it); this can be seen in the surely genuine utterance in 3:2: "You only have I known of all the families of the earth; therefore I will punish you for all your iniquities."[17] Whenever their appeal to the guidance out of Egypt gives this sinful people cause to relax, not only will this misguided rhetoric about their history with Yahweh be struck from them, but also in light of Yahweh's special nearness to Israel they will face exactly the opposite consequence of this intimacy. It is dangerous to come near to Yahweh, who even in his intimacy with Israel remains the free Lord who is resolved to bring its sins to judgment.

Amos mentions in a special manner the tradition of the wilderness period and the conquest. In both cases he turns them in accusation against the people. In 5:25 the time of Israel's wandering in the wilderness appears in polemic against the present: that earlier period was free of the cultivated sacrificial system, replete with sacrifices and gift offerings, of the present day.[18] The remembrance of the time of conquest in 2:9 confronts Israel in a different manner. Here the prophet has in mind the tradition, found also in the story of the spies (Numbers 13–14), about the people of great stature who once occupied the land but then were destroyed by Yahweh. For the prophet, this tradition becomes the occasion to make manifest the ingratitude of the people who repay Yahweh's great deed with disobedience.

really? [handwritten margin note]

Hosea

Much better versed in Israel's ancient tradition and citing it copiously, Hosea also makes no explicit reference to the Sinai tradition. In its stead, however, the patriarchal tradition appears here for the first time. Moses, the unnamed "prophet" in Hos 12:13 [MT 12:14] through whom Yahweh effected the Exodus from Egypt, is contrasted with the patriarch Jacob in 12:3, 12 [12:4, 13] who possessed the same traits of untruthfulness and dishonesty that later on characterized Israel. While still in the womb he cheated his brother, and later he fought with God. It is striking to note this sharp antithesis between, on the one hand, the valuation of Moses and the Exodus, which also emerges distinctly elsewhere in Hosea,[19] and, on the other hand, the assessment of the figure of Jacob, who despite all his questionable aspects is nonetheless one of the bearers of promise in Genesis. According to the prophet, the patriarch represents the present people in their sinfulness. Thus this time-honored tradition becomes a subject of polemics.

In comparison, Moses and Israel's trek through the wilderness are bright memories for Hosea (12:13 [14]; 13:5). On closer analysis, though, we can see that this clear picture is painted not in order to provide in Hosea's day a firm foundation, here in its cultically guarded tradition, on which Israel could recline undisturbed. Rather, as in Amos 5:25 and Jer 7:22 the prophet introduces the wilderness recollection as a picture contrasting with his present age. Unlike Amos, Hosea does not have in mind solely the previous lack of contact with contemporary sacrificial practices. With more historico-theological insight, he contrasts, on the one hand, the wilderness period as a time of poverty with, on the other, the period beginning with the entrance into the land when the people became wealthy, opulent, and forgetful of God. While in the creedal formulation the remembrance of the divine guidance in the wilderness and the divine gift of land merge together in a positive emphasis, Hosea puts the two periods, wilderness wandering and settlement of the land, in radical contrast with each other. It is obvious how existing tradition does not retain and develop its own momentum here, but is rather fashioned anew by the prophetic preacher and thus becomes material, a plastic structure, for the prophet's specific proclamation about Yahweh's imminent assault against Israel. Would Hosea have known nothing of this in Hosea's view of history?[20] We can detect nothing of this in Hosea's view of history. With his preaching the prophet intended for the people who had sinned with the powers (the Baals) in the land to be confronted with the full impact of Yahweh's coming to set things right. This led him to use the keyword "wilderness" (= area away from the land of Baals) as an extremely colorful contrast to the keyword "land" (= territory of the Baals).[21] We will see in Ezekiel that also the elements "Exodus from Egypt" and "guidance through the wilderness" experience a new shift in character in the context of a yet more sharply radicalized accusation of sin.

Another development occurs in Hosea that has great significance for later prophecy. As we already mentioned, this prophet proclaims Yahweh not, in the first instance, as the One who encountered Israel in antiquity, but as the One who is prepared to come anew. Consistent with this, Hosea takes the traditional elements that appeared questionable in retrospect and thrusts them into his announcements of the future. Thus we find that references to Egypt, to the guidance in the wilderness, and to the conquest receive surprisingly new use in the prophet's future-oriented utterances. While Yahweh once called his son out of Egypt,[22] now the pronouncement of imminent judgment declares: "Now he [Yahweh] remembers their iniquity and punishes their sins; they will return to Egypt" (Hos 8:13). In 9:3 it is connected with the simultaneous threat of exile in Assyria: "They will not remain in Yahweh's land; but Ephraim will return to Egypt, and in Asshur they will eat unclean food" (compare Amos 7:17). The same double threat is also to be found in the original text of 9:6: "For behold, they will go to Asshur; Egypt will gather them, Memphis will bury them" (also Hos 11:5 LXX). Both can also be linked together in an utterance that looks beyond the judgment to a future pardon: "Like a bird they will come trembling from Egypt, and like a dove from the land of Assyria; and I will return them to their houses, says Yahweh" (11:11).[23] Here the language of the period, with the antipodal powers being Assyria and Egypt, is connected with the singular idea, seen clearly in 8:13, about Israel's "return" to Egypt—in a sense, the removal of the history of salvation (*Heilsgeschichte*) back to its beginning, from which point a new start can then occur.

We find a more obvious allusion to a traditional element of salvation history in the passage where the approaching judgment is pictured as the fetching of Israel back into the wilderness: "But I, Yahweh, your God from the land of Egypt—again I will make you dwell in tents, like in the days of the [initial] encounter (12:9 [MT v. 10])."[24] Yet here in Hosea the wilderness period is also esteemed as the time of Yahweh's special closeness and pristine love to his people, and as such it is inserted into an announcement about the future. For in 2:14-15 [MT vv. 16-17] the threat of being fetched back into the wilderness joins with a statement about a new effort by Yahweh to woo Israel, to "speak to her heart." And then this is followed by a new gift of land, the renewed bestowal of vineyards from the desert. Here it is not only old tradition as the heritage from the past that is "interpreted," but the transmitted remembrance is also turned antitypically into promise that is to be validated when Israel truly returns to her God.

Isaiah

In Isaiah we can also observe the same transformation of transmitted proclamation into announcements about the future. Recent scholarly effort has determined clearly that Isaiah moves within a different sphere of tradition than does Hosea. To be sure, Isaiah is concerned with no other Lord than the *one* Yahweh. Called the "Holy One of Israel," Yahweh is considered to be associated in a special way with Israel, which at the time of the prophet's early preaching existed politically as "both houses of Israel" (8:14). But Isaiah is a Jerusalemite. As such he is not so preoccupied with Yahweh's activity in the exodus from Egypt, wilderness wandering and conquest, as much as with Yahweh's dwelling in Jerusalem.[25] It was here, during his call, that he had a direct experience of the presence of Yahweh, the Holy One. Thus it is no accident that the messianic expectation of a savior-king from the house of David breaks forth in the prophecy of this resident of the City of David, for this promise made to the house of David belongs to his background of tradition.

Yet Isaiah preaches the Coming Lord as well. The category of the Holy One, who alone is exalted and who humbles everything on earth that becomes haughty, is central for him, and for this reason his announcement of the coming Day of Yahweh issues also into the image of a tumult that devastates everything that is lofty in the natural and human world (Isa 2:11-22). From his own call he is familiar with the burning power of the Holy One wherever he encounters impurity. Thus for Isaiah the account of the judgment against Jerusalem, the city that became a harlot,[26] does not take the form of a story about a return to Egypt or to the wilderness or about a new conquest. Rather, it is a report about a consuming fire that will smelt the base metal, purge the impurities, and thereby create the future for a city that will again deserve the name "faithful city" (1:21-26).

Among the traditions in Jerusalem associated with the Holy One of Israel, in whose presence Israel had believed since the time of David and Solomon, was apparently also one about the kingdoms that assaulted the mountain of God and were dashed to pieces on it.[27] The people of Jerusalem spoke perhaps in mythical language about this guarantee of security at the place where God resides. Psalms 46, 48, and 76 give evidence that this security of the place was praised in light of past assaults, and that it was confidently expected for the future as well. One is inclined to connect this with the security that Jeremiah, a century after Isaiah, found so objectionable in the people who came to the temple: not only did they emphasize it liturgically in triplicate form—"This is the temple of Yahweh, the temple of Yahweh, the temple of Yahweh" (Jer 7:4)—but they also drew from this a comforting conclusion— "We are safe" (7:10).

Just like Micah (Mic 3:12) in the time of Isaiah, Jeremiah responded to this comfortable security by proclaiming a catastrophe that would bring the same fate of the temple in Shiloh to the Jerusalem temple as well. Both Micah and Hosea stem from a background of tradition different from that of Isaiah. It is instructive, therefore, for us to see how this Jerusalemite Isaiah in his prophetic message transforms the traditions that come down to him. This is most obvious in the Davidic promissory tradition as well as in the Zion tradition.

Concerning the promise to the Davidic house, we might first conclude from the account in Isa 7:1-9 that Isaiah permits this promise to remain valid and completely unbroken into the present. In his earlier preaching he had proclaimed that judgment would soon come upon Jerusalem—the consequence of the burning wrath of the Holy One of Israel against all arrogance and all unrighteousness in this city. Then in the so-called Syro-Ephraimite War in the year 733 B.C.E., two kings from the North, Rezin the king of Aram-Damascus and Pekah the king of Northern Israel, went to battle against Jerusalem for the sole military purpose of setting a man on the Jerusalem throne who would have leanings in favor of their anti-Assyrian coalition efforts. Because of his father's Aramean name Tabeel, it seems likely that the new king was to be an Aramean. In this situation with cold fear gripping Jerusalem, Isaiah is charged to approach King Ahaz and to announce to him in the indicative mood: "That will not happen, nor will it come to pass" (7:7). It is striking that the "house of David" is expressly mentioned several times in the account in 7:1-9. So Würthwein is surely correct in assuming that behind Isaiah's utterance and assurance can be perceived the Davidic tradition reflected in the promise of Nathan in 2 Samuel 7.[28] In this does not Isaiah simply join the ranks of the ones who through retrospection take refuge wholly in the old tradition esteemed so highly in David's court?

The conclusion to the episode in Isa 7:1-9 and its continuation in 7:10-25 are informative at this point: "If you do not believe (*ta'aminu*), you will not remain (*te'amenu*)."[29] The first scene ends with this polished wordplay, an exhibit-piece of all the splendor of Isaianic diction.[30] The simple indicative assurance, which seemed to impart so much certainty, is thereby set into the context of prophetic openness toward future conduct. Its truth and validity will hold good if "belief" is present—and that means only at those points where people do not presume that their refuge and security lie simply in their possession of the tradition (*traditum*) from the past, but where they open themselves in expectancy and obedience to God's approaching activity and set their whole security in him who is speaking here.

The episode that follows in 7:10-25 shows clearly how reluctant King Ahaz is to accept this assurance, which is to be confirmed by a sign. He declines the offer of a sign and attempts throughout to preserve his own freedom of action over against what is expected from Yahweh. So Isaiah holds indeed to his promise that the immediate danger will not be fatal. But after this comes a judgment against David's house that is all the more ominous: there will come "days the like of which have not existed since Ephraim broke from Judah" (7:17).

We can detect a similar treatment of the *traditum* revered in Jerusalem about the invulnerability of Zion. Probably at a later historical period when the Assyrians had already come dangerously close to Judah, the authorities in Jerusalem relied on their secret negotiations with allies, rather than on protection by Zion. In this situation comes the puzzling divine utterance of Isa 28:16-17a in which the prophet seems to take up the belief about Zion without disrupting it: "Behold, I am laying in Zion a stone, a tested stone, a precious cornerstone for a firm foundation." But again he turns to the future and makes the additional observation that in all of this Yahweh has in mind not simply the empirical Jerusalem, but his just city: "I will make justice as the plumb-line and righteousness as the level." Yet above all there is again a demand for faith here: "He who believes will never waver." Again there is no simple reliance on "tradition." Again mention of the tradition about unshakable Zion empties into the free future of God. The declaration of "tradition" can retain its validity only if there is complete, open trust in Yahweh.

The same point is formulated somewhat differently in another passage. Isaiah 14:28-32 indicates that messengers from the Philistines were in Jerusalem at the time of a change in rules in Asshur, and with confidence and even joy because of the opportune situation they wanted to include Jerusalem in their planned security network. To this Isaiah states: "What should one answer the messengers of this people? This, that Yahweh has founded Zion. The poor among his people will take refuge there" (v. 32). Again in this utterance all obvious security is shattered. The tradition about Zion as the place of

safety is not cast aside, but is reestablished with a divine proviso. One cannot simply flee into this shelter. Zion is a refuge only for the "poor." This is to be understood as the "believers," as used elsewhere. The prophet has in mind those people who do not rely, with firm security perhaps quite piously expressed, on the salvific tradition about Zion, but rather who are sure only of their own poverty—yet thereby also of the certain future of Yahweh. It is stated that Zion will be a shelter only for these "poor."

The Ariel prophecy in Isa 29:1-7 illustrates this declaration from yet another perspective. The city that celebrates its feasts where David once encamped is told of its greatest degradation. All details remain in the semi-darkness of inti-mation. This arrogant, festal city must sink deep into the dust even though it bears the name Ariel, "Hearth," after the altar of God that is found in it. But then, when it has reached the lowest point of degradation (might we interpret this according to 14:32—"will have become poor"?), then God will turn its fate and will cause the foes encamped against it to be scattered like a nocturnal apparition, a dream in the night.

For all of this, Isaiah clearly appropriates more of pious tradition than does, for example, Amos. But nowhere does he regard tradition simply as self-evi-dent *traditum* that is to be honored because of its origin. In all of these pas-sages the freedom of Yahweh, who desires that his personal will be recognized in everything, is reckoned into the element of tradition. As long as Yahweh remains true to character, he will always show himself to be the One who is free, who holds all future in his hands. This will not simply sweep aside a promise handed down in tradition—but it may well transform it.

The same thing can be said of the messianic statements in Isa 8:23aβ²?; 9:1-6 [9:1aβ², 2-7]; and in 11:1-9. Bright light breaks over the greatest need of the people who sit in darkness, who have become poor; the king appears in whom the righteousness demanded by Yahweh will be fully realized. According to 11:1-9 this new king of righteousness is a shoot growing out of the chopped-down stump of Jesse. In this case also, Yahweh prepares his new thing only for a later period, after judgment has caused the people to despair of their own power.[31]

Isaiah's language, just like the place from which his traditions stem, is quite different from that of Hosea. While Hosea spoke of a return to the wilderness, Isaiah speaks of the poor, of faith, as the only way by which the promises in received tradition can attain reality.

Ezekiel

Ezekiel leads us into yet another world. Although he was probably from Jerusalem, it is no longer possible for us to assign him exclusively to the Israelite or the Jerusalemite sphere of tradition. His preaching is a blend of tradition streams. The allegorical speech in Ezekiel 16 refers to Jerusalem as the unfaithful wife. To describe her origin, v. 3 seized upon elements remembered from Jerusalem's Canaanite prehistory. On the other hand, it is Israel in its entirety, during its Egyptian origins that is the subject of the metaphorical speech about the two whoring women in chap. 23, as also in the non-metaphorical theology of history in chap. 20. The location of the city and the temple is not identified by the name of Zion, a word that appears nowhere in the whole book, but as the "high mountain of Israel (*har merom yiśra'el*; 20:40). The same name is given the place where, according to 17:23, the messianic twig will be planted anew.

But especially impressive is the relentless daring with which Ezekiel is able to shatter revered elements of tradition in their original meaning and instead make them serve the prophetic message.

Of the five themes identified by Martin Noth, the patriarchal history never occurs in a positive way in Ezekiel's own words. We have evidence that it was not unknown to him: he cites a statement current among the people remaining in the land after 587 B.C.E., a statement in which they looked to Abraham for consolation. Although Abraham was only one man, he received the land. "But we are many, and the land is given us as a possession" (Ezek 33:24). The prophet sharply rejects such efforts of the still sinful people to comfort themselves by remembering the promise to the Fathers.[32]

We can observe Ezekiel's radical transformation of revered tradition most clearly, however, in his use of the other Pentateuchal traditions. In Ezekiel 23 the element of the exodus from Egypt is shriveled into the assertion that Yahweh had taken as wives two young women with Bedouin (tent) names who, while yet in Egypt, had been promiscuous and evil and who later continued to play the whore with foreign lovers—Asshur, Babylon, Egypt. "Egypt," the element remembered from the past, is reassessed in terms of Judah's impious politics of coalition during Ezekiel's time. Judah refuses to learn anything from the fiasco that resulted when her elder sister Northern Israel whored after Asshur. Rather, the Southern kingdom whores first with the Babylonians, turns then to renew her old, illicit love affair with the Egyptians, and so incurs the vengeance of her older lovers. What remains intact of the good assertions in the credo?

There is analogous poignancy in the literal description of Israel's early history in Ezek 20:1-31. This passage treats the themes of the exodus from Egypt and the wilderness period, with allusion as well to the giving of the commandments. But what is left of the creedal statements? In Egypt Yahweh swore to the house of Israel that he would lead them out from there, and he commanded them to abandon the Egyptian gods. Yet even at that point they would not let themselves be separated from the gods of Egypt. Nevertheless,

Yahweh led them out of Egypt "for the sake of his name, that it might not be profaned in the sight of the nations." And he gave them his commandments in the wilderness, but the people in turn disregarded them, with the result that God refused to allow the first wilderness generation to enter the land.[33]

Despite renewed appeal for obedience to the laws, the next generation remained rebellious also, so that Yahweh, while not destroying them in the wilderness for his name's sake, nonetheless decided then to scatter the people later into all the world—and in fact gave them commandments on which they could only run aground.[34] At this point the account breaks off.[35] Quite clearly it jumps over additional historical phases in order to get to the immediate motivation in the fate that is coming to pass in Ezekiel's days. The old history of salvation themes in the tradition—exodus, Sinai events, guidance in the wilderness, conquest—are all completely recast in the service of the divine "No," which combats firmly any of Israel's self-assurance of her creedal tradition. The same history that confirms salvation and is esteemed in tradition is here transposed into history that confirms disaster.

Ezekiel 16 demonstrates the same process with the Jerusalem/Zion tradition, which is recapitulated at the conclusion of Ezekiel's symbolic actions to announce the fall of Jerusalem:

> This is Jerusalem: I have set her in the center of the nations, with countries around her. And she has wickedly rebelled against my ordinances more than the nations, and against my statutes more than the countries round about her. (Ezek 5:5-6)[36]

Ezekiel 16 shows Jerusalem's ignoble origin: "According to your ancestry and your origin you stem from the land of the Canaanites. Your father was an Amorite, your mother a Hittite" (16:3). Lacking nobility, she acts thereafter with the unfaithfulness of a foundling whom Yahweh had picked up, raised, made honorable, and married but then who became proud of her beauty and gave herself to foreign lovers. In the behavior of this woman we can recognize the essence of Baalism for which Hosea had reproached the Northern kingdom and with which later Jeremiah in his early preaching had also charged Judah/Jerusalem.

In Ezekiel, however, we can also see how old tradition in altered form is introduced, after the catastrophe of 587, into the announcement of future salvation. In a new supplementary passage (20:32-44), formulated after 587, the prophet confronts a people who think that theirs is the lot of assimilation to the idolatrous cults of their neighbors (20:32). With exodus terminology and in oath form Yahweh announces his royal reactions, the new exodus, the new encounter with Yahweh in the wilderness, and the new conquest, at the center of which will be the new cult on the "lofty mountain of Israel." The history of salvation message, handed down as *traditum* from Yahweh's previous salvific actions, is formulated in the future mood as the anticipation of things yet to come for Israel—the community's tradition transformed into hope. In chaps. 40–48 the new temple constitutes the object of the last great visionary description in the Book of Ezekiel. It undoubtedly contains significant secondary additions, and in its present form the concluding section describes a new, ideal division of the land—a fully righteous allotment corresponding antitypically to Joshua 13–24.

In the second half of the Book of Ezekiel, in chaps. 34 and 37, the *traditum* "David" occurs within a promise about the future. Chapter 34 is a retrospective condemnation, sharply polemical, of previous "shepherds of Israel." Somewhat in tension with this, the new situation promised by Yahweh includes the name of David, familiar from the past:

> I will set over them one shepherd, my servant David, and he shall feed them. . . . And I, Yahweh, will be their God, and my servant David shall be a prince among them; I, Yahweh, have spoken. (34:23-24)[37]

In this passage the old traditional promise to David is thrust intact into an announcement of the future.

Deutero-Isaiah

The prophet during the final years of the exile, Deutero-Isaiah, appropriates fully the promissory theme of the new exodus, treated earlier in Ezek 20:32-44. He makes use of a typological correspondence between old and new in his descriptions of the path through the wilderness where water flows forth from the rock (Isa 48:21), and Yahweh himself accompanies his people (40:10-11). As in Ezekiel 20, these traditions about exodus, wilderness wandering, and new conquest are transposed into anticipation of the coming acts of Yahweh, and in this they are conjoined with an expected glorification of Zion. Thus it is impossible for us to distinguish sharply between traditional backgrounds or "streams," as we could between Hosea and Isaiah.

Yet in comparison with Ezekiel 20, there is something novel in Deutero-Isaiah's reflection on the category old/new—tradition about the past and announcement about the future. In connection with this, we need also to direct attention to Jer 31:31-34, certainly a post-Jeremianic piece. This pericope contrasts the two covenants: the old covenant stemming from the exodus from Egypt, with the law mediated in imperative form to Israel; and the new covenant, replacing the old, with the law to be written upon the people's hearts so that imperative instruction is no longer needed. Thus the new will do away with the old, that which had been handed down in tradition. In Isa 43:16-21 the old exodus from Egypt is compared to the new exodus, with the words: "Do not think about the former things; behold, I am doing something new." However, this is not to be understood as a polemical invalidation of the old. Rather, the greater "new thing" simply surpasses the old, and this renders unnecessary any "remembrance," that is, the process of transmission of old tradition in the cultic "memory" (compare parallel passages in Jer 16:14-15 = 23:7-8).

Nonetheless, we can see elsewhere that Deutero-Isaiah sets aside the previously intended import of ancient traditions and boldly recasts them in terms of the "new." While he appropriates the patriarchal tradition (Abraham in Isa 41:8 and 51:1-2) in its old sense as narrated in Genesis, and while he appeals to the Noah tradition as an example (54:9-10), he does not deal similarly with the Davidic tradition. In a daring manner, the latter tradition in 55:3-5 is redirected toward the future and widened to include the whole people. The David of the past is no longer esteemed as the founder of a great kingdom to which the people, newly liberated and guided back to Zion, can return; rather, he is Yahweh's "witness." In the imminent future the promise given to David (ḥasdê david) will now be fulfilled for the people; their political liberator Cyrus is even given the title "Yahweh's anointed one" (45:1). The people will then be "Yahweh's witness" among the nations and will increase "Yahweh's empire" in that other persons will come running to give glory to Yahweh. This would also be the sense of 44:1-5, a description of how, through Yahweh's poured-out spirit, that is, his blessing, the people will be increased, persons will come and say, "I am Yahweh's," will call themselves by the name of Jacob and will tattoo Yahweh's name (as a sign of belonging) on their hand.

There is another matter that we can only present in the form of a question here: Deutero-Isaiah's preaching is characterized by copious flashbacks to Israel's older traditions about salvation. Aside from the creation statements, it begins with the Noah tradition, which is mentioned in Isa 54:9-10 for comparative purposes; its connection with the statement about the covenant seems to suggest that the prophet had in mind a narrative form related to the Priestly source tradition. He appropriates the tradition about Abraham (and Sarah) in a positive way (41:8; 51:2), whereas he seems to refer to Jacob in 43:27 in the same critical fashion as Hosea does. In Deutero-Isaiah the exodus, wilderness wandering, conquest, and Zion appear, in part antitypically, thrust into the future. We spoke also of the way he recast the Davidic tradition. In light of all of this, we might well ask whether the Mosaic tradition also reverberates in Deutero-Isaiah. Might such a correspondence be concealed behind the mysterious figure of the Servant of Yahweh, the one who brings forth justice to the nations (42:1, 3-4), after he had first been charged with the prior task of leading

Israel home? Deutero-Isaiah's own office is perhaps also delineated behind this assignment. This question about a Moses typology hidden here deserves serious consideration, but since the problem remains unresolved it will not be reckoned into our final evaluation of the matter of prophetic proclamation and interpretation.[38]

THE THEOLOGICAL IMPORT

By way of conclusion, we must now attempt to summarize what we have observed in concrete texts. In terms of "Tradition and Theology," our task is to reflect on discernible features of the phenomenon of "interpreting" pre-given tradition especially in the area of prophetic proclamation, as seen in the examples treated.

To begin with, it is obvious that one can speak of "traditions" on a narrower and on a wider horizon. In the *narrower sphere,* clear relations among the individual prophets came to light. Prophetic proclamation about the Day of Yahweh, the origin of which as a confrontation with popular faith can be recovered in the work of Amos, is transmitted through later periods as a special prophetic theological term (*theologoumenon*). The image of the destroyed marriage between Yahweh and Israel, which finds its roots in the symbolic act demanded directly of Hosea, becomes part of the prophetic message in the preaching of Jeremiah and Ezekiel.[39] And reference to the "Holy One of Israel," for which Isaiah 6 seems to be the place of prophetic origin, reoccurs in Deutero-Isaiah.[40]

What does it mean for the understanding of the great prophets that they live like this within an inner-prophetic "tradition"?[41] Does this lead to the picture of a specific "office" with an "officially" regulated sermon, and do the great literary prophets fit also into such a picture?[42] Does not even such a prophet as Jeremiah refer to this when he opposes Hananiah with the reproach: "The prophets who were before me and you from ancient times— they preached of war, famine, and pestilence against many countries and great kingdoms" (Jer 28:8)? Does not this presuppose a prophetic norm of preaching, a "tradition" in which each prophet stands?

There is opposition to this as early as Amos's hefty protest against Amaziah, who wanted to fit him into a "school": Amos contradicts him by referring to the commission he received directly from Yahweh. Jeremiah's polemic against the prophets who steal each other's words (Jer 23:30) is also opposed to this. Moreover, this same Jeremiah, who reflected on the legitimacy of prophetic proclamation more intensively than any other prophet, was the very one to accentuate "Yahweh sent me" (26:15; compare 1:7) as well as the polemically defensive charge, "Yahweh did not send you" (28:15 and elsewhere). This itself counsels against our tying prophetic legitimacy with a general office, which in turn would be bound to a specific tradition.

Jeremiah 28 is an especially impressive text for elucidating the prophet's peculiar freedom from "school ties"—while still being demonstrably determined by "older prophetic tradition." Isaiah preaches (in 14:25) that Asshur will be broken and its yoke and burden eliminated from the people. Isaiah 9:4 [MT v. 3] formulates it with corresponding language: "The yoke that burdens him, the rod that strikes his shoulder [or: the collar on his shoulder?], the rod of his oppressor, you shatter as on the day of Midian." Jeremiah 28 then reports that in the fourth year of Zedekiah Jeremiah put a yoke upon his neck and proclaimed the necessity of surrendering to Babylon. The prophet Hananiah confronts him in the temple. He tears the yoke from Jeremiah's neck and smashes it to pieces while declaring solemnly in Yahweh's name: "Thus will I break the yoke of Nebuchadnezzar, the king of Babylon." With these words Hananiah is standing fully in the tradition of Isaiah and simply repeating what his predecessor had said before him. Yet, so we are told, Jeremiah departs without a word, although he had just previously warned Hananiah by referring to an opposing prophetic tradition (quoted above). Could it be in the end that Hananiah's actualization of the tradition from Isaiah is truly legitimate? The text then reports tersely that Jeremiah receives a new message from God to tell Hananiah: "Within the year you shall die." And the account ends without commentary: "And the prophet Hananiah died in the same year, in the seventh month." This episode shows clearly how little shelter a prophet can actually find in tradition, even where this happens to be a previously valid prophetic message. It demonstrates well how little the prophet, even within the inner-prophetic process of tradition, can dispense with the fact that Yahweh in his freedom can utter his word anew.

Such ties in view of inner-prophetic transmission of the prophetic message are paired with, on the other hand, the great freedom with which a prophet, despite considerable dependence on the proclamation of another prophet, can nevertheless treat the message handed down from this predecessor. Such sovereignty is perceivable, for example, in the use made by Ezekiel of the tradition about the exodus-wilderness period: whereas Hosea and Jeremiah sketched this in brilliant colors as the time of Israel's closeness to her God, Ezekiel (in chaps. 20 and 23) transforms this into an exactly opposite picture of total recalcitrance.

This last example leads us into the *wider sphere*: ancient pre-prophetic tradition about Israel's salvation, and its treatment in the context of prophetic proclamation.

The entire discussion in this essay took its starting-point in Amos's "No" to all revered tradition in which the people of his day sought shelter. Alongside Amos, Hosea issued a "No," formulated in the name given his third child, against the central affirmation of Israel's "covenant formula," the awareness that Israel is Yahweh's people; this "No" thus exceeds the warning in Amos 3:2.

It also became clear right at the beginning, however, that this "No" stems from an equally impassioned "Yes"—a "Yes" to Yahweh, known by this name in Israel's pious tradition, the God who had now mobilized against his people. Amos's "No," like that of Hosea, is to be understood in terms of Yahweh's uprising against Israel, against the people "known" by Yahweh (Amos 3:2) and identified by him as "my people" in Amos 7:8 and 8:2 within a proclamation of judgment, indeed within a message about the "end." In speaking of Yahweh, whose name they knew from Israel's tradition, these prophets were not expounding a neutral *traditum* but rather the personal God designated in his very name, the One who lives, who comes.

Yet this One, whose ominous approach is proclaimed, became also the subject of all that was commonly recounted from older Israelite tradition—that which occurred in the exodus from Egypt, in the wilderness wandering, in the conquest (the patriarchal tradition recedes well into the background) in dwelling on Zion, in David's kingdom with the promise associated with him. But Israel's faith sought refuge in these as declarations of assurance, of historical promise, and of Yahweh's gracious presence in the midst of his people. And for this reason all of these traditions had to take on a different complexion.

We could see that the individual prophets spoke very differently about these *traditia*. The memory of Yahweh's gift of land could become an illustration of Israel's current deep ingratitude toward the God whose will for justice was known well, yet was disregarded (Amos). With perceptible sublimation of actual recollection, the wilderness period could become a time of virtuous poverty and full loyalty to Yahweh—in sharp contrast to the neglect of the present, when Baalistic opulence in the land had eclipsed the knowledge of Yahweh (Hosea). When Yahweh's people relied more on current political agreements than on the Holy One in their midst, then the fact that Israel's Holy One dwells on Zion could become a threat, and deliverance was to be expected only for those who relied on and believed in Yahweh and who recognized their own deficiency before the One who alone is exalted. Insolent assault against the statutes of the Holy One in the Davidic house established by him could, though, also spell the ruin of an external power (Isaiah). For Ezekiel, however, the entire tradition from the people's past merged, in light of their present rebellion against Yahweh, into a single history of disobedience. The initial events during the exodus from Egypt and the wilderness period were declared to be the true cause of the immediately impending catastrophe.

For all of this, is it appropriate to speak of "interpretation" of historical traditions? To be sure, old traditions emerge throughout. Yet in terms of the actual function which "tradition" should serve, namely, the function of wholesome assurance for the present in "memory" and in "actualization" of past events,[43] the *traditum* crumbles to pieces wherever the great pre-exilic prophets take hold of it. In their preaching it becomes the accuser of the present. And even at the price sometimes (especially in Ezekiel) of radical recasting with all beneficial aid eliminated, the *traditum* is made to serve entirely the prophets' immediate proclamation of judgment, the sole locus of emphasis. The God who comes in judgment emerges from the entire pious tradition. He is to be known in his impending judgment, and no longer in tradition about previous deeds (a proof-saying, *Erweiswort*). Alongside this, the old traditions have nothing of their own to emphasize. "Tradition," in the salutary sense of the word, shatters and becomes an empty shell of mere historical recollection, over which a completely different word of God is proclaimed.

But then something else happens. The ancient tradition can experience a peculiar transformation that one cannot properly call "interpretations of traditions": in an antitypical fashion it can express what Yahweh pronounces as judgment (return to Egypt, a new period in the wilderness) and as the sequel to judgment (new exodus, new covenant, new conquest, new presence of Yahweh, new kingdom on Zion). Israel's old tradition offers the vocabulary with which the impending action can be described. Yet as such it is still more than just a graphic illustration. Tradition discloses the constancy of the One who is free, who remains committed to act "for his own sake" (Ezek 36:22; Isa 43:25; 48:11), who "takes pity on his own name," as Ezek 36:21 formulates it with sober objectivity.

These summarizing comments have not attended adequately to points of connection or to distinctions that could be made between, for example, Amos and Isaiah. Israel's great prophecy does not speak with one voice—and especially not in terms of the traditions available to it and treated by it. Yet it happens that upon every historical tradition that may be cultically transmitted as revered *traditum* the prophets, despite all individual differences, impose their message about the One who is known by the traditional name of Yahweh and who is about to rise up again within Israel's history. He cannot be captured in some citation about a past event—and thus be put at our disposal. "Tradition history" must not be evaluated unthinkingly as "theology."[44] The "No" of such prophets as Amos remains firm and relentless. Nevertheless, God is the One who is free—free then also to begin anew after the great catastrophe. Since old material in new form seems to reappear in the proclamation of this new beginning granted freely by Yahweh, it becomes evident that the One acting in Israel remains unchanged. In proclaiming this new deed Ezekiel declares:

"You will know that I am Yahweh when I open your graves and lead you up, my people, out of your graves" (37:13). The *traditum* "Yahweh," which is more than just a *traditum,* becomes an indicator, pointing to the One who, in freedom and yet also in faithfulness, can begin anew—and desires to begin anew.

Prophetic proclamation thus shatters and transforms tradition in order to announce the approach of the Living One.

From Prophetic Word to Prophetic Book

Introduction

Amos has conspired against you in the midst of the house of Israel; the land is not able to bear all his words. For thus speaks Amos: "Jeroboam will die by the sword, and Israel must go into exile away from its own land." (Amos 7:10-11)

This, according to Amos, was the high priest's report to King Jeroboam II of Israel at the national sanctuary of Bethel. The report was followed by Amos's immediate expulsion from the land at the priest's own initiative. We read in Jer 26:8-9 that priests and prophets seized Jeremiah at the temple in Jerusalem after one of his speeches, saying:

You are doomed to die! Why did you prophesy in the name of Yahweh that this temple will be like Shiloh [an earlier sanctuary in northern Israel that lay in ruins in the days of Jeremiah] and the city will be desolate and without inhabitants? As both of these passages from the Old Testament prophetic books demonstrate—and more examples could easily be given—a prophetic word entails a concrete reference to history. Prophecy is critically spoken into a particular context and, in turn, generates a specific response at a given time in history.

By the same token, the prophetic commission is always subordinate to the sovereignty of God, who sends when and where he desires and who always remains lord over the content of the prophetic message. It is evident from Isaiah's words that this prophetic commission might be configured very differently if the historical circumstances were different. Indeed, the wording may actually appear to be almost the opposite of what had been said earlier.[1] Thus the commission cannot simply be used word for word in an attempt to apply it to a new historical situation.

Jeremiah 28 shows how the prophet Hananiah reuses a word of the prophet Isaiah, who had prophesied more than a century earlier. Faithful to his predecessor, Hananiah uses Isaiah's message in the Jerusalem temple during the final decade prior to Jerusalem's destruction. He confronts the prophet Jeremiah, who was running around with a yoke on his back, proclaiming, "You should bear the yoke of Nebuchadnezzar's foreign rule according to the will of God." In an impressive symbolic gesture, Hananiah tears the yoke from his neck, breaks it, and announces, "Thus says Yahweh, 'Even so I will break the yoke of Nebuchadnezzar king of Babylon from the neck of all the nations within two years'" (Jer 28:11). This, of course, is very similar to Isa 9:4 [MT v. 3], which reads, "For the yoke of his burden, and the staff for his shoulder, the rod of his oppressor, you have broken as on the day of Midian." And Isa 14:25b, "His yoke will be taken from them, and his burden from their shoulders."

In response, however, Jeremiah confronts what appears to be firmly grounded in the prophetic word by saying: "Listen, Hananiah, Yahweh has not sent you, and you have given false confidence to this people. Therefore Yahweh declares, 'Behold, I am sending (sweeping) you away from this country. You will die this very year.'" This is followed by the laconic statement, "And the prophet Hananiah died in the seventh month of that year" (28:15-17).

What all of this shows is that a prophetic word is always a message that is highly relevant to a given historical context, a message that is invariably characterized by the freedom of God. It can turn into a treacherous lie if someone lifts it out of its context by even the most pious biblicism in an attempt to perpetuate the word merely by quoting it without sharpening his ear to hear God's will anew for his or her own time.

But now we have books in our Bible that do not merely tell us what happened to the prophets in ages past. The books of the so-called classical prophets of the eighth through the sixth centuries are for the most part collections of the prophets' words that were simply recorded without comment and transmitted in written form.[2] What benefit can we derive from this word that was written down and transmitted for later time? Should the fate of a Hananiah not raise suspicion in us—indeed be a warning for us not to take up these words in a different time? (It should, of course, be self-evident that our present is in many respects different from the times of the prophets in ancient Israel and Judah.) What, we continue to ask, occasioned the writing down of these words, words that clearly had relevance for a particular point in time? Are they not robbed of their actual life by having been written down? Does the recorded prophetic message not take on an archival character, that is, material that is of interest to the historian but irrelevant for the life of the later community?

All of these questions introduce the topic of the following discussion. What can be said regarding the progression from the oral, situation-bound prophetic word to the written message, which was lifted out of its original context and has apparently become timeless? What can be said, moreover, regarding the relevance of the written prophetic word for the community that has transmitted this word in its holy scriptures and doubtless will continue to pass it on in the future?

RECORDING PROPHECIES

Here, then, is the first question: Can we learn something regarding the recording of the prophetic word from the wording of the writings of classical prophecy of the eighth to the sixth centuries? In the following discussion, we will focus on the prophecies that were collected in the actual prophetic books of the Old Testament. Our answer will indeed be in the affirmative. It will be shown that there is clear evidence in the prophets' own contemporary proclamation.

Isaiah

Isaiah 8:1-2 records a peculiar event. The prophet reports,

> Then Yahweh said to me, "Take a large tablet and write upon it with a human pen: Maher-shalal-hash-baz" [this has been translated as 'rob soon, hasten spoils']. And I got reliable witnesses, Uriah the priest and Zechariah the son of Jeberechiah to attest for me.

The particular issue of what is meant by "human pen"—that is, whether one should read, with Wildberger[3] (following Gressmann), with a slight change of vocalization, "with (a) hard (pen)" or "with a pen of destruction"—does not need to be discussed further at this point. Morenz has plausibly suggested that this curious expression that Isaiah was told to write down originated in the language of Egyptian soldiers, referring to the spoils won in a quick victory.[4] I consider it probable that this emphatic expression, posted publicly with the aid of witnesses, originally was intended to be a message of calamity directed toward Judah by the prophet Isaiah. However, when the text continues a son of Isaiah is given a symbolic name in a second act that was apparently accomplished some time after the first, and this second act is, in changed circumstances, turned polemically against both of the enemies of Judah, who are approaching Jerusalem in the Syro-Ephraimite War:

> And I went to the prophetess, and she conceived and bore a son. Then Yahweh said to me, "Call his name Maher-shal-al-hash-baz; for before the child knows how to cry 'My father' or 'My mother,'[5] the wealth of

> Damascus and the spoil of Samaria will be carried away before the king of Assyria." (8:3-4)

We may note here that the prophet himself is urged by Yahweh to write down a terse, initially mysterious, but unmistakably calamitous message that has relevance for anyone who reads the words written on the tablet. The use of witnesses, one of whom is also named as a high priest of the Jerusalem temple in 2 Kgs 16:10-16, underscores the importance of this tersely phrased, written pronouncement.

The account in Isaiah 8 finds a parallel in Hab 2:1-4, where a prophet of the second half of the seventh century reports:

> I will take my stand to watch, and station myself on the tower, and look forth to see what he will say to me, and what I will answer concerning my complaint. And Yahweh answered me: "Write the vision; make it plain upon tablets, so he may run who reads it. For still the vision awaits its time; it hastens to the end—it will not lie. If it seem slow, wait for it; it will surely come, it will not delay.

When this is followed by the statement, "Behold, the unrighteous person languishes [thus the Zürcher Bibel, but the text is uncertain], but the righteous person will live by his faithfulness," what is at issue once again is the announcement of a crisis in which only that person can be saved who remains faithful to God. Standing on the rampart and watching for the divine revelation, which is called a "vision," may reveal something of a stereotyped prophetic office. We may perceive that, as in Isaiah, the revealed word is recorded and publicly posted, so that everyone is able to read it.[6] The people are not merely to hear the prophets' message from God with their ears, but to read it with their own eyes. In both cases, we find a divine message that is to be proclaimed into a particular situation, a message that is valid even if its fulfillment is delayed, as appears to be the case in the present circumstance. God wants people to know his word, in any event, and ensures that the message is written down for the purpose of unmistakable proclamation.

In another place in Isaiah, one finds another motif regarding the writing down of the prophetic message. Isaiah 8:16 provides a possible example of this. We find here the final pronouncement of a series of statements made by Isaiah in the context of the Syro-Ephraimite War. In a surprising development, the prophet is authorized at this point by his God to promise to Judah, to whom he had previously announced judgment, deliverance from the threat represented by a coalition of the two kings of Aram and northern Israel. This promise has only one condition, which is that Israel's king must be prepared to rely on Yahweh's promise: "If you do not believe, you will not remain" (Isa 7:9). The king, however, is not ready to do this. The assistance of the Assyrian king, who had been summoned to help, seems more reliable to him. Thus Isaiah views the Assyrians as the more dangerous enemy of his people, and the danger is imminent. The prophet himself feels condemned to silence and waiting. His final message in these days is:

> Bind up the testimony, seal the teaching among my disciples; I will wait for Yahweh, who is hiding his face from the house of Jacob, and I will hope in him. (Isa 8:16)

Duhm, Smend, and others find in this verse a hint regarding the writing down of the prophetic words from this time and their committal to the prophet's circle of disciples. But it is not impossible that this is merely a symbolic reference to the fact that Isaiah no longer appeared or spoke but felt compelled to remain silent. However the message may have been preserved by his disciples, it remains a living indictment of a disobedient people.

The subject of Isaiah 30:8-11, on the other hand, is clearly the writing down of a message from the prophet's later period. Yahweh says to the prophet:

> And now, go, write it before them on a tablet, and inscribe it in a book, that it may be for the time to come as a witness for ever. For they are a rebellious people, lying sons, sons who will not hear the instruction of Yahweh; who say to the seers, "See not [visions]"; and to the prophets, "Prophesying not to us what is right [the truth]; speak to us smooth things, prophesy illusions, leave the way, turn aside from the path, let us hear no more of the Holy One of Israel."

Once again, the topic of discussion is the writing down of a prophetic word. Opinions differ regarding the precise content of what is to be written down.[7] But one thing is clear, namely, that we are dealing with something other than a person's memoirs. When the prophet is instructed to "go in," that is, probably to retreat from public proclamation and to write down his message, the purpose is different from the purpose in Isaiah 8 and Habakkuk 2. The prophet is to be a concealed accuser and witness of the people's guilt for "the latter day." When calamity finally strikes, the nation will not be able to resort to the excuse, "We never heard of it." In the form of written word, God will be present even in the later hour of judgment.

At this point one may ask whether or not this may also have been the motive for recording the prophetic word in other instances. Amos was banished from the northern Kingdom. People did not want to listen to his message any longer. Should one perhaps interpret the recording of, say, the cycle of visions in Amos 7–9 in this way, which, despite expansions, can still be recognized? There the prophet speaks in the first person, so that it is reasonable to assume that he was personally responsible for writing down his message. It may be assumed that Amos obeyed the command to leave the country. In the hour of calamity, however, the word recorded by him will accuse the people. No one will be able to say at that time that Yahweh had not spoken. Yahweh himself will stand before the nation as its accuser by his written prophetic word. The disaster is not a result of destiny but of culpability. God has spoken actively in history.

The passage regarding the Syro-Ephraimite War in Isaiah 7–8, which probably has the prophet's own records as its basis, is preceded by Isaiah 6, another section that is told in the first person. Since the unit of Isaiah 6:1—9:6 clearly interrupts a previously existing context of so-called strophic poetry and perhaps also a collection of seven cries of woe, one should consider it to be an already-formed, coherent, subsection.[8] The placement of the prophetic commission before the pronouncements of the year 733 B.C.E. thus appears to conform to the prophet's own preference. This, however, leads to the fact that not even the writing of the commissioning narrative in the first person should be seen as the writing of memoirs. This call narrative with its mysterious statements confirms Isaiah's realization that the failure of his proclamation and his lack of success in the offer of divine grace do not constitute an incidental mishap caused by the prophet's own incompetence. The lack of response is rather an integral component of the judgment, which was why Yahweh had sent him to "this people." It was precisely the offer of grace that hardened the nation all the more toward its God.

Thus the prophet reports how he was already told the following message at the hour of his call by Yahweh, the one whom he had seen in the temple and who had sent him thence to his people as his messenger:

> Go, and say to this people: "Hear and hear, and do not understand; see and see, but do not perceive! Make the heart of this people fat, and their ears heavy, and shut their eyes; lest they see with their eyes, and hear with their ears, and understand with their hearts, and turn and be healed." (Isa 6:9-10)

This is the message given to the prophet by Yahweh on the occasion of his call. As Isaiah himself experiences his own impurity and cries out when entering the light of the Holy One at the hour of his call in the temple, it is precisely the message regarding God's gracious suspension of judgment in the year 733 that reveals the people's profound obduracy.

> Woe is me! For I am lost;[9] for I am a man of unclean lips and I dwell in the midst of a people of unclean lips; for my eyes have seen the King, Yahweh of hosts! (Isa 6:5)

That their obduracy is already revealed at the prophet's call is probably the most profound motive underlying the prophet's narration of his call. The written account does not seek to confront the reader with the prophet as an individual or with his life story, but rather with God himself, before whom God's people can only be revealed in all of their faithlessness and guilt.

Amos

From here we may turn to the other prophetic call narratives, asking whether or not similar motives led to their being recorded in writing. Amos does not give an account of his call. The information that Yahweh had taken him from his flock and had given him a prophetic commission (Amos 7:15) is part of an extraneous report that originates from the circle of his followers. The cycle of visions, however, even though one should not interpret it as a call narrative, indicates nonetheless that the severe message of Yahweh's judgment upon his people should be distinguished from the backdrop of his initial willingness to forgive, which is still perceptible in the first two visions in chapter 7. Should not the writing down of this personal experience of visions serve the intention of recording irrevocably the inexcusable condition of the nation against which Amos prophesies?

Once again this occurs by means of the written word, since the people refused to listen to the prophet's oral message. "The lion has roared; who will not fear? The LORD Yahweh has spoken; who can but prophesy?" (Amos 3:8). This word, also recorded by Amos, manifests the total unavoidability of the prophetic mandate, as well as the menace posed by the Lord who approaches the people with his word.

Jeremiah

One could make similar observations regarding the investigation of the call narratives of Jeremiah and Ezekiel, whose records also betray, apart from the validation of the prophetic call, the purpose of confrontation with the Lord, who approaches for the purpose of judgment. But regarding the issue of the recording of the prophetic word, we may instead look at the curious episode reported in Jer 51:59-64. There we learn that Jeremiah sent his prophetic words against Babylon with Seraiah, the quartermaster of King Zedekiah, when he accompanied the king to Babylon in the fourth year of the latter's reign.

Jeremiah wrote in a scroll [RSV: book] all the disasters that should come over Babylon. . . . And Jeremiah said to Seraiah: "When you come to Babylon, see that you read all these words. . . . When you finish reading this scroll, bind a stone to it, and cast it into the midst of the Euphrates, and say, 'Thus shall Babylon sink, to rise no more, because of the evil that I am bringing upon her.'" (51:60-61, 63-64)

The written prophetic word therefore has a dual function. In the first place, it is in the possession of the man who is going to Babylon. He can read it there on location, in the country of the recipients of the prophetic word. Second, it is the subject of a symbolic prophetic act that is to be enacted vicariously by the king's companion, who is sent on his journey with the written prophetic word. The sinking of the scroll in the Euphrates, which is accomplished by weighting it with a stone, surely does not serve only the function of the diligent destruction of a document that is dangerous for its bearer to possess in Babylon itself. The scroll's lowering in the Euphrates, the great river of Babylon, also represents the imminent total destruction of Babylonian power, which will never be restored. And since symbolic prophetic acts are more than mere graphic illustrations, since they always also exercise an influence of their own in the form of a kind of anticipation of the coming event, so all the power of the written prophetic word casts its shadow forward by this act. One might be tempted to speak of a kind of magical act if it were not that, especially in Jeremiah, the divine word that touches him personally also reveals itself to him as a crushing force. "Is not my word like fire, says Yahweh, and like a hammer which breaks the rock in pieces?" (Jer 23:29). The prophet hurls these words toward those who think they can disguise their own dreams as God's word. Thus Jeremiah himself, by his own admission, when considering whether to remain silent, experienced God's word in his heart like burning fire shut up in his bones. "I am weary with holding it in, and I cannot" (Jer 20:9).

The episode recounted in Jeremiah 51, of course, raises a number of questions. How can Jeremiah, who in his letter to the exiles urges them to pray for the well-being of their captors' country and who predicts that they would live in the land of their exile for a long time (Jeremiah 29), at the same time speak harsh words of warning against Babylon? Consequently, these must be words that would only take effect in the distant future seventy years on (25:11; 29:10), after the time of Nebuchadnezzar, his son, and his grandson (27:7). On the other hand, the fact that it is Seraiah (the brother of Jeremiah's closest associate, Baruch) who features as the king's companion during a trip by Zedekiah to Babylon (which is not mentioned elsewhere, though Zedekiah's motives may be easily explained) instills confidence in this report as the narration of an actual event in the prophet's life.

With the account of Jeremiah 36, we enter historically reliable territory. According to this narrative, Jeremiah had already, in the fourth year of Jehoiakim, the second predecessor of Zedekiah, received the divine command to dictate to Baruch the scribe all the words Yahweh had commanded him during the last few years. A day of repentance was held some time later in connection with the unexpected invasion by Nebuchadnezzar of the world of Syria and Palestine, which only recently had been controlled by the Egyptians. On this day, Jeremiah commissioned Baruch to read the words of the scroll in the temple. Jeremiah himself could not enter the temple; whether this was due to temporary ritual impurity or to a permanent prohibition from entering the temple is unclear. At this point, we may discern a further reason for the writing down the prophetic word that had initially been spoken orally. We see nothing here of the intrinsic power of the written word of Jeremiah 51. Nor does the writing serve the purpose of recording an accusation of inexcusable disobedience at the hour of imminent judgment, in the sense of Isaiah 30. The word read by Baruch to the community gathered in the temple was designed instead to shake them, just like the orally spoken prophetic word, so that the people might still be induced to return to Yahweh through a fresh hearing of Yahweh's prediction of judgment. Here as well, it is entirely clear that the divine word, which had been proclaimed at an earlier time, is designed to address the circumstances of the community directly and to confront the people with their God.

The recording of the word is, therefore, not understood in terms of a historicizing documentation of earlier proclamation but as an attack on the present—this time by the mediation of a third party who holds the written prophetic word in his hands and reads it. One can see, then, that this form of transmission of the word stirs up excitement among the people, that the royal government officials themselves are touched, and that they ensure that the king himself is informed. The word, however, has no effect on the king. What is more, Jehoiakim commits the blasphemy of throwing the divine word in its written form into the fire. And only the fact that both Jeremiah and Baruch hide themselves saves the prophet and the mediator who read his word from sharing the fate of the written divine word at the hand of the king.

Jeremiah 36 signals a new stage of the prophet's ministry through his word. He is no longer merely entrusted with prophetic speech in the form of direct, oral discourse, which may or may not be reasserted in concise, public, written form; but he also issues written summaries of messages that had been delivered in a variety of contexts and now can be read by a third party. This shift marks a gradual change in the prophetic ministry at the end of the seventh century in relation to the prophecy of the eighth century.[10] One should not conceive of this as an abrupt change. The transmission of words that had originally been written down for different reasons, and also the collections of the messages of the eighth-century prophets, may have been significant in this regard.

But it is the end of the seventh century that illustrates the attempt of contemporary prophecy also to reach its audience by means of written proclamation. Whether the introduction of the so-called "Book of Comfort for Ephraim" in Jeremiah 30–31, where Jeremiah is commanded by Yahweh to "write all the words I have told you in a book," is indeed original with Jeremiah is doubtful in the light of the strong deuteronomic form of the final collection.[11] What cannot be disputed, however, is the fact that Jeremiah, after Jeremiah 29, proclaimed Yahweh's command that the people accept obediently the divine judgment in a letter that was written by him, taken to Babylon by a royal delegation, and there read by a third party to the Judeans who had been deported to Babylon in the year 597 B.C.E.

why?

Ezekiel

The call narrative of the prophet Ezekiel furnishes clear proof that the prophetic word was normally understood in terms of a written word at the beginning of the sixth century. When the prophet is commissioned by Yahweh, who calls him to eat a scroll handed to him (Ezek 2:9—3:3), it is evident that the prophet was already familiar with scrolls of this kind, inscribed with the prophetic word. When Jeremiah, in one of his confessions before Yahweh, admits, "Your words were found, and I ate them" (Jer 15:16a), it should be understood metaphorically. In Ezekiel, the word written in a book becomes tangible reality that is experienced in the form of a vision.[12] Prophetic writing has become a visible entity. Did Ezekiel the priest perhaps see with his own eyes the dramatic scene in which Baruch read Jeremiah's scroll in the temple? When he more closely describes the scroll that lay before him with the words, "and it had writing on the front and on the back, and there were written on it words of lamentation and mourning and woe" (Ezek 2:10), it becomes apparent that the word he is to proclaim will likewise be the word of judgment that needs to be announced harshly at that very hour, only a few years before the complete destruction of Jerusalem. This calamity will evoke nothing but "lamentation and mourning and woe" in the house of Israel. But when it is determined immediately thereafter that the scroll devoured by the prophet becomes "sweet as honey," one is reminded initially of the continuation of the sentence quoted in Jeremiah's confession, "Your words became to me a joy and the delight of my heart" (Jer 15:16aβ). While the message is harsh, the prophet delights in the very fact that God is speaking at all, even though the word uttered by God may lead the prophet himself into suffering and misery, as can be observed immediately thereafter in Jeremiah.

If we wanted to pursue these thoughts further, it would now be necessary to establish to what extent written material can be found in the books of the prophets from Neo-Babylonian to Persian times. It would also be necessary to consider to what extent faithful records of a prophet's oral address to the people surrounding him can be found in this written version, which may even have been composed by the prophet himself. We dare not overlook the fact that the Book of Ezekiel, which is consistently portrayed as a report by the prophet himself, clearly reflects a later revision, as is the case, for example, in the words by which Yahweh initially addresses the prophet himself before he commissions him to speak to the "house of Israel." Thus in Ezek 37:1-14, for example, the prophet is authorized to proclaim to the nation, which languishes and sighs in the throes of the death of political destruction, the coming awakening to new life and the return to the land in the incredible vision of the raising of the dead bones. Here the detailed narration of the visionary experiences is placed prior to the three final verses that contain the actual commission to deliver the prophetic message. The explicit message the prophet is given to proclaim is very short (vv. 12-14). In Ezek 36:16-22a, the announcement Yahweh commands Ezekiel to make to the people—that Yahweh would make a new beginning for the sake of his own name, that he would bring the nation back from exile, and that he would purify it and give it a new heart—is preceded by a recapitulation, directed personally to the prophet, of the past evil history of the desecration of the divine name among the nations. Can anyone imagine all of this as the prophet's primarily oral proclamation? The extent to which Deutero-Isaiah's message of salvation in Isaiah 40–55 contains a simple reproduction of an oral prophetic word, without at least occasionally containing the reflected-upon written deposit of the prophet's word, is disputed.[13] (Should we in this case think of a pamphlet-like transmission of the prophetic word?) And in the case of the great, systematically arranged cycle of night visions of Zechariah,[14] later expanded from seven to eight, we can barely avoid the supposition of a conscious literary composition that was probably never proclaimed orally in this form. This fact cannot conceal the notion that, in Zechariah as well, brief individual expressions are repeatedly interjected among the visions and may best be interpreted as oral proclamation using the same style.

With this we turn to the second kind of question that will be entertained in the following discussion: What can be said regarding the process by which the prophetic word was transformed into a definitive book, a process in which the original features of the proclamation are clearly removed far from the original occasion of their utterance? That is, what can be said about the formation of the unified book and the theological implications of this?

Composition of Prophetic Books

With this second thought, we enter the arena of the method called redaction criticism. This approach no longer pursues the "actual voice" (*ipsissima vox*) of the individual prophet, that is, regarding what is "genuine" (as is often said in ambiguous language) in the individual prophetic book. Instead, it begins with the entirety of the book's text and asks what the book's redactor or redactors themselves sought to emphasize. The method first became familiar to us from the New Testament Gospels: What is the particular *kerygma* of Mark, Matthew, or Luke that is recognizable in their respective shaping of the Jesus tradition?

In recent times, the prophetic books have increasingly been approached with this kind of question. Does not the book have a dignity of its own in the form in which it was received into the canon of biblical literature? Can one not discern a particular message of the book in its entirety beyond the things explained by historical criticism and beyond the things said by the prophet who gives the book its name?

Later Additions and the Book of Amos

We may start with the book of the oldest prophet of scripture, Amos, whose work has already been analyzed frequently in this regard.[15] Without aiming at comprehensiveness, we may select three facts.

The first pertains to the observation that can be made regarding the first part of the book. The first two chapters of the Book of Amos contain the so-called "Cycle of Foreign Nations." Here, in a peculiarly stereotypical style, words of judgment are assembled against a number of Israel's neighbors. Such warnings against neighboring nations may constitute an ancient prophetic practice. Prophetic discourse of this kind is found in the story of Elisha, during the period before the writing prophets. There the promise of victory for Israel implies the defeat of Israel's enemies (2 Kgs 3:18-19; 7:1-20; 13:14-19; but compare 8:11-13).[16]

The novel element in Amos's "Cycle of Foreign Nations," however, consists in the fact that the charges against the neighboring nations develop into an initially similar, but eventually incomparably broader, word of accusation and judgment against northern Israel, to which Amos had been sent as a prophet. Israel must not presume that it will escape Yahweh's judgment and expectantly and complacently look for Yahweh's judgment on its neighboring nations.

> You only have I known of all the families of the earth; therefore I will punish you for all your iniquities. (Amos 3:2)

This is how the prophet expressed the same idea in a different passage. Today one can still read in the "Cycle of Foreign Nations" immediately before the stanza concerning Israel, a stanza regarding Judah:

> Thus says Yahweh, "For three transgressions of Judah, and for four, I will not revoke the punishment; because they have rejected the law of Yahweh, and have not kept his statutes, but their lies have led them astray, after which their fathers walked. So I will send a fire upon Judah, and it shall devour the strongholds of Jerusalem. (Amos 2:4-5)

Linguistic usage and conceptual development clearly distinguish this stanza from Amos's style and conceptual world elsewhere and place it in the sphere of deuteronomic speech and thought, which had spread widely in post-Josianic times.[17]

The most important thing, however, has not been said with the mere assertion that the stanza is "inauthentic" within the framework of Amos's ancient "Cycle of Foreign Nations." Rather, we encounter here a later Judean addition that lends the entire cycle a new direction at a later time and in a different environment: Let no one in Judah (after the northern kingdom has been subdued, while Judah, for the time being, survived) point to the northern kingdom, saying, "There is the sinful kingdom that has rightly been judged." Your case, Judah, is likewise addressed by Yahweh in all of this! This is how the Judean addition applies the older prophetic word to more recent circumstances or to a different group of listeners. Yahweh's word does not die when the situation that had originally been addressed ceases to exist.

A similar case is Amos 6:1, where a reference to those living in Jerusalem is placed prior to the word that attacks the blasphemous self-confidence of those living in luxury in Samaria: "Woe to those who are at ease in Zion." Since Amos never attacks Jerusalem elsewhere in his own words, we should see this as an expansion, which turns against Jerusalem the threatening word that was once spoken by the prophet against Samaria.

Similar traces of a Judean interpretation, which document how the written prophetic word receives new relevance in changed circumstances, can be found in the book of the prophet Hosea, who also prophesied in the northern kingdom. Thus when Hosea in 5:5 speaks of Israel's stumbling over its guilt and adds the statement, "Judah shall also stumble with them," the message of the prophet of the northern kingdom, when read in book form in the southern kingdom, turns with surprising directness against the Judean audience as well. As the living judge, God unexpectedly steps out of his ancient word in new immanence. This is also the case in Micah where, in a context originally directed against the northern kingdom, the question is asked, "What is the transgression of Jacob? Is it not Samaria (the capital of the northern kingdom)?" and the question put right beside it is, "And what is the sin of the house of Judah? Is it not Jerusalem?" (Mic 1:5 LXX). Thus the prophetic word in the prophetic book illumines new contemporary circumstances that transcend the original prophet's historical situation.

A second observation can be made regarding the Book of Amos. In three different passages, brief, entirely different hymnic pieces are inserted into the prophetic words. These pieces speak of Yahweh's creative power, describing it participially, and all climaxing in the phrase, "Yahweh is his name" (Amos 4:13; 5:8; 9:5-6). Drawing on Josh 7:19, Horst has rendered plausible a very specific life-setting for these doxologies.[18] In this Joshua passage, after the taking of Jericho, a man named Achan transgressed the strict prohibition and secretly took a bar of gold from the spoils. Joshua says to Achan, "Give honor to Yahweh, the God of Israel, and render praise to him; and tell me now what you have done," a statement that is followed by Achan's confession of guilt. It becomes clear from this statement that a confession of guilt before God could take on the form of praise. According to Horst, in such expressions of praise, which seem like lost fragments in the Book of Amos, we encounter the fact that the later community that reads and hears the prophetic word here confesses its own guilt and thus praises Yahweh. However doubtful the theory of Wolff that these doxologies always occur when Yahweh's judgment has previously been threatened against the altar at Bethel and that, specifically, in these doxologies one is able to hear the voice of the community at a time when the altar of Bethel was destroyed under Josiah,[19] we nonetheless have found another instance where an older prophetic word is affirmed as valid in a new setting contemporary with its transformation into a book, at a time when praise is given to God by a later community. People confess that Yahweh deserves honor and glory precisely when he acts as a judge.

After these partial observations regarding individual additions to the book, we may note a third element pertaining to the book in its entirety. In his own words, Amos announced judgment over Israel without mercy. The book named after him, however, climaxes in 9:11-15 in two words from Yahweh that promise future salvation. Amos 9:11-12 speaks of the fact that Yahweh will restore the fallen booth of David, that he will repair the breaches in its wall and restore the ancient rule over Edom and over all nations belonging to Yahweh; in other words, Amos refers to the restoration of the Davidic kingdom. In the second word (9:13-15), on the other hand, it is the blessing of nature that is in view alongside the promise of restoration and the people's return to the land.[20] In both cases the one who speaks is someone who already has in view God's judgment of his people and of the house of David. How should one evaluate these two final sections of the Book of Amos? The mere assertion that we are dealing here with later additions does not suffice, and neither does their simple removal from the Book of Amos. This expansion has been consciously added to the Book of Amos during the course of the book's further development. The explanation that is frequently given, that the intention was to give a more positive ending to the Book of Amos in the light of all the warnings it contains, is unduly superficial. Rather, this expansion, whoever may have formulated it, seeks to place Amos's proclamation in a larger context and wants it to be read in the light of a more comprehensive knowledge of God's will for his people. This comprehensive knowledge of Old Testament faith, however, entails the assurance that Yahweh is committed to his promise, even when he must proclaim only death and judgment in Amos's particular context. This also entails the knowledge that Yahweh will fulfill his promise to the house of David, even though it has collapsed into a heap of rubble. This is without doubt maintained at this point entirely within the framework of Old Testament faith. Yahweh will once again say a decided "yes" to the kingdom of David, which reaches beyond the mere borders of Israel. The second addition (9:13-15) affirms this "yes" of God to his people with regard to the blessing of all of nature as well. Yahweh asserts anew that "the mountains shall drip sweet wine, and all the hills shall flow with it (with the abundance that grows on their slopes)."

This arrangement of a prophetic book, by which words of salvation follow the complete collection of the prophet's words of doom, can also be discerned in the Book of Hosea. The words of salvation cling to the divine promise that remains valid for Israel even in the midst of and beyond the calamity. Hosea 14 gives a preview of the eventual return of Israel to her God and God's renewed provision of salvation. Once again, this may stem from the later hand of a redactor. And in the Book of Micah we note that this change, from a proclamation of doom to a proclamation of salvation, can be found twice in the juxtaposition of chapters 1–5 and 6–7. It should also be noted that we find at the very end of the Book of Hosea the pensive remark of a man speaking in the style of wisdom, saying:

> Whoever is wise, let him understand these things; whoever is discerning, let him know them; for the ways of Yahweh are right, and the upright walk in them, but transgressors stumble in them. (Hos 14:9 [MT v. 10])

In both expansions, the ones who speak are the individuals who are directly affected: first, the one affected by the imminent judgments of Yahweh, the one who looks beyond the judgment into the future; then, the one who wisely meditates and ponders everything, the pensive pious one, who maintains that everything that has been said in the preceding book should not be seen as archival history but as a message that calls for proper understanding.

Macro-Structure and Ezekiel

Alongside the two-fold structure of the prophetic book, one also finds tripartite structure that likewise entails a very definite message and that can be clearly discerned in the books of Ezekiel, Isaiah, and Zephaniah, and also in the Greek version of the Book of Jeremiah. It can be seen most clearly in the Book of Ezekiel. The first large main section, Ezekiel 1–24, the "destruction section" (*pars destruens*), in which primarily words of judgment are found, is followed by a collection of words against foreign nations in chapters 25–32, directed against seven addressees. The fact that the last of these seven groups (that is, the collection of words against Egypt and the Pharaoh) is evidence of the deliberate arrangement of the entire collection. This middle section is followed by a third part, chapters 33–48, the "constructive section" (*pars construens*) which contains for the most part promises of salvation for the house of Israel, particularly in its long concluding section, chapters 40–48, the great vision of the new temple and the new land.

It is not hard to understand the message of this arrangement: the words referring to Yahweh's intervention against the nations surrounding Israel announce, together with Yahweh's judgment against Israel's neighbors, Yahweh's renewed turning to his own people.[21] The rich details found in conjunction with the words against Egypt in the Book of Ezekiel show that five of the six units where a specific date is given belong in their original state precisely to the period of Judah's final days. The order "words of doom / words of salvation" is marked also in Ezekiel's message by the date of the comprehensive judgment of Israel in 587. Thus the order "proclamation of doom / words against the nations / proclamation of salvation" suggests itself to Ezekiel by the chronological sequence of his proclamation. The Book of Ezekiel could therefore have provided the example par excellence for the arrangement of additional prophetic books, such as the books of Isaiah and Zephaniah, where this historical sequence and the distribution of proclamations of doom and of salvation cannot be demonstrated as clearly and where the material organized by the redactor, especially in the case of the Book of Isaiah, proves to be rather resistant to this kind of arrangement. As mentioned, this principle of arrangement also penetrated very late into the Greek transmission of the words of Jeremiah. The words against the nations that are found almost at the end of the Hebrew text (Jeremiah 46–51) have been inserted in connection with Jeremiah 25.

It should further be mentioned that final narrative elements were added to the books of First Isaiah (Isaiah 1–35) and Jeremiah during a later stage. In Isaiah, this unequivocally represents a borrowing from 2 Kings 18–20. Jeremiah 52 likewise betrays a proximity to the final narratives of 2 Kings. The driving force behind these two additions is not the contemporization of the message but rather a historical interest that led to expansions of the books with portions that further illumine the times and circumstances of the prophetic proclamation. In the expansion of the Book of Isaiah it is also no doubt a matter of the completion of the prophetic message with clearly legendary traditions from the Isaianic school.

Why ?

Internal Expansions and Jeremiah

While the factors just mentioned pertain to the total conception of the prophetic book, we now need to draw attention to the internal expansion of the collections of original prophetic words as a feature of subsequent history and ponder its theological significance. We are dealing with a phenomenon that can especially be found in the Book of Jeremiah but that is also not entirely absent from other prophetic books. Regarding the Book of Jeremiah (the book that is at present probably the most difficult prophetic book to interpret), it was noted as early as the turn of the century that it consists of peculiarly disparate parts. Subsequently, in 1914, Mowinckel sought to explain this lack of homogeneity by demonstrating that four entirely different collections or sources are brought together.[22] Source A contains the prophet's original words. Source B includes narratives about Jeremiah that could come from the pen of his friend Baruch. Source C is discourses of Jeremiah in deuteronomistic revision. And Source D is the so-called "Book of Consolation for Ephraim" in Jeremiah 30–31. The sayings regarding the nations in chapters 46–51 are not included in this analysis.

Mowinckel's theory has stimulated Jeremiah research in many ways and has remained a major subject of discussion until Rudolph's commentary.[23] It was Mowinckel's Source C that particularly attracted attention. What was one to think of the words of the Book of Jeremiah that reveal such an unmistakable proximity to deuteronomistic language and conceptuality? A stage of research that focused on the mere delimitation of deuteronomistically colored chapters was followed by a period of more detailed analysis of this material. This analysis now seeks to identify potential Jeremianic material within the deuteronomistically colored sections. The analysis of Winfried Thiel represents a showcase of this kind of work.[24] Thiel dealt with this subject in part of his dissertation, which treated the entire Book of Jeremiah. The question that is significant for the present discussion can by crystallized on the basis of the partial publication of Thiel's work. I would like to illustrate this in the case of Jeremiah's temple discourse, which has already been mentioned, and by its revision by deuteronomistic redaction.

Jeremiah 26, a chapter that belongs to the second part of the book, which primarily contains narratives, reports the events surrounding Jeremiah's discourse in the temple. The juxtaposition of a discourse section (chapters 1–25) and a narrative section (chapters 26–46) may possibly reveal a structural principle of the deuteronomist that does not, however, appear to contain any particularly profound theological implications. This also applies to the addition of Jeremiah 52 to chapters 1–51 in a later connection. The narrative of Jeremiah 26 indicates the commotion that was caused by Jeremiah's proclamation when he equated the coming fate of the Jerusalem temple with the fate of the temple at Shiloh. Jeremiah's life is threatened by the irate priests and prophets in the temple, who are initially also followed by the people gathered there. He only escapes with his life because the government officials intervene, forcing an orderly hearing, and because elders of the land remind others that, in the days of Hezekiah, Micah of Moresheth had likewise proclaimed:

> Thus says Yahweh of hosts, "Zion shall be plowed as a field; Jerusalem shall become a heap of ruins, and the mountain of the house a wooded height." (Jer 26:18b)

Hezekiah did not kill Micah but sought to appease Yahweh. The entire context, like the reference to the word of Micah in Mic 3:12, indicates that Jeremiah openly proclaimed the temple's destruction. Thiel's freeing of the text of Jeremiah 7 from the redactional additions of the deuteronomist reveals this apodictic proclamation. It reads:

> Do not trust in these deceptive words: "This is the temple of Yahweh, the temple of Yahweh, the temple of Yahweh." . . . How? Lying, murder, adultery, swearing falsely, burn incense to Baal—and then come and stand before me in this house and say, "We are delivered." Has this house become a den of robbers in your eyes? . . . Go now to my place that was in Shiloh . . . and see what I did to it for the wickedness of my people Israel. Therefore I will do what I did to Shiloh to this house in which you trust. (Jer 7:9-14)

This original text experienced a telling change during the time of the exile, when the deuteronomistic redaction did not merely arrange the text but also revised it. Thus the charge of false confidence in the temple was further developed by the following pronouncements:

> For if you truly amend your ways and your doings, if you truly execute justice one with another, if you do not oppress the alien, the fatherless, . . . and if you do not go after other gods to your own hurt, then I will let you dwell in this place, in the land that I gave of old to your fathers for ever. (Jer 7:5-7)

What has happened here? The apodictic prophecy of doom has been transformed into a hypothetical threat. Thiel coins the term "preaching of alternatives" for this. The people are offered an alternative to calamity. Salvation will be the reward for obedience, and calamity will be the consequence of disobedience. One may initially object that this destroys the original prophetic message and that the original apodictic word of Jeremiah is no longer heard. The historian who reads the text with the intention of reconstructing the past proclamation of Jeremiah cannot avoid this verdict. Once again, however, it would be completely wrong to close the case regarding this word and to consider the message of Jeremiah to be material for the archives.

In reality, something totally different has happened. The redactor who revised the transmitted text lived during the time of the exile. The judgment has occurred, the temple has been destroyed, the nation's sovereignty was lost. In the midst of these circumstances, the bearer of the tradition of Jeremiah's word adapts it by clinging to the divine promise (in the way of those who added the conclusions to Amos and Hosea) that God's dealings with his people are not a thing of the past, even at this point of apparent complete hopelessness.

He also knows, however, that the word of the living holy God, spoken by his prophet, is nothing but abiding truth. Thus he continues to transmit this message. At the same time, he knows that this message is not done away with by the events of the year 587 but rather has abiding validity, since it is the word of the living God. In 587, God spoke in history and proved the truth of his word. A person endangers his life if he does not heed God's righteousness. Thus he expands the transmitted discourse of Jeremiah by a direct appeal in a conditional formulation. Only when the people of Yahweh are willing to listen to Yahweh's requirements can they receive a future. This results in a peculiar parallel to Ezekiel 18, a word probably spoken by the prophet himself after the collapse of 587. This word, likewise, albeit in stronger priestly coloring, ties the possibility of "life" to the call to repentance, which needs to find concrete expression in the keeping of God's commandments.[25]

Did the deuteronomistic redactor falsify the divine word? For the historian, it is clear that he changed Jeremiah's original message. For the one who attempts to hear the divine call anew from that earlier word, it should be clear that the redactor provides Yahweh's truth with new relevance in his new circumstances. Once again, the text of the Book of Jeremiah, at this as well as at other places where the apodictic proclamation turns into the "preaching of alternatives," becomes evidence for the fact that the valid call of Yahweh to his people was maintained in a new and different situation. And no doubt whatsoever is cast on the knowledge that God is the same today as he was yesterday. The issue is listening to the prophetic message in a new day.

Apocalyptic and Isaiah

We should say a brief word regarding one final phenomenon that is evident as we consider the development from prophetic word to prophetic book. Again, we can merely illustrate the general principle, and the Book of Isaiah may serve as an example. Otto Kaiser, in his treatment of Isaiah 13–39, when considering the development of the prophetic word, initially maintained that one should distinguish between an eschatological, proto-apocalyptic, and an apocalyptic period.[26] Expectations "that reckon with a decisive turn in the destiny of Israel and of the nations without ceasing to be historically grounded are 'eschatological.' They are called 'apocalyptic' when they expect a change of people's circumstances by way of supernatural or cosmic intervention, while the connection to specific historical powers remains obscure or fanciful, or finally calculations regarding the time of the last events are made." In the majority of the Isaiah texts analyzed, one finds an intermediate layer "that pertains to the transitional stage between historical-eschatological and cosmic-apocalyptic elements."[27]

At this point the issue is not the analysis of individual texts in order to determine whether or not Kaiser's specific interpretations are supported by the text in every case. We must be content with determining the basic tendency that can doubtless be observed in several instances. This coincides with comments made by Paul D. Hanson, from a different perspective, regarding texts in Trito-Isaiah and in Deutero- and Trito-Zechariah.[28] Thus, for example, the so-called "Isaiah Apocalypse" in Isaiah 24–27 joins onto the collection of oracles against the nations in chapters 13–23. Yahweh's activity regarding the individual nations expands there to the great assize of the nations and the description of the earth-shattering doom of Israel's enemies. This is followed in context by a description of the great meal that Yahweh will prepare on his mountain for the nations, when the veil will be taken away from the faces of the nations. The collection of chapters 28–35, in turn, leads in chapters 34–35 from the wrath of Yahweh, which is described as his great day over the entire world of nations as demonstrated by the destruction of Edom, to the description of salvation, which is narrated in the clear colors of Deutero-Isaianic proclamation. Lebanon and the desert are transformed when Yahweh brings salvation to his people. The conclusion of the entire Book of Isaiah speaks expansively of the divine judgment upon all flesh and of the new heavens and the new earth that God will create for the well-being of his people. "From new moon to new moon, and from sabbath to sabbath, all flesh shall come to worship before me, says Yahweh"—while the enemies will perish in eternal fire (Isa 66:23-24). This is the final image in the Book of Isaiah. Similar things can also be seen in the postexilic Book of Joel and in the Book of Zechariah, which was treated by Hanson. They likewise conclude with a worldwide perspective of a final judgment and final salvation.

CONCLUSION

While we cannot discuss this in detail, we need to ask the principal question, which concerns the inner legitimacy and theological validity of this redaction of certain parts of prophetic books or of entire books. Traces of this can already be detected in the early prophecy of Amos regarding a day of Yahweh, a proclamation that continues through Isaiah, Zephaniah, and Ezekiel, all the way to Joel and Malachi. In this way, the prophetic word is interpreted as a phenomenon that is relevant for the whole world. In the historical Isaiah as well as in Amos, this prophetic word proclaims Yahweh's presence in the judgment of his people, addressing very concrete times and circumstances. This is certainly not merely a matter of sketching a worldwide historical framework that people can complacently acknowledge, just as Ezekiel's audience could say to him, "The vision that he sees is for many days hence, and he prophesies of times far off" (Ezek 12:27b). Rather, the apocalyptic expansion in the arrangement of the final elements of certain prophetic books seeks to show that the world in its entirety will be confronted with Yahweh's presence not on a distant day, but soon—a presence by which Yahweh, through his judgment, brings salvation to his own. This is a final unleashing of the prophetic message, which is relevant even in a new situation.

Even more apropos, we may say that it is an unleashing that comes about because of the knowledge that Yahweh will continue to accomplish a work of judgment and salvation that cannot be escaped by any realm, people, or period. However much apocalypticism may later become entangled in the thicket of calculations, in the end it is rejuvenated by the confidence that the Lord of all the world and of all of history is committed to his word, the word initially spoken by the prophets, addressing clearly demarcated circumstances in the life of the people of Israel.[29] The increasing significance of the world's confrontation with its God—which can never be addressed as a thing of the past, however much past events may reveal traces of his activity regarding his people and the world—can be revealed to us when we pay attention to the path of development from the prophetic word to the prophetic book in all of its various stages. The transformation of the divine word into a book never sent into retirement the living call of the living Lord. It is able to speak unexpectedly to a new day. God never retires.

3

The "Land" in the Prophets

The classical prophets of the pre-exilic period were the great disturbers of the peace within the world of Old Testament Israel. This was not because of any particular individual characteristics that could be attributed to them, but because they had been encountered by the reality of Israel's God.

> The lion has roared;
>   who will not fear?
> The LORD Yahweh has spoken;
>   who can but prophesy? (Amos 3:8)

Thus, everything that they say is bound up either expressly or implicitly with this address of Israel's God. That applies also to their speech about the land, which is my focus here.

AMOS

Already the earliest of the writing prophets, Amos, makes clear that Israel recognizes that it is not indigenous to its land. The land was first given to Israel in the brightness of its early history by Israel's God. As it is expressed in the words of God,

> Yet I destroyed the Amorite before them,
>   whose height was like the height of the cedars,
>   and who was as strong as the oaks;
> I destroyed his fruit above, and his roots beneath. (Amos 2:9)

Where Israel is guilty of self-confidently presuming itself to be secure behind this knowledge as a barricade of religious insurance, even though it refers to God who brought it out of the land of Egypt, there is to be heard in the mouth of God whose sovereignty extends in the same way to the nations the biting formulation:

> Are you not like the Ethiopians to me,
>   O people of Israel . . . ?
> Did I not bring up Israel from the land of Egypt,
>   and the Philistines from Caphtor
>   and the Syrians from Kir? (Amos 9:7)

At the same time, Amos knows of his God's close relationship with Israel: "You only have I known of all the families of the earth." But precisely because of this he draws the terrible consequence: "therefore I will punish you for all your iniquities" (Amos 3:2). This consequence has also to do with the land. The message of Amos entails that Israel will again be removed from the land. Because of this message he is denounced and expelled from the land by the high priest of the royal shrine at Bethel, with the observation: "the land is not able to bear all his words" (Amos 7:10). While the pre-classical prophets occasionally threatened kings and their courts with divine judgment, in the case of Amos the threat is expanded with radical intensity to the entire people: Jeroboam will die by the sword and Israel will be led into exile, "away from its land" (Amos 7:17). Addressing himself directly to the priest who wants to prohibit his speaking, Amos says, "You yourself shall die in an unclean land." As Gerhard von Rad has shown, accompanying the historical component of the gift of the land, there is the cultic assessment: the land is "Yahweh's land."[1] Life outside the land given to Israel is life away from the "pure" land—that is, the only land in which the priestly conduct of worship can be performed. Only those who are in the land are near to Yahweh, or in the realm of "life."[2]

The proclamation of Amos is based on knowledge of the legal demands of Israel's God. The debate about whether Amos has before him an already codified law, ultimately of amphictyonic origin, or whether he possesses a legal consciousness rooted in the clan, or whether he independently articulates a general moral knowledge of God's desire for justice, need not be taken up here. I am still inclined as before to believe that he was acquainted with a specific understanding of Israel's more ancient divine law.[3] In addition to general references to legal violations against the poor, he also offers concrete formulations: "They lay themselves down . . . upon garments taken in pledge . . . ; they drink the wine of those who have been fined" (Amos 2:8). These are intended to call to mind the older stipulations of the Covenant Code:

[margin handwritten note: How about a covenant?]

If you lend money to any of my people with you who is poor, you shall not be to him as a creditor, and you shall not exact interest from him. If ever you take your neighbor's garment in pledge you shall restore it to him before the sun goes down; for that is his only covering, it is his mantle for his body; in what else shall he sleep? And if he cries to me, I will hear, for I am compassionate. (Exod 22:25-27)

To practice justice and righteousness is, in sum, the legal demand of God who brought Israel into its land. That is what is to be done in Israel. The most zealous worship at the holy place in the pure land is no substitute for it:

I hate, I despise your feasts,
    and I take no delight in your solemn assemblies. (Amos 5:21)

Let justice roll down like waters,
    and righteousness like an ever-flowing stream. (Amos 5:24)

ISAIAH

His younger contemporary, Isaiah, is strongly reminiscent of Amos in his early proclamation—his attack on the cult, the wanton feasts, the women of the capital city, the violation of the rights of the underprivileged. His demand to "Seek justice, correct oppression; defend the fatherless, plead for the widow" (Isa 1:17) is addressed to the zealous activity of the cult in Jerusalem.

Isaiah's talk of the land, however, is perceptibly different from that of Amos. In the authentic words of this prophet, who speaks of the "Holy One of Israel," one hears nothing of the exodus from Egypt or the destruction of the Amorites.[4] There is no hint of the consciousness of not being indigenous to the land. His conception of the land is shaped by his familiarity with Zion as the site of God's presence. If the formerly "faithful city . . . full of justice" could be described in retrospect with the words "righteousness lodged in her" (Isa 1:21), it may be that behind the possible memory of the prosperous time of David there still echoes the pre-Israelite memory of a divinity Ṣedeq, whose name is preserved in the names of the pre-Israelite kings Melchizedek and Adonizedek.[5] For Isaiah, it is the early period of the righteous city, the city of Ṣedeq, that stands at the beginning, not the wilderness period nor the entry into the land.

Thus in the portrayal of judgment, which Isaiah proclaims no less than Amos, the destruction of the city and its surrounding territory is much more in view than the loss of land brought about by the deportation of the population. This can be seen clearly in the prophecy against Ariel, "the city where

David encamped" (Isa 29:1-8). In Isa 5:13 there is a reference to the removal of the people, which has in view, according to the details that follow, not the loss of the land but the perishing of the noble and the humble because of hunger and thirst in the process of deportation. At the center of the call narrative stands the threat of the devastation of the land.[6]

To this corresponds what Isaiah says of salvation. In passages that differ from similar passages in other pre-exilic prophets, the view can shift unexpectedly in the middle of a judgment speech to the possibility of deliverance. Beyond refining by fire, the "city of righteousness" stands once more, according to Isa 1:26. He announces to the Philistine ambassadors, whose land rejoices in the hope of freedom at the death of the Assyrian king, a new invasion of destructive power from the North, but adds: "What will one answer the messengers of the nation? 'Yahweh has founded Zion, and in her the afflicted of his people find refuge'" (Isa 14:32).[7] The enigmatic prophecy of salvation in Isa 28:16-17 points in the same direction. In the midst of a threat against those in Jerusalem who consider themselves secure in their policy of alliance it states: "See! I am placing on Zion a foundation stone, a *bohan* stone, a precious foundation-cornerstone. One who believes must not run in fear" (author's trans.). This is the reconstruction of Zion. But it is true of this new structure that "I will make justice the line, and righteousness the plummet."[8] In Ezekiel as in Deutero-Isaiah this expectation of a new Zion as the site of God's presence is combined in a new synthesis with the expectation of a new exodus (Ezek 20:32-38; Isa 52:7-10). Here we must mention again the Ariel prophecy where, after Ariel is lowered into the deepest dust, there is a sudden divine turn toward precisely this place, and the multitude of the enemy is scattered like chaff.[9]

"Justice and righteousness"—that was also the norm on which Amos saw his people run aground. In the case of Isaiah it can now be seen how this norm was immediately related to ownership of land. In Isa 5:8 he says,

> Ah, you who join house to house,
>   who add field to field,
> until there is room for no one but you,
>   and you are left to live alone in the midst of the land! [NRSV]

Behind this cry stands a distinctive knowledge of the property laws at work in Israel. Every Israelite is entitled to his particular share of the land. In the jubilee legislation of Leviticus 25, which is probably later, the attempt is made in the "year of release" to reinstate the arrangement that was distorted in the intervening years. In Isaiah's day this distribution of the land in accordance with the will of God was being grossly violated by the accumulation of landed estates (however the development of this state of affairs should be explained historically).[10]

MICAH

It is remarkable that Isaiah's contemporary Micah, coming from Moresheth in the territory of Judah, attacks in his prophecy precisely the same distortion in land distribution:

> Alas for those who devise wickedness
> and work evil deeds on their beds!
> When the morning dawns, they perform it,
> because it is in their power.
> They covet fields, and seize them;
> houses, and take them away;
> they oppress householder and house,
> people and their inheritance. (Mic 2:1-2, NRSV)

The key word *naḥalah* (inheritance), which also appears with striking frequency in the deuteronomic sphere, shows in what the problem consists: destruction of the beneficial divine distribution of the land, attention to which is paid by Naboth, who refuses to sell the portion that belongs to his family. "Yahweh forbid that I should give you the inheritance of my fathers" (1 Kgs 21:3).

Isaiah and Micah attack unjust dealings in property. It is then instructive to note how differently the two of them speak of the divine response of punishment. In Isa 5:9-10 there is first the destruction of the houses of the great landowners who perpetrated the injustice. Next appears the refusal of the land to provide an adequate harvest. In the case of Micah the allusion to the division of the land within the "congregation of Yahweh" (*qhl Yhwh*) is more concrete. Unfortunately, the text in Mic 2:4-5 is not intact. Albrecht Alt finds here a new redistribution of the land (*anadasmos gēs*), in which the landowners no longer have anyone who can cast the measuring line to determine an allotment for them, while the oppressed will again receive their lost portion.[11] Hans Walter Wolff, on the other hand, understands the statement more generally to mean that "whoever has been dispossessed of his land can no longer expect his lost property to be returned in a future sacral distribution of the land."[12] The present text, which he regards as containing secondary expansions, refers in any case to the exile that deprives the entire people of the land.

HOSEA

If with Isaiah the emphasis falls on Jerusalem and the complete absence in Israel's history of a basis for possession of the land, then Hosea, the only prophet actually from the northern kingdom, stands most clearly in opposition to this view. In his prophecy there is no mention of Jerusalem-Zion. None of the sanctuaries of the northern kingdom mentioned by him has a central status corresponding to that of Jerusalem for Isaiah. Instead, the traditions of Egyptian origin, wandering in the wilderness and Israel's conquest emerge as the most important. Knowledge of the land as God's gift receives from Hosea a fundamentally critical significance. Admittedly one does not recognize in his words the social demand for just property laws observed in Isaiah and Micah. The social component of prophetic criticism is not completely lacking in Hosea, but it does recede perceptibly. On the other hand, emphasis falls on the polemic against the common belief that the gifts of the land—grain, wine, and oil—are from the local Baals, or at least from Yahweh worshiped in a baal-ized form. For that reason Hosea offers a passionate indictment of the priests in chapter 4. They were supposed to be the guardians of genuine knowledge of Israel's God. To the contrary, they had led the nation into vegetation worship with its form of cultic prostitution.

> The men themselves go aside with whores,
>   and sacrifice with temple prostitutes,
> thus a people without understanding comes to ruin. (Hos 4:14, NRSV)

The significance of the land comes to light not only in this critique, however. It leads to the formulation of a specific theology of history, encompassing the past and the future, which had its effect on Jeremiah and was radically expanded by Ezekiel. Thus Hosea speaks of the call of Israel out of Egypt, the bright period of wandering through the arid wilderness, and the fall into sin, which occurred in the entry into the rich and fertile land.

> Like grapes in the wilderness,
>   I found Israel.
> Like the first fruit on the fig tree . . .
>   I saw your ancestors.
> But they came to Baal-peor,
>   and consecrated themselves to Baal,
>   and became detestable like the thing they loved [as their lover?].
> (Hos 9:10, NRSV)

It was I who knew you in the wilderness,
>   in the land of drought;
But when they had fed to the full,
>   they were filled,
>   and their heart was lifted up;
>   therefore they forgot me. (Hos 13:5-6)

Corresponding to this early history rooted in Egypt is the history of judgment into which God will lead his people. He brings them back precisely to the beginning: "they shall return to Egypt" (Hos 8:13; 9:3). Considering the immediate threat of Assyria, which already in Hosea's day had broken into Israel's neighboring territory, the Assyrians are suited to this purpose.

They shall not remain in the land of Yahweh;
>   but Ephraim shall return to Egypt,
>   and in Assyria they shall eat unclean food. (Hos 9:4)

This is literally "those who eat shall make themselves unclean; see Amos 7:17. Assyria can be seen as the climax of the threat. If the division of the text in 9:6 is correct, it reads: "For behold, they are going to Assyria; Egypt shall gather them, Memphis shall bury them" (see also Hosea 11). But then Hosea can also simply speak of God's judgment forcing his people back into the wilderness period:

I, Yahweh, am your God
>   from the land of Egypt;
I will again make you dwell in tents,
>   as in the days of the feast [of tabernacles?] (Hos 12:9; MT 12:10)[13]

But God's intention to judge is most completely interwoven with his intention to be gracious in Hos 2:14-15a [MT 2:16-17a]:

Therefore, behold, I will allure her,
>   and bring her into the wilderness,
>   and speak tenderly to her.
And there I will give her her vineyards,
>   and make the Valley of Achor a door of hope.

The land with its precious produce will again be given to a people returned to its God. Thus the return of the land is also part of the expectation of salvation by the prophet who himself may have experienced the terrible catastrophe of Israel/Ephraim under the attack of Assyria.

JEREMIAH

Jeremiah and Ezekiel, whose reference to the land will be examined further, belong to the period of the late seventh and early sixth centuries. In the east, the Babylonians had displaced the Assyrians. Of the "two houses of Israel" of which Isaiah spoke (Isa 8:14), the smaller—Judah, which now applied the designation of God's people, Israel, to itself—still existed and preserved the treasures of the Jerusalem temple and the Davidic dynasty.[14] As a result of the politics of the reform-minded king Josiah, who took over the political vacuum left in the province of Samaria when Assyria's power was broken, the hope for reunification flamed anew. Traces of this hope can be recognized in Jeremiah and Ezekiel (Jer 3:6-25; 30–31; Ezek 37:15-28).

Jeremiah's pronouncements about the land have been more precisely investigated by Peter Diepold in *Israels Land*.[15] It must be recognized that the Book of Jeremiah stands firmly in the deuteronomistic stream of tradition and has been expanded and revised by that tradition. Winfried Thiel, whose analysis Diepold takes over, has pursued this problem.[16] Here, where it is a matter of the prophet's stance toward the land, I can restrict myself to those pronouncements that in all likelihood stem from Jeremiah himself.

With respect to his theology of history and its bearing on his evaluation of the possession of the land, Jeremiah is dependent upon Hosea, as has already been mentioned. Though not with the emphasis of Hosea, he speaks of deliverance from Egypt (Jer 2:6) and, much more colorfully, of the divine guidance through the wilderness, "in a land of deserts and pits, in a land of drought and deep darkness, in a land that none passes through, where no man dwells," into "a plentiful land, to enjoy its fruits and its good things" (2:7a). As in Hosea the time when "you followed me in the wilderness, in a land not sown" is seen as the shining period of the first "love as a bride" (2:2), which is then followed in the land by the time of unfaithfulness: "But when you came in you defiled my land, and made my heritage an abomination" (2:7b). "My land" it is called here in the mouth of God. The land is often spoken of in precisely this personal way (Diepold). It is pictured in expressions of highest praise: a desirable land, a "heritage most beauteous of all nations," as it is expressly designated in 3:19—a designation that recurs in Ezek 20:6, and is used as a secret code name for the land in Daniel (Dan 8:9; 11:16, 41, 45). Yahweh designates his land as "my heritage." The frequent use of the designation "my heritage" already marks it as characteristic of Jeremiah's speech. And it is in the use of this designation to refer almost indistinguishably to the land and to the people that the close connection between this, God's land, and the people called by God is recognized. In the cultic defilement of God's land, Israel encroaches upon God's own possession and compels him to pass judgment on people and land.

I have forsaken my house,
  I have abandoned my heritage;
I have given the beloved of my soul
  into the hands of her enemies.
My heritage has become to me—
  like a lion in the forest,
she has lifted up her voice against me;
  therefore I hate her.

. . . .

Many shepherds have destroyed my vineyard,
  they have trampled down my portion.

. . . .

The whole land is made desolate. (Jer 12:7-8, 10, 11b)

In his view of the future Jeremiah no longer stands in the footsteps of Hosea. In his case nothing can be seen of a new leading into the wilderness or a return to Egypt from which Israel will again come into possession of its land. The land will suffer devastation. Nebuchadnezzar, called by God "my servant," is summoned to execute punishment. The nation is to acknowledge him, so long as God gives him power. To the deportees in Babylon Jeremiah writes that they are to build houses there and live in them, to plant gardens and eat their fruit, to take wives and bear sons and daughters, to give their sons wives and their daughters husbands, who will then themselves bear children so that they will multiply and not become fewer. They are to seek the welfare of the city [Greek: "of the land"] to which they have been deported, and to pray for it, "for in its welfare you will find your welfare" (Jer 29:7). Only in a completely hidden way can the prospect of a further future in the land be recognized in that peculiar, yet unmistakably authentic episode in which Jeremiah, in the midst of the invasion of Jerusalem at the command of his God buys a field outside Anathoth that is already occupied by the enemy and carefully concludes the purchase legally with a public and private bill of sale. "Houses and fields will again be bought in this land" (Jer 32:15). The word concerning a seventy-year period of punishment (Jer 25:11-12; 29:10) cannot convincingly be denied Jeremiah. Is the reluctance of Jeremiah to abandon the land for Egypt, together with an anxious group of those left behind following the murder of Gedaliah, also to be understood on the basis of that certainty that there would once again be life in the devastated land? According to the symbolic interpretation of the two baskets of figs in Jeremiah 24, of course, the hope for the future lies in the first instance with those who suffer judgment in exile. The great promise of the new covenant in Jer 31:31-34, which speaks of God's gift of a new posture toward the Torah but says nothing of the possession of the land, is probably not to be attributed to Jeremiah. To draw conclusions about Jeremiah's hope for the future after 587 B.C.E. on the basis of those parts of the so-called "Book of Consolation for Ephraim," which are currently held to be authentic, is (contra Diepold) hardly advisable.

EZEKIEL

In the book of the somewhat younger priestly prophet Ezekiel, already deported in 597, it is first of all linguistically striking that alongside the infrequent designation "land of Israel" (*'ereṣ yiśra'el*) is found the more frequent designation "earth/territory of Israel" (*'admat yiśra'el*). Both expressions refer to the remainder of Israel in Judah under the theologically important, overarching name Israel. Bernard Keller has undertaken the attempt to discern a conscious differentiation in this duality.

> *'Erets* Israel is formerly the combination of *'adamah,* the earth; of the people and of the divine presence; the glory of YHWH. *'Admat* Israel is simply the earth that bears the mark of the absence of the people and of the glory.[17]

The second part of the book speaks of the return of the people and of the glory of Yahweh. "*'Admat* Israel gives way to the *'ereṣ* Israel, the reunion of earth, of the people, and of the divine presence."[18] The differentiation, however, cannot be sustained upon closer examination.[19] No theological conclusions can be drawn from the dual formulation. The specifically Ezekielian designation is *'admat yiśra'el.*

Ezekiel lived in the time of the great crisis, during which parts of the population of Judah were taken into Babylonian exile in two or, according to Jer 52:28-30, three groups. Among the surrounding nations the saying dishonoring the God of Israel circulated: These are the people of Yahweh, and yet they had to go out of his land" (Ezek 36:20). Speaking directly to the land, understood by Jeremiah in almost human terms, the enemies say, "You devour people, and you bereave your nation of children" (Ezek 36:13). This formulation is strikingly similar to the evil report the spies brought back following their reconnaissance of the land, a report that brought punishment upon the entire nation: "The land, through which we have gone, to spy it out, is a land that devours its inhabitants" (Num 13:32).

In his severely accusatory proclamation prior to 587 B.C.E., Ezekiel had attributed the cause for the punishment not to the land but to the nation Israel and to Jerusalem. In both of the historical-theological summaries in Ezekiel 16 and 23, in which Jerusalem and then the two kingdoms of Israel are pictured as abandoned women, wanton from the beginning (according to Ezekiel 23, already in Egypt), their histories unfolded with expansive imagery, neither the land nor the conquest of the land is mentioned. Canaanizing sexual cults (in Hosea's sense) and political alliances (in Isaiah's sense) are here the grounds for the consequent judgment in 587, which provoked ridicule from neighbors and vilification of the land from elements of the population. But in Ezekiel's words, discussion of possession of the land now commences in new ways.

From other reports we know that the neighboring Edomites participated in the destruction of Jerusalem. They were themselves perhaps forced from the East by the pressure from Nabatean groups, and thrust into the land from the South. In Ezek 35:10 the undisguised claim to the land in the mouth of the Edomites is reported: "These two nations and these two countries shall be mine, and we will take possession of them," and the text adds, "although Yahweh was there." And in a prophecy of salvation directed to the mountains of Israel, which corresponds to a prophecy of judgment against the same addressees in Ezekiel 6 and renders it ineffective, the prophet says: "But you, O mountains of Israel, shall shoot forth your branches, and yield your fruit to my people Israel; for they will soon come home" (Ezek 36:8). For the sake of his own honor, the God of Israel remains true to his promises. This is developed in the historical-theological speech in Ezekiel 20, which is composed without use of imagery.

> On the day when I chose Israel, I swore to the seed of the house of Jacob, making myself known to them in the land of Egypt, I swore to them, saying, I am Yahweh your God. On that day I swore to them that I would bring them out of the land of Egypt into a land that I had searched out for them, a land flowing with milk and honey, the most glorious of all lands. (Ezek 20:5-6)

The land has been promised, not to Edom, but to Israel. The divine message of the prophet maintains persistently, whether the stiff-necked rebelliousness of the people is portrayed for the first time in Egypt and then also in the wilderness or is told in an unprecedented redescription of history, that already in the wilderness period God had decided to scatter his people among the "lands." But after the catastrophe, the vision of the valley of dry bones proclaims God's message: "Behold, I will open your graves, and raise you from your graves [as my people] in the land of Israel" (Ezek 37:12).[20] The expansion in 20:32ff., coming probably after 587 B.C.E., and taking up in revised form Hosea 2, shows how the nation will be led out in a new exodus from the nations into "the wilderness of the peoples" (Ezek 20:35). In a new "face-to-face" encounter God will carry out the division. The rebels will not be permitted to enter the land again, but the rest will bring offerings pleasing to God "on the mountain height of Israel" (again an Ezekielian expression). Contrary to Hosea 2, there is no mention of the renewed bestowal of vineyards. That is the decision of Israel's God over against any other nation that would attempt to lay claim to possession of the land.

The division in the wilderness, however, makes clear that, with reference to possession of the land, new divisions are announced that cut through the midst of the nation itself. More can be seen of this in other parts of Ezekiel. The pericope in Ezek 11:14-21 speaks to the situation between 597 and 587 B.C.E., however one judges the literary-critical problems.[21] Here something is heard from those remaining in Jerusalem about the deportees: "They have gone far from Yahweh; to us this land is given for a possession" (Ezek 11:14). This claim to possession is answered with a word from God, which promises that the deportees will return and will be given a new heart and a new spirit, "that they may walk in my statutes and keep my ordinances" (Ezek 11:20).

This is formulated even more sharply against those remaining in the land after 587: "Son of man, the inhabitants of these waste places in the land of Israel keep saying, 'Abraham was only one man, yet he got possession of the land; but we are many; the land is surely given us to possess'" (Ezek 33:24). In response to this apparently pious recourse to the ancient promise of land to the patriarch Abraham, which here appears for the first time among the writing prophets (Isa 29:22; Mic 7:20; Jer 33:26 belong to post-exilic expansions) follows the blunt repudiation:

> Thus says the LORD Yahweh: You eat flesh with the blood, and lift up your eyes to your idols, and shed blood; shall you then possess the land? You resort to the sword, you commit abominations and each of you defiles his neighbor's wife; shall you then possess the land? (Ezek 33:25-26)

Here the point is developed polemically that possession of the land and disobedience toward God's commandment are mutually exclusive. In the concrete unfolding of the commandment we recognize the priest, who has the ritual prescriptions for purity before him. But there are also reminders of Amos: the shedding of blood and social injustice; and of Isaiah: reliance on their own strong arm, and trust in power.

Concluding the Book of Ezekiel is the great vision of the new temple to be erected according to the appropriate measurements. The vision is dated in the twenty-fifth year,[22] and it includes a sketch of a new distribution of the land with precise geographical limits bounded by the Jordan. Following the settlement of the land comes the new distribution, according to specific allotments

(Ezek 47:13-14)—a new Joshua event. The text displays a remarkable mixture of archaizing elements joined to earlier traditions and the bold placement of new accents. The use of the old tribal system is archaizing. In the arrangement of tribal territories, every tribe (Joseph is spread across Manasseh and Ephraim) receives a strip of land of equal size. This arrangement takes up old geographical traditions but in places revises them radically. It is expressly prescribed that also the resident aliens (*gerim*) shall be given the right of residence and property among the respective tribal territories (Ezek 47:22-23).

Approximately in the middle (the distribution of seven tribes in the North and five in the South is further reminiscent of the earlier reality of the northern tribes' greater importance) there lies a thirteenth strip of land, proportioned as the rest, which is named *terumah* ("lifted up"), the term used of what is offered in sacrifices. The land is lifted up as a sacrifice offered to God. At its two outer boundaries lies the land of the prince. At the center is the region containing the temple, in land reserved for the priests. North of it is the region of the Levites, and south of it is the region for the city. The divine instruction, which stands over everything as Torah, is not to be ignored: the sharp separation of the most holy, in which Yahweh dwells, from that which is less holy, and the latter from that which is profane. In addition, there is the appropriate distribution of the profane. But all of it is distinguished by that which is "lifted up" in the midst of it, the offering through which the giver of the land is honored.

That is how the attempt is made in this utopian sketch to fashion the land of Israel obediently in relation to the concrete geographical boundaries previously set out. There is no possession of the land without attention to the just arrangement of it, which gives honor to the Lord of the land and provides to every part of the nation including the *gerim* living in the land, its proper portion.

I may be permitted to conclude by citing the observation of Moses Hess from the nineteenth century, an observation, which—using different terms—comes particularly close to the prophetic view. He says,

> The first commandment of God that he has implanted in our hearts as the creator of all the races, the source and basic principle of all the others that have fallen to the lot of our people, is that we are ourselves to practise the law that we are commissioned to teach the other historical peoples. The greatest punishment that has been inflicted on us for deviating from the path traced out for us by divine providence, that which has always oppressed our people the most, is that, since we have lost the land (*la terre*), we can no longer serve God as a nation through institutions that cannot be continued and developed in our present exile, since they presuppose a society founded in the land of our ancestors. Yes, it is the land (*la terre*) that we lack, in order to practise our religion.[23]

4

Visionary Experience in Jeremiah

INTRODUCTION

To appreciate Jeremiah's prophetic experience it is essential to keep in mind the auditory element that is a particularly important feature of his prophecies. This is to be found not only in the introductory formulas of the passages shaped according to a deuteronomistic understanding (Mowinckel's "Source C," differently presented by Thiel; see also Wildberger): Jer 7:1; 11:1; 18:1; etc.[1] In addition, the account of Jeremiah's call and the collection of Jeremiah's own early oracles (chapters 2–6) stand under the rubric of a personally shaped formula for the coming of God's word (*Wortereignisformel*; Jer 1:4; 2:1).[2]

In a similar way, the coming of God's word is also significant in the narrative sections of the book (Mowinckel's "Source B," differently presented by Wanke).[3] Here it is stressed that Yahweh's word to Jeremiah did not always come immediately. Jeremiah 28 and 42 tell how the prophet was in acutely oppressive situations in which he had to speak directly and yet wait in obedience for the word of God. According to chapter 28, his message that Judah would have to bear the yoke of the king of Babylon appeared to be negated by the contrary preaching by Hananiah of an apparently certain message supported by an impressive act of symbolism. He left the scene in silence (28:11b), but later as a result of the reception of a new word, he announced God's message to Hananiah that his death was imminent as divine judgment for his disobedient preaching. In the "Passion narrative," chapter 42 sketches the situation after the murder of Gedaliah.[4] In fear of Babylonian revenge the survivors wanted to flee to Egypt but were unwilling to do this without a divine decree. Jeremiah waited ten days in a situation full of anxiety until the word came to him anew, which he then announced (42:7).

56

This impression persists even for the most distinctively personal words, which were probably recorded by the prophet himself (Mowinckel's "Source A").[5] In his "Confessions,"[6] he describes his experience of the reception of the word in the midst of his bitter complaint and its importance for him:

> Your words were found, and I ate them,
>> and your word became to me a joy,
>> and the delight of my heart,
> For I am called by your name. (Jer 15:16)

Corresponding to this is his polemic against frivolous prophetic proclamation according to which human dreams can be equated with the word of God:

> Let the prophet who has a dream tell the dream, but let him who has my word speak my word faithfully. What has straw in common with wheat? says Yahweh. Is not my word like fire, says Yahweh, and like a hammer which breaks the rock in pieces? (Jer 23:28-29)

Already in those passages from the early period,[7] which are structured in a form comparable to that of the "Confessions" and speak of the coming of a "foe from the North," it is possible to trace how the prophet is overwhelmed by the divine proclamation. Even physical convulsions are implied. He knows that the divine word repeated by him has itself the power to kindle a fire: "Behold, I am making (*notēn*) my words in your mouth a fire, and this people wood, and fire shall devour them" (Jer 5:14).

In the light of this passage the possibility cannot be excluded that the one feature of the call narrative that goes beyond mere audition—"Then Yahweh put forth his hand and touched my mouth; and Yahweh said to me, 'Behold, I have put (*natattî*) my words in your mouth" (1:9)—was from the first a constituent element in the narrative. In his analysis of Jer 1:4-10, Thiel has rightly drawn attention to the related statement of Deut 18:18.[8] Here Yahweh promises Moses: "I will raise up for them a prophet like you from among their brethren; and I will put (*wenatattî*) my words in his mouth." But Thiel's conclusion is not convincing. He argues that there is a "somewhat abrupt transition from a mere audition to a previously unimplied account of a vision because the specific words of introduction to the vision itself are lacking here (contrast Ezek 2:9).[9] On the other hand, it is inadequate to refer only to an "impression of feeling" (*Gefühlseindruck*), as Seierstad does.[10] Jeremiah is aware of the way in which his lips have actually been touched. References to the "hand of Yahweh" in the prophetic experience are found not only in Jeremiah (Jer 15:17, in the context of a "Confession"), but also in Isaiah (Isa 8:11), and especially in

Ezekiel. In this Ezekiel took over speech forms characteristic of the pre-classical prophets.[11]

AUDITION AND VISION

Considerations of this kind make it probable that Jeremiah's bewilderment when confronted by the word of Yahweh is not adequately described as an "auditory experience." The hammer that breaks the rock in pieces, the fire that is kindled through the prophet against the people, the touching of his mouth by Yahweh at the time of the commissioning with the prophetic message, imply an experience that seized the prophet totally in all his different senses.

> My heat is broken within me,
>   all my bones shake;
> I am like a drunken man,
>   like a man overcome by wine,
> Because of Yahweh
>   and because of his holy words. (Jer 23:9)

When Jeremiah describes in his "Confessions" how he has attempted to resist the necessity of proclaiming words that bore oppressively upon him, "If I say, 'I will not mention him, or speak any more in his name,'" he had to admit, "there is in my heart as it were a burning fire shut up in my bones, and I am weary with holding it in, and I cannot" (Jer 20:9). The coming of God's word completely shatters him and its effects go far beyond auditory experience.

It is therefore not surprising that, in one of the most impassioned of the prophet's oracles from his early preaching relating to the announcement of the foe from the North, reference is also made to the bewilderment of the prophet at the vision he experiences. To the auditory affliction of the prophet, to which the words "Violence and destruction" (Jer 20:8) must refer, there is added a visual distress, which has the effect of seeming to shatter the whole of his bodily sensation:

> My anguish, my anguish! I writhe in pain!
>   Oh, the walls of my heart!
> My heart is beating wildly;
>   I cannot keep silent;
> For I hear the sound of the trumpet,
>   the alarm of war.
> Disaster upon disaster is summoned,
> [or: *Disaster follows hard on disaster?*]

the whole land is laid waste.
Suddenly my tents are destroyed,
   my curtains in a moment.
How long must I see the standard,
   and hear the sound of the trumpet? (Jer 4:19-21)

Here it is not simply words that the prophet articulates; the reality of war breaks in upon all his senses. His ears actually hear the trumpet blast and the battle cries; his eyes actually see the war standards raised. In the liturgy for a time of drought (Jer 14:1-22), there is an extract going back to Jeremiah himself, which incorporates a comparable terrifying vision:

Let my eyes run down with tears night and day,
   and let them not cease,
For the virgin[?] daughter of my people is smitten with a great wound,
   with a very grievous blow.
If I go out into the field,
   behold those slain by the sword!
And if I enter the city,
   behold, the diseases of famine! (Jer 14:17aβ-18a)

In vision the prophet perceives the impending disaster, which he must proclaim to the people.[12] In the most profound personal bewilderment he announces it and writhes with pain on account of what he sees. Thus the prophet who is characterized particularly as one who receives God's word is appropriately also called a "seer."[13]

COMPARISON TO EZEKIEL

It is naturally to be expected from this that among the words in the Jeremiah tradition there should also be found specific accounts of the visions he experienced, as is also the case with his slightly younger contemporary Ezekiel. In Ezekiel it is even more clearly the case than in Jeremiah that the great majority of the utterances of the prophet employ the formula for the coming of God's word in the first person. The theology of the coming of God's word is more obvious in Ezekiel than in any other prophetic book. There are fifty passages with the formula "the word of Yahweh" (*debar Yahweh*) in Ezekiel as against thirty in Jeremiah.[14] But interspersed between these *debar Yahweh* passages there is also to be found material of a visionary kind, arranged in four or perhaps five major units: Ezek 1:1—3:15; 8–11; 37:1-14; 40–48 (less certainly, 3:16-21, 22ff.). These visions are structured on a grand scale in a manner

comparable to the purely verbal proclamations of Ezekiel (chap. 7: the Day of
Yahweh; chap. 16: the faithless woman; chap. 23: the two faithless women;
chap. 27: Tyre's ship of state; chap. 34: the shepherds of Israel; etc.). In these
visions the formula for the coming of God's word is missing.[15] The specific
structure of the visionary description is to be found in the introductory formula, which is literally: "I looked, and lo!" In each case it is introduced by a
more precise description of the character of the visionary act by the use of the
prophetic theolegoumena of the "hand" or "spirit" of Yahweh. For the most
part the visions are dated, but in 37:1 the date appears to have been lost.

In the Book of Jeremiah there are, in fact, three reports of visions. These
constitute, first, the two visions of 1:11-15(16), secondly, the unit 4:23-26, and
finally, chap. 24, which in its present form is unmistakably deuteronomistic. It
is on these three passages that we shall concentrate in what follows.

THE VISION IN JEREMIAH 4:23-26

So far as redaction is concerned, Jer 4:23-26 is attached, without any transition
or distinctive introduction, to words that enable us to perceive the whole
drama of the invasion of the "foe from the North" (Jer 4:11-14, 15-18), which lead
into the anguished cry of distress that reveals the personal bewilderment of
the prophet (4:19-21, discussed above). As justification for the judgment that is
about to occur, an oracle is added in 4:22, which, in terms reminiscent of Isa
1:3, depicts the folly of the people in their lack of knowledge as the cause of the
strange judgment. The visionary oracle, 4:23-26, is then followed by a
sequence with a new introduction by means of the messenger formula (4:27-
28). Verse 28 is a variant on the pronouncement in Amos 1:2 concerning the
mourning of the land, combined here also with the threat that the skies will be
made black. The preceding statement in v. 27b that Yahweh will not bring
about a complete annihilation corresponds to the similar passages in 5:10 and
5:18 and is to be understood as a mitigating gloss from the hand of a later editor; alternatively, the negative might be deleted as not original,[16] or understood as a nominal form.[17] Verse 28a, however, should be accepted as original.
The section 4:29-31 reverts to the drama of the picture of the enemy breaking
in, and v. 31 reveals the deep feeling of vulnerability on the part of the prophet
as he describes what he has heard:

> For I heard a cry as of a woman in travail,
>> (a cry of) anguish as of one bringing forth her first child,
> the cry of the daughter of Zion gasping for breath,
>> stretching out her hands,
> "Woe is me! I am fainting before murderers."

Between these passages there now stands 4:23-26, the unity of which is achieved by the repetition of the stereotyped sequence, "I looked . . . and lo!" as a means of presenting the visionary experience:

> looked on the earth, and lo, it was waste and void;
>> and (I looked) to the heavens, and they had no light.
> I looked on the mountains, and lo, they were quaking,
>> and all the hills moved to and fro.
> I looked, and lo, there was no man,
>> and all the birds of the air had fled.
> I looked, and lo, the fruitful land was a desert,
>> and all its cities were laid in ruins
>> before Yahweh, before his fierce anger.

In this description there are no specific elements associated with the description of the enemy invasion of the land of Judah. The direct drama of the words of 4:11-14, 15-18, 19-21 and 29-31 is not to be traced here. There is no cry of distress to betray the personal bewilderment of the prophet. In its place comes a deathly silence. Instead of the limited horizons of Judah and Jerusalem, which can be recognized as underlying the surrounding passages, the scene is here a universal one: earth/heavens, mountains/hills, birds of the air, (fruitful lands with) orchards, lands containing cities. It is a more than human emptying, darkening, laying waste—it is complete and universal.

In his discussion of this passage, Fishbane has drawn attention to its similarities with the depiction of creation in Genesis 1.[18] With minor variations in the sequence he finds in this passage the use of the same elements as in Genesis:

Pre-creation	"waste and void" (*tohû wabohû*)
first day	light
second day	the heavens
third day	the earth, mountains and hills/the earth, dry land
fourth day	the heavenly bodies (no equivalent in Jeremiah 4)
fifth day	birds
sixth day	humanity

In the equivalent of the passage relating to the Sabbath day Jeremiah speaks of God's "fierce anger," in which Fishbane sees a distant allusion to the regular return in the Babylonian hemerologies of an *ūm ibbu* (or *ūmu limnu*), a day of ill omen. It is advisable to remain cautious about the acceptance of a "pattern," especially where we are dealing with a concluding statement about Yahweh's anger; but it is not to be denied that Jer 4:23-26 does indeed speak of the anger of Yahweh in the context of allusions to creation. This perception led Friedrich Giesebrecht,[19] following earlier scholars, to state that he could not suppress his doubts about the genuineness of 4:23-26. Similarly, Paul Volz rejected these verses,[20] which he regarded as speaking the language of apocalyptic and characterized with the keyword "world catastrophe," from the range of the genuine words of Jeremiah, since, he maintained, Jeremiah nowhere speaks of a great dramatic catastrophe, of the Day of Yahweh, or of the break up of the established world. In contrast to this, Bernhard Duhm had already stated:

> The vision has a symbolic character; chaos signifies the devastation brought about by the Scythians. So-called second sight often shows a tendency of this kind. As to the interpretation of one recent scholar, who translates the perfect tenses with present tenses and regards the poem as not genuine, one can only say that he has not understood it, and that further words are unnecessary.[21]

In view of these diverse assessments of the authenticity of the vision what judgment can be offered?

In redaction-critical terms, Jer 4:23-26 stands at the conclusion of a collection of oracles. The new introduction by means of the messenger formula marks 4:27 as the beginning of a new sequence. At the beginning of this sequence—whatever decision is taken about v. 27b—there occurs in v. 28 a statement that once again concentrates on the mourning of the earth and the darkening of the heavens; this is followed in 4:29-31 by a fresh series of threats relating to the "foe from the North." The conclusion (4:23-26) of the preceding redactional unit, which was introduced at 4:5, had the function of a final climax of the words of threat that were based on the anger of Yahweh.

In form-critical terms, the passage consists of a four-times repeated and monotonous "I looked . . . and lo!" Such repetitions are not in any way unusual in Jeremiah. Not only is there the mocking threefold repetition of "I have dreamed" in the polemical quotation of the prophets' words (23:25-26, emended text), but also the equally polemical threefold repetition of "the temple of Yahweh" in the temple speech (7:4). Another threefold repetition of words from the prophet's own mouth is contained in 23:30-32: "Behold, I am against the prophets." If 15:2 stems from a genuinely Jeremianic setting,[22] this would be a fourfold enumeration of the plagues of judgment, a form that is particularly characteristic of Ezekiel as a means of expressing completeness.[23] The present passage could then also be grouped with the preceding list.

Nevertheless, it is clear that the four "I looked . . . and lo!" passages are not in all respects parallel to one another. In 4:23-24 the verb "I looked" is followed by an accusative (preceded by *'et* in v. 23 only) denoting the area encompassed by the prophet's vision; this accusative is lacking in vv. 25-26, and the content of the vision is introduced directly by "lo!" (*hinnēh*): in v. 25, no men and no birds of the air; in v. 26, the desolation of the fruitful land and the ruin of cities. The description of destruction is much more direct in vv. 25-26 than in vv. 23-24. In vv. 25-26 there is no longer any mention of a specific place toward which the seer looks, but instead the great void of heaven and earth is set before him directly, with the destruction of the fruitful land and of all human habitation before his very eyes.

It is particularly important to bear in mind that the two pairs of sentences with their broadly parallel form reach their climax in the closing phrase, which is not part of the formal structure, v. 26bαβ: "before Yahweh, before his fierce anger." Just as the four "I looked" sentences (beginning with *ra'îtî-*) have been juxtaposed in an asyndetic construction, so this final announcement consists formally of two elements joined asyndetically, in which the second element functions as an explanation of the significance of the first. This interpretive closing phrase unmistakably recalls the close of the first unit within the redactional section 4:5-26, that is 4:8. The theme of the dramatic and vivid oracle in that passage was the summons to flight before the invading enemy, a retreat into the fortified cities, into Zion itself. Yahweh himself (at this point the threatening words of the Yahweh speech are presented in first-person forms) is bringing destruction from the north, destruction through a lion that has broken out of its thicket, made the land a waste place and emptied the cities of their inhabitants. So the speech demands that the people should break into laments and wailing as a result of what is taking place. To this is added a motif that is reminiscent of the repeated refrain of the poem found in Isa 9:8—10:4 [MT 9:7—10:4]: "For all this his anger is not turned away," found here in the form "for the fierce anger of Yahweh has not turned back from us." What is found here in 4:8, expressed by means of a double use of the construct state, emerges in 4:26 as the asyndetically expressed "before Yahweh, before his fierce anger," and so supplies the justification for the vision. The whole formula, with minor variants, is characteristic of Jeremiah: compare 12:13, as well as secondary passages such as 25:37-38; 30:24; 51:45; see also 49:37. Its prototype may be Hos 11:9, and in other pre-exilic prophetic collections it is found in Nah 1:6; Zeph 2:2; 3:8.

These redaction- and form-critical observations, as well as the wordlinks in the final phrase of the vision, make it not improbable that we are dealing in 4:23-26 with a genuine vision of Jeremiah himself. Its distinctiveness lies in the fact that it envisages the irruption of the fierce anger of Yahweh first of all in cosmic dimensions: the laying-waste of the earth reducing it to chaos, the darkening of the skies, the shaking of mountains and hills, the disappearance of all living creatures from earth and heaven; only after this does it mention the orchards laid out by men and the cities built by them. It is a terrifying vision, which brings the terror of the prophet into view in a quite different way from the visions normally seen by him of the destruction of the land in war. In the final statement, however, this visionary oracle is linked with the oracle in 4:5-8, which proclaims an actual emergency brought about by war.

Jeremiah, unlike Amos, Isaiah, Zephaniah, and Ezekiel, does not speak explicitly of the "Day of Yahweh,"[24] and is thereby once again linked particularly closely with Hosea. But links with Amos and Isaiah are also not wholly lacking in Jeremiah, as we have already noted in our treatment of Jer 4:8, 22 (so also Berridge). It is therefore possible that themes that elsewhere have their setting in passages dealing with the "Day of Yahweh" (darkness—Amos 5:20; perhaps also 8:9; the confusion of the mountains and of all that is lifted up in nature—Isa 2:11-17) are here also influenced from that source.

It remains open to question whether it is appropriate, with Duhm,[25] to speak simply of the "symbolic character" of the vision. When Horst lists this in his series of "event-visions," he correctly emphasizes that for the prophet the anger of God is an actual event, which confronts him as a ghostly, paralyzing sight with worldwide implications. In contrast to the other passages of Jeremiah referred to earlier, the personal emotions of the prophet under the impact of his vision are not expressed.

THE VISION IN JEREMIAH 1:11-15

Of quite a different character is the pair of visions in Jer 1:11-15(16). Dependence on the series of visions in Amos is obvious enough, particularly in their formal structure. If specifically Jeremianic features are more clearly characteristic of this passage than of the vision in 4:23-26, it is also striking that we have here the phenomenon, by no means fully explained, of an inner-prophetic tradition-link specifically involving the report of a visionary experience, in which one might have expected that the most personal and distinctive characteristics of the prophet would be revealed.[26]

In redaction-critical terms, the first chapter of the Book of Jeremiah reveals a structure deliberately shaped by a secondary editor. Siegfried Herrmann has worked out the most probable pattern of composition that can be discerned as underlying the present form.[27] The formula for the coming of God's word (v. 4) leads into the closely integrated words of commission, which make clear to Jeremiah the fact that he had been set apart for the prophetic vocation even before his birth, with no possibility of refusal (vv. 5-7); these words are followed by God's promise of help and the actual event of ordaining by Yahweh (vv. 8-9), with a repeated underlining of the magnitude of the prophetic task

(v. 10). A carefully balanced pair of visions reveals the validity and the contents of the prophetic commission (vv. 11-16).[28] The conclusion (vv. 17-19) recalls once more the circumstances of the commissioning and, with words similar to those used in the first section, reminds the prophet once again of the extent of his task and of Yahweh's help in it. Our own particular subject of interest within this total composition has to be confined to the two visions in vv. 11–12 and 13-15. The latter is followed in v. 16 by a further amplification.

In their linguistic structure the two visions represent a twin entity, the two parts of which possess a common form, however much their contents may be different. This form is foreshadowed in the four visions, also arranged in two pairs, of Amos 7:1-8; 8:1-2, which may represent, along with 9:1-4, a cycle of visions originally put together by Amos. Whether this in its present form can legitimately be seen as referring to an older "seer tradition," as supposed by Reventlow in his proposed reconstruction of the prophetic role in Israel's covenant liturgy,[29] does not need to be considered further here.

It is peculiar to Jeremiah that the two visions should each be preceded by the formula for the coming of God's word (1:11, 13), which from the outset brings the vision that has been seen into relation with the encountered word. In Amos this association with a theology of the word is lacking, however much the visions that he had seen are related directly to his proclamation to Israel. The purely visionary presentation is maintained there to the extent that all four visions are introduced by "Thus the LORD Yahweh showed me: behold!" (*koh her'ani adonai yhwh wehinneh*). Yahweh himself stands unequivocally as the author of the real vision that underlies what is actually seen. The "presence vision" of 9:1-4 betrays a form that is different in its presentation of subject and object.[30] It lacks the reference to Yahweh as the revealer of the vision. As in Isaiah 6, Yahweh is the object of the verb of perceiving, and the vision itself is described in the first person singular as in Jer 4:23-26. The second pair of visions, Amos 7:7-8 and 8:1-2, differs from the first in that after the vision itself a question is directed to the prophet: "Amos, what do you see?"; the prophet's answer, which describes in an explicit way the vision he has seen, is followed by God's explanation of the meaning and a statement of his intentions. The pattern of the second pair of visions in Amos is extended in the early post-exilic period in Zechariah. There the question concerning the content and significance of what has been seen comes no longer from God's side, but from the prophet himself, who learns its significance by means of an interpreting angel. The visions in Jeremiah 1, by contrast, are closer to those in Amos. The linking together of the two visions is very explicitly stated: "The word of Yahweh came to me a second time." As against the Amos passages, however, it is only in the first of the two questions that the prophet is directly addressed by his own name. Moreover, the answer of the prophet in the first of the Jeremiah visions is specifically endorsed by Yahweh himself: "You have seen well." The lack of this endorsement in the second Jeremiah vision, which like the third and fourth of Amos's visions leads directly into the divine announcement of the implications of the vision, creates a formal imbalance between the two Jeremiah visions that distinguishes them from the pairs of visions in Amos with their more uniform structure. These small variations, however, ought not to diminish the impression of the very great similarity of the form of the Jeremiah visions to that of the Amos visions, particularly the second pair.[31]

The similarities between the first Jeremiah vision and the first of the second group of Amos visions can be taken one stage further. Jeremiah sees a branch or wand of almond. After the divine summons to state what he has seen and the word of endorsement from Yahweh himself there follows a further elaboration of the divine speech in which the word *šaqed* ("almond") is surprisingly changed into the similar-sounding participial form of the verb *šqd* ("to watch"). This verb is used in Jer 5:6 to describe the cunning lying-in-wait of the leopard for its prey. (Allusions to 1:12 are found in 44:27, where Yahweh is watching with a view to destruction, and in 31:28, where the watching will bring salvation.) In the language of the Psalms, *šqd* is used in parallelism with *šmr* (Ps 127:1; RSV: "watches" [*šmr*] / "stays awake" [*šqd*]), and it is also found in Prov 8:34, again in parallelism with *šmr* (RSV: "watching" [*šqd*] / "waiting" [*šmr*]), and in a negative sense in Isa 29:20 (RSV: "watch to do evil"). A similar type of vision, which, by the deliberate requirement of having to give a name to what has been seen, is transformed on the basis of assonance into a word of judgment, is to be found in Amos 8:1-2. Horst lists these as the only two examples of what he describes as "word-play visions."[32] In this subgroup what is seen in the vision is not significant in its customary sense as a eloquent symbol, but the proclamation derives from what is seen only after its transformation by means of an aural association of words. But any idea of a mere game must be dismissed. The word has its own "bodily existence" even in the shift from the visual to the aural means of recognition. It proclaims itself in the vision.

Yahweh is "watching over (his) word to perform it." This manner of expressing the message that arises from the vision leaves many questions unanswered. Which "word of Yahweh" is here implied? Is it the word of earlier prophets—of Amos, for example, with whose prophecy the vision we are considering has so many similarities? Is it the word of Hosea, whose influence on Jeremiah's own message has been convincingly demonstrated by Gross?[33] But Amos and Hosea had preached against the Northern Kingdom, which in Jeremiah's day was no longer in existence. Is it then the word of the Jerusalemite Isaiah, who had combined a message of salvation and of disaster in a distinctive way? A link with Isaiah seems to be indicated by Jer 4:22. Or is it the word that, according to the call narrative, Jeremiah himself received when the hand of Yahweh touched his lips (1:9)? In any case, there is no doubt that the reference must be to a word that is pressing toward its realization in event. Once again there is a striking similarity between Jeremiah and Ezekiel, where the verbal expression in the mouth of Yahweh, "I Yahweh have spoken, and I will do it," is frequently repeated (Ezek 17:24; 22:14; 36:36; see also 5:13) and where the theme of the fulfillment of God's word is presented in a polemical fashion in the speech passages of Ezek 12:21-25 and 26-28. Deutero-Isaiah, at the end of the exilic period, should also be borne in mind; in the account of his commissioning he makes a distinction between the transitoriness of "all flesh" and "the word of our God (that) will stand forever" (Isa 40:6, 8; see also 55:10-11). In any case it is clear that the first vision of Jeremiah leads him directly into his basic knowledge of the effective word—to the experience that, according to the evidence of the "Confessions" of Jeremiah, is both his deepest joy and his deepest distress (Jer 15:16; 20:8).

The question is thereby immediately raised whether Jeremiah understood this "word" to be a word of salvation or of judgment. An unambiguous answer to this question is provided by Jer 1:13-15, verses that were apparently linked by the prophet himself with vv. 11-12 to form a twin pair of visions. This second vision presents greater difficulties than the first to an immediate understanding. The almond branch is a clearly discernible objective reality. But what can be meant by "a blown pot (that is, presumably, one under which a fire has been kindled), and whose face (front?) is from the north" (RSV: "a boiling pot, facing away from the north")? Is it implied that it has been tilted or poured out from this direction, as suggested by Bright's translation: "It is tipped from the north"? What is clear is the message that this vision, which is to be included among the "symbol-visions" in the more general sense, contains within itself: "Out of the north evil shall break forth upon (or more probably, "shall be kindled against," reading *tuppah* or *tenuppah*) all the inhabitants of the land." This is then developed in an announcement in which Yahweh himself is the subject: "For, lo, I am calling all the tribes/kingdoms of the north, says Yahweh; and they shall come and every one shall set his throne at the entrance of the gates of Jerusalem, against all its walls round about, and against all the cities of Judah" (Jer 1:15).

It would be wise to refrain from any overimaginative description of a specific situation in which Jeremiah might have seen the cooking pot (or indeed, the almond branch or wand).[34] In the same way it is meaningless to ask whether Jeremiah knew clearly in which direction the pot that he saw before him faced. As with Hosea's marriage or many of the symbolic actions of Ezekiel, we find ourselves in a position where the significance of the vision or symbolic action has made what the prophet actually saw or did complicated and unrecognizable, so that while the announcement of the meaning of the vision or symbolic action is completely clear, the biographical details that would be of special interest to modern ways of thought are obscured and remain out of reach. So it must be left as an open question whether the pot boiling over (or indeed, the almond branch) would also have been a visible reality to an external observer or whether it was a "vision" that had no actual counterpart in the clear light of day. The question is also not susceptible of an answer in the case of the visions of Amos. For the symbolic actions it is, of course, true that the carrying out of the action, in whatever way this was done, was an essential part of them. With regard to the vision of the boiling pot, it may be asked whether the underlying text of Ezek 24:1-14 ("the pot on the fire") was not inspired by it.[35]

The two visions, which in their formal structure seem identical, do not appear to have any discernible association of content. At the same time, it is possible to see the basic point of reference in the way in which the second vision makes it clear what "act" of Yahweh the word put in the mouth of the prophet (Jer 1:9) must announce. The second vision is obviously in a close relation with the early preaching of Jeremiah concerning an invasion by a "foe from the North." This foe remains unnamed, both in the vision and the words from God that explain it, and in the oracles concerning the invasion, which are found especially in Jeremiah 4–6. The victory of Nebuchadnezzar at Carchemish in 605 B.C.E. provided this proclamation with a clear historical realization. According to Jeremiah 36, the events of which took place at the same period, Jehoiakim condemned the early preaching of the prophet, which had been written on the scroll that was burned with the words: "Why have you written in it that the king of Babylon will certainly come and destroy this land?" (v. 29). Whether or not one accepts the authenticity of these words as actually spoken by Jehoiakim,[36] the "foe of the North" is here named by virtue of the historical fulfillment. From then on, as far as we can make out, Jeremiah also spoke openly of the Babylonians. In Ezekiel, who stands in the succession of this proclamation of Jeremiah, this open manner of speaking of the Babylonians and their king, Nebuchadnezzar, is merely continued. The time for veiled speech is done. Even so, its secret character subsequently inspired the prophecy concerning God (Ezekiel 38–39), with its development toward apocalyptic.

There is no reason from the content of the two visions in Jeremiah 1 to deny them to the prophet himself. How far the visions belonged from the outset to the events connected with the call of the prophet is not clear. In any case the redactor who brought Jeremiah 1 together into its present form did not entirely miss the mark when he inserted into the total picture, which in its present form anticipates both the prophet's oracles against the nations and the expectation of reconstruction after the period of judgment and destruction, the two visions with the genuinely Jeremianic themes of the unshakable effectiveness of the word of Yahweh and the threat of the invasion of the "foe from the North."

THE VISION IN JEREMIAH 24

The vision in Jeremiah 24 presents even greater problems. It is reminiscent of Ezekiel in that here, by contrast to Jer 1:11-15 and 4:23-26, the vision is given a date.

It differs, however, from Ezekiel in that there is lacking here the precise dating of the event by means of year, month, and day. The statement is more general, that the prophet's vision took place "after Nebuchadnezzar king of Babylon had taken into exile from Jerusalem Jeconiah the son of Jehoiakim, king of Judah, together with the princes of Judah, the craftsmen, and the smiths, and had brought them to Babylon." Because this dating (which does in fact fit the following vision) destroys the connection between vv. 1a and 2 and makes use of information from 2 Kgs 24:14, it should be regarded from a literary point of view as a supplementary insertion.[37]

The prophet sees "two baskets of figs placed before the temple of Yahweh" (perhaps better to emend the text to "standing before . . ."). Once again we cannot decide whether the two baskets, with their different kinds of figs, would have been visible to any profane eyes, or whether it was a disclosure to be seen only by the eyes of the visionary. The introduction, "Yahweh showed me, and behold," which is the same introductory formula for a vision that we have noted in Amos, leaves both possibilities open. The specific naming of the location, "before the temple," implies that the figs will have been a gift presented before God (Deut 26:10ba); in the normal procedure for bringing an offering there will then have followed the priestly decision, whether the offering was "acceptable" (*leraṣôn*) or "not acceptable" (*lo' leraṣôn*); see Lev 22:20-21, and compare also Gen 4:4-5, the *š'h* of Yahweh (RSV: "the LORD had [no] regard"). As in the second pair of visions in Amos and in Jer 1:11, 13, the vision is here followed by the question of Yahweh to the prophet, "What do you see?"—the pointedness of this question is emphasized by the calling of the prophet by his own name, "Jeremiah, what do you see?" (Jer 1:11), just as in Amos 7:8 and 8:2.

The immediate context does not provide any further clue as to the nature and origin of this vision. It is preceded by two blocks of material, the extent of which can be recognized by the titles: "Concerning (RSV: to) the house of the king of Judah" (Jer 21:11—23:8) and "Concerning the prophets" (Jer 23:9-40). In Jer 25:1ff. there follows a complex unit consisting of oracles against the nations. Its date ascribes it to the time of Jehoiakim. Jeremiah 25 appears to be the conclusion of an originally independent collection of oracles, to which the narrative material in chaps. 26ff. has been appended.

Form-critically considered, Jeremiah 24 consists of an elaborately constructed account of a vision, containing within itself elements of the deuteronomistic preaching of alternatives.[38] It differs from Jeremiah 1 in that the appended explanation is introduced by a new formula for the coming of God's word (24:4). The messenger formula of v. 5 is superfluous in that the personal address to the prophet has already been given in the formula for the coming of God's word, and should perhaps be regarded as a clumsy later insertion. The explanation that then follows is introduced by the comparative particle "like" (ke). In two roughly equal sections it sets out, on the one hand, the judgment of Yahweh concerning those who have been deported to Babylon and, on the other, that concerning Zedekiah, his ministers and those who remained in the land, as well as those who were living in Egypt. It contrasts the unconditional condemnation of the second group with the promise of salvation, which is conditional upon their conversion (v. 7b), for those living in Babylon. The reference to those who had escaped to Egypt presupposes already the events after the fall of Jerusalem that are referred to in chaps. 42ff. Consequently, this exposition cannot be thought to have a Jeremianic origin.[39] Indeed, Siegfried Herrmann and Thiel have shown in detail how both the vocabulary and the theological outlook here are the work of deuteronomistic redaction.[40]

The introduction to Jeremiah 24 explicitly names Yahweh as the author of the vision, and in this respect it is closer to the four visions in Amos 7:1-8 and 8:1-2 than is Jer 1:11-15. On the other hand, the arrangement of paired visions employed both in Amos 7–8 and in Jeremiah 1 is not present here. The fact that Jeremiah sees two baskets of figs functions here to characterize the two different conditions in which Judah found herself after the partial deportation of 597 B.C.E. The preaching of alternatives, which, according to the closing phrase (v. 7b), makes the salvation alternative of vv. 4-7 dependent on the conversion of those deported in 597 B.C.E., is formulated with only the first of the two groups in mind upon whom Yahweh's judgment is pronounced through the visionary experience. For the second group no possibility of salvation seems to exist any more.

The whole passage gives, therefore, a disunited impression. The vision of the two baskets of figs seems at first to lead to an unconditional verdict in the situation of 597 B.C.E.: for those in exile future salvation, for those remaining in the land, and for those who escaped to Egypt (in the situation of 597 envisaged proleptically) future condemnation. But then through the preaching of alternatives a conditional element is introduced into the promise of salvation, which is envisaged by the whole structure of the vision, in that the announcement of salvation to the exiles is linked to the condition of their conversion.

This double emphasis leads to recognition that the same feature can also be traced in the Book of Ezekiel. There the polemic against those who remained in the land is very bitter in the passages dating between 597 and 587 B.C.E. They had concluded from the fact that they had not been carried off into exile that "to us this land is given for a possession," whereas the exiles "have gone far from Yahweh" (Ezek 11:15). Ezekiel 33:24 shows the claim to the land being further developed after 587, since here it is even founded upon an allusion to the saving history of Abraham: "Abraham was only one man, yet he got possession of the land; but we are many; the land is surely given us to possess." In Ezekiel also, therefore, it is to those far away from the land that the divine promise is made that Yahweh would once again lead them back into the land. No reference is made in Ezekiel to the Jewish community in Egypt. The promise of return for those exiled in Babylon is set out quite unconditionally in some passages (Ezek 36:24-32; 37:1-14). But at the same time it is noteworthy that Ezekiel, in his words to the exiles amongst whom he found himself, can call for repentance and conversion (14:1-11; 18).[41] Ezekiel 14:1-11 is particularly reminiscent of Jeremiah 24, in that in both instances the covenant formula[42] is associated with the call to repentance. On the other hand, Jeremiah 24 recalls terminology to be found in Ezekiel inasmuch as Jer 24:7aα—literally, "I will give them a heart to know me that I am Yahweh"—links together in a striking way the assertion of recognition followed by the accusative ("know me") with the typically Ezekielian combination of the assertion of recognition ("you will know that . . .") and the formula of self-introduction ("I am Yahweh").[43] In the Book of Jeremiah the same linking is to be found in the wisdom saying, 9:23-24 (MT vv. 22-23); see also 16:21.

Is it possible, therefore, to find a point of attachment in Jeremiah's own preaching for the vision of chap. 24? To investigate this question it is essential to engage in a more basic examination of the chapter.

As against the vision passages considered previously, which may be attributed to Jeremiah himself, the main characteristic here is not an announcement of Yahweh's intentions for the future, but an evaluation of the disastrous events for Judah that had already taken place. What would seem to be the obvious assessment of them is to be turned upside down. Yahweh's future belonged not to those who appeared in these events to have been preferentially treated by Yahweh's judgment but to those who had already been judged—provided that they returned to Yahweh, as the condition attached to v. 7 states. By means of the vision, according to the present text, Yahweh's judgment upon two groups of people is represented; and inasmuch as it makes use of the picture of two baskets of figs it recalls, as far as the basket is concerned,

Amos's vision of a basket of summer fruit (*kelûb qayiṣ*) from which Amos had made a link with the word meaning "end" (*qēṣ*). Since in Jeremiah 24 the word *dûd* is used for the basket, it is not possible to postulate a direct dependence of Jeremiah 24 on Amos 8:1. In a similar way comparison of the two visions brings out the structural differences between them. Whereas Amos 8:1-2 reveals the coming end of Israel in an ominous way, the basis of Jeremiah 24 is the statement of a comparison: "like these good figs" (v. 4) and "like these bad figs which are so bad they cannot be eaten" (v. 8). It is at the same time true that a reference to the work of Yahweh is also added: "so will I regard . . . the exiles" (v. 4)—"so I will treat Zedekiah" (v. 8).

It is proper to raise at this point the question whether there may not lie behind the vision, as its real point of origin, a simple word picture that Jeremiah could well have used. In Jeremiah 2–6 we find words of Jeremiah in an elevated style, which are generally agreed to be those words of the prophet himself that can be identified as such with the greatest confidence. These make vivid and abundant use of word pictures. Thus Jer 2:20 uses the metaphor of an animal breaking its yoke; 2:21 of a choice vine; 2:22 of washing oneself with lye; 2:23 of a restive young camel; 2:26 of a thief. We must ask whether the vision of Jeremiah 24, with its setting out of alternatives, which has been shaped by the rich use of polished language, does not have as its nucleus a simple pictorial comparison, expressed in Jeremiah's own words, which Jeremiah had used with reference to those who had been exiled in 597 B.C.E. The oracles referring to Jehoiachin (Coniah) in 22:24-30, which have been much elaborated, and especially v. 28, which by its use of the characteristically Jeremianic formal device of the triple question is shown to be an original formulation of Jeremiah himself, betray a remarkable sympathy on the part of Jeremiah for the deported king, and appear to provide evidence of a high estimation of the deported leaders of society (to whom Ezekiel also belonged). In any case, as Ackyrod has rightly emphasized,[44] we must assume for Jeremiah 24 an entirely ad hoc comparison, directed to a particular situation, which is not to be amplified into a fixed assessment of the value of those who remained in Palestine and those who had been deported to Babylon in the way that the present form of the vision has done. The sense of security of those who had not been deported in 597, to which Ezekiel's words bear witness, would then have been challenged by the prophet with his picture of the inedible figs, just as he had characterized his people in 2:21 by the picture, even more firmly rooted in Israel's sacral language, of a choice vine that had degenerated into a wild vine.[45]

We are here, naturally, in the realm of the consideration of possibilities. But in any case we may discount the rather unlikely assumption that the deuteronomistic redaction of Jeremiah could have arrived at the (by no means common) picture of good and bad figs without there being any support for such a picture in the transmitted words of Jeremiah himself.

This raises the question whether a further step may legitimately be taken. Did the original words of Jeremiah already contain a report of a visionary experience, in which the prophet saw baskets of figs that had been brought to the sanctuary, of which one was "acceptable" (*leraṣôn*) or "not acceptable" (*lo' leraṣôn*; compare on the same point Mal 1:7-9), which then was changed into Yahweh's word for him concerning the two groups of people?

Whether this is so or not, it can scarcely be doubted that the present form of the text of Jeremiah 24 is the responsibility of a later hand. A polemic of Jeremiah that was originally directed at a particular wrong attitude in a concrete situation has, at a later stage, in which it was a question not only of the two groups, those who remained in the land and those who were deported to Babylon in 597 and 587 B.C.E., but also of a third group, those who formed an Egyptian diaspora, become an absolute judgment: salvation will come through the Babylonian exile (*golah*). Such a verdict would have been anachronistic in the situation of 597. What is reported elsewhere of Jeremiah's words in the period between 597 and 587 (esp. chaps. 27–29) shows the prophet concerned in other ways with the survival of those who remained in Jerusalem, without forgetting those who had already been deported in 597.

Thus the assumption of an original Jeremianic background for the vision of Jeremiah 24 remains surrounded by many uncertainties.

CONCLUSION

In summary, it can clearly be established that the preaching of Jeremiah certainly did not lack a visionary element. The utter bewilderment of the prophet at the way in which he had been seized by Yahweh cannot be mistaken in the oracles of the early period, to which belong both the twin visions that are linked with the narrative of his call (1:11-15) and the vision of 4:23-26.

The main emphasis has, however, shifted in Jeremiah entirely to the transmission of preaching—at least so far as we can see from the text that has been handed down. Indeed one can pose the question, to which a certain answer is impossible, whether the visionary element does not diminish in importance in the course of the prophetic proclamation of Jeremiah. The reason for this could well have been the conflict of Jeremiah with the prophets of salvation, who recounted their dreams and emphasized in them the visual element in order to boast of the mysterious character of their prophetic experience. Jeremiah reproaches them with preaching "visions of their own minds" (23:16).[46]

But what do we know of the actual character of the prophetic experience of Jeremiah's later years? Where a third person reports of his career in the times of Jehoiakim, Zedekiah, and finally the hopeless closing stage of the history of Judah, there the oracular judgment decides everything. But neither do the passages that are traditionally classified as "Confessions" (Jer 11:18—12:6; 15:10-21; 17:14-18; 18:18-23; 20:7-18) contain any clear allusions to visual experience.[47]

Jeremiah, therefore, represents a transitional stage in the direction of the preaching of Deutero-Isaiah, in which no visionary elements are to be found. There the word of Yahweh that "will stand forever" (Isa 40:8) is in control of everything. The divine confirmation in history establishes "the word of his servants,"[48] that is, the prophets (Isa 44:26). Here is the effective cause of what happens (Isa 55:10-11). But this complete lack of a visual element is already characteristic of Hosea, with whose message Jeremiah shows close links. On the other hand, Jeremiah is different in this regard from his younger contemporary Ezekiel, with whom in other respects connections can be traced.[49] Despite the emphasis on the power of Yahweh's word, the great significance of the visionary element in Ezekiel cannot be mistaken. This aspect is developed in Zechariah after the exile and in this way is a preparation for the apocalyptic technique,[50] when that reached its full maturity in Daniel after the long period of the silence of prophecy. The validity of such a development is not a matter for judgment here. With Jeremiah the validity of the experience as reflecting his own distinctive knowledge is not to be doubted.

5

The Message of the Prophet Ezekiel

DATE AND LOCATION

Ever since the second quarter of the twentieth century, a storm of critical challenges has surrounded the person and book of the prophet Ezekiel, which long appeared to offer no particular problems. Since Gustav Hölscher "rescued" Ezekiel the "poet" by reducing his authentic words from the 1,273 verses of the existing text to 144, and C. C. Torrey in 1930 judged the entire book to be a pseudograph from the third century B.C.E., discussion on the prophet and his book has continued.[1] Volkmar Herntrich contributed yet another question to this discussion: Would Ezekiel, who was, according to the text, one of those deported to Babylon with King Jehoiachin and yet so outspokenly addressed Jerusalem and its inhabitants, be better understood as a prophet active in Jerusalem?[2] Of course the question immediately arose whether some words ought not to be located in the time of the exile. If so, then Ezekiel must have worked in both places.[3] Finally, there came the thesis that Ezekiel worked first with the exiles, then came to Jerusalem, and later returned to preach among the exiles again.[4]

Various solutions have been examined in the course of this critical investigation. New critical schemes, however, which eliminated difficulties on one side turned up new problems on the other. Recently, therefore, the question has been raised again whether the book's own assertions about the place and time of the prophet's proclamation ought not to be considered very seriously.[5] According to the book, the prophet went into exile with King Jehoiachin following the capitulation of Jerusalem. From the Neo-Babylonian Chronicle,[6] this can be precisely dated as the second day of Adar of the seventh year of Nebuchadnezzar (according to Parker and Dubberstein's calculations, March 16, 597 B.C.E.).[7] According to Ezek 3:15, Ezekiel lived there in an exile district named Tel Abib. This name comes from the Akkadian *til abūbi*, "hill of the deluge."[8] It is to be understood as a hill that had not been inhabited for a long time. Obviously the place had been given to the deportees for a new residence. In the following discussion, we assume that the book's own assertions are correct.

TRADITION HISTORY

The critical work on Ezekiel has not, however, been in vain. Even where the new syntheses have not endured, a number of insights were reached that prohibit a simple return to the views held prior to Hölscher and Torrey. In 1880 Smend still understood the Book of Ezekiel as "the logical development of a series of thoughts in a carefully thought-out and, in part, quite systematic plan" from which one could not remove a piece "without destroying the whole ensemble."[9] He believed that in the evening of his life Ezekiel "wrote his summary of Israel's situation at that period, as well as its past and future." In contrast, criticism has revealed a lively history of tradition, editing, and additions to the prophet's words as the book took on the form we know today.

Whoever reads the book carefully must conclude that the prophet's words have been collected and transmitted within the framework of a circle of disciples, a sort of "school" of the prophet.[10] The transmission brought more than expansions and explanatory additions. A peculiar characteristic of the process by which the words of Ezekiel were passed on is that individual passages were developed and expanded in terms of new perspectives. Thus, for example, the allegory of Jerusalem as the unfaithful wife in Ezek 16:1-43, already here enriched by several elaborations, is taken up in a quite new form in vv. 44-52. Here the two sisters, Samaria and Sodom, not mentioned in vv. 1-43, are added to the unfaithful wife, Jerusalem. This is not an independent speech that the collectors placed next to vv. 1-43. Rather, the theme introduced in vv. 1-43 is taken up again with a new start and is further developed from a new perspective. Comments are added in vv. 53-58 that indicate an impending change and probably belong to the sphere of the prophet's proclamation of salvation that was first uttered after Jerusalem's final fall in 587 B.C.E. Finally, in vv. 59-63 a fourth exposition is attached whose theme, "oath and covenant," dominates chapter 17. This raises the question whether it has not been added with a view to the continuation in chapter 17.

Whether this final supposition proves true or not, one can scarcely avoid the conclusion, both here and in other speech complexes (compare, for example, chapter 34), that the apparatus of a school, a "teaching house," stands behind this process of taking up words anew and further elaborating certain themes.

We might add that where reference is made to the more precise conditions of Ezekiel's work, he is often presented as sitting in his house and receiving people (Ezek 8:1; 14:1; 20:1; and 33:30-33 also seems to presuppose this situation).[11] Nowhere is the prophet portrayed as speaking and preaching in the streets. These facts are illumined by the history of schools in preclassical, preliterary prophecy, according to which Elisha is described in a remarkably similar manner as a teacher of groups of disciples or elders gathered around him (2 Kgs 4:38; 6:1; and esp. 6:32). It is easy to demonstrate, as materials of chapters 16 and 34 presume, the scholastic development of various prophetic themes within such a group.

At the same time, however, this process makes it difficult to decide in particular cases the question of how far the prophet himself partook (shared) in the further development of his words, and how far the development was independently taken over after his death by his disciples. The distinction between genuine and nongenuine is in every case incomparably more difficult, and the transitions much less sharply defined than in the case of the proclamation of Isaiah. The polishing of his public speeches distinguishes Isaiah's proclamation much more clearly from that of his disciples, who are expressly mentioned in Isa 7:16-18.

Consequently, any presentation of the message of Ezekiel must always keep in mind this peculiarity in the process of tradition by which the prophet's words became the materials now deposited in his book.

EZEKIEL AND PRELITERARY PROPHECY

The relationship of Ezek 8:1; 14:1; and 20:1 to 2 Kgs 6:32 (and 4:38; and 6:1) points to a certain closeness between Ezekiel's prophecy and that of preclassical, preliterary prophecy. This relationship in the history of tradition, however, comprehends much more than mere references to the prophet and his circle of hearers. It invests several features of the prophecy of Ezekiel with a pronounced archaic character.[12]

The phenomenon of the "spirit" was of central importance for the preliterary prophecy, which understood it, not as intellectualism or speculative, inquiring reason, but rather as the moving power that comes from Yahweh. We see this in the account of the prophet band that descended from the heights of Gibeah and from whom the spirit sprang over to Saul so that he became ecstatic and was changed into another person (1 Sam 10:5-6). Also, after Elijah was taken away, his disciples assumed the "spirit of Yahweh" had snatched up the master and cast him down on one of the mountains or in one of the valleys (2 Kgs 2:16).

Classical literary prophecy before Ezekiel—Amos, Hosea, Isaiah, and even Jeremiah—resolutely avoids speaking of "spirit" as that power that authorizes the prophet. Was this because the "man of the spirit" was connected so strongly with outward oddness that attracted attention and caused the prophets to appear as "crazy"? "The man of the spirit is mad" was the opinion of the people with whom Hosea was confronted (Hos 9:7). And the young prophet who anointed Jehu king was immediately and derisively called mad by Jehu's companions (2 Kgs 9:11).

Ezekiel, by contrast, does not hesitate to speak of the "spirit." He speaks exactly as Elijah's disciples presumed concerning their master. He says that the spirit seized him, picked him up, carried him from the place of his calling by Yahweh back to Tel Abib (Ezek 3:14-15) and later (8:3) to Jerusalem and, according to 11:24, still later returned him again to the exiles.

Alongside "spirit" and almost synonymous with it, the term "hand of Yahweh" also occurs in the Elijah story. After God's judgment on Carmel, the "hand of Yahweh" comes upon Elijah so that he runs swiftly alongside Ahab's chariot as far as Jezreel (about 30 kilometers, as the crow flies; 1 Kgs 18:46). Ezekiel also speaks in exactly the same way of the "hand of Yahweh" that fell on him and removed him from the sphere of daily life (8:1). A man's hand seized him by the hair, and the spirit lifted him through the air to Jerusalem.[13]

The remarkable features of vision at a distance are closely related to the effects of seizure by the spirit or by the hand of Yahweh. Ezekiel views what is happening in the temple in Jerusalem, the abomination that vaunts itself there, and God's consequent punishment through the mysterious agents of vengeance (9–10). He sees the newly built sanctuary in Jerusalem (40–48). This recalls the story of Elisha's servant Gehazi, who secretly ran off to collect a payment his master had turned down. When he returned with innocent countenance, Elisha said to him, "Did I not go with you in spirit when the man turned from his chariot to meet you? Was it a time to accept money . . . ? Therefore the leprosy of Naaman shall cleave to you" (2 Kgs 5:26-27).

Furthermore, one also finds in Ezekiel the peculiar form of a *Qibla,* facing the addressee of a message in order to establish optical contact: "Son of man, set your face toward the mountains of Israel, and prophesy against them" (Ezek 6:1; see also 17:17; 21:2, 7; 25:2; and others). This does not occur in the classical prophets before Ezekiel, although it is found in the ancient story of the seer Balaam who was called to curse Israel and who then had to stand at a place where he had Israel before his eyes and could then deliver his message (Num 22:41; 23:13; 24:2).

These contacts with preliterary prophecy behind classical literary prophecy could be multiplied.[14] Ezekiel is, therefore, special among the classical prophets in his use of older materials.

Ezekiel and Prophetic Books

On the other hand, we cannot fail to recognize that Ezekiel also knows the earlier great literary prophets and their word and that he updates their message in his own way. In Amos, an assonance of words leads (from one of his visions) to a short statement of proclamation: "The end has come" (Amos 8:1). In Ezekiel 7 there is something like an extensive sermon on this sentence that is now broadly developed in various forms. Similarly, a number of other themes that Ezekiel develops undoubtedly derive from preceding prophecy. Compare, for example, Ezekiel 16 with Hosea 2; Ezek 22:17-22 with Isa 1:22, 25 and Jer 6:27-29; Ezekiel 23 with Jer 3:6-14; and Ezekiel 34 with Jer 23:1-8.

Here we may point to a unique transposition of such stimuli that discloses something of this prophet's particular sensibility and power of experience. In one of the so-called confessions of Jeremiah in which he both laments and extols before God the pain and sweetness of his distress, the prophet says: "Your words were found, and I ate them, and your words became to me a joy and the delight of my heart; for I am called by your name, O Yahweh, God of hosts" (Jer 15:16). In Jeremiah this is a figure of speech, as comparison with Pss 19:10 [MT v. 11]; 19:11; 119:103; and Prov 16:24; 24:1-3 will show. Ezekiel, however, in telling about his calling, reports that he was given a scroll, written on the front and back with words of lamentation, mourning, and woe, which he ate at Yahweh's command, and that in his mouth it became as sweet as honey (Ezek 3:1-3). In an unusual transposition, Jeremiah's figure of speech becomes experienced reality for Ezekiel.

Similarly with an image from Isaiah, the prophet Isaiah employs a striking image at the time of the Syro-Ephraimite war, when a sharp observer could already discern in the background the dark shadow of the brutal Assyrian conqueror: "In that day, the LORD will shave with a razor which is hired beyond the River—with the king of Assyria—the head and the hair of the feet, and it will sweep away the beard also" (Isa 7:20). Yahweh is portrayed as a barber! A daring picture becomes again in Ezekiel a dramatic, experienced reality. As a symbolic act, Ezekiel, at Yahweh's behest, cuts off his hair with a sword (knife). He throws a third of his hair into the fire, he cuts up a third with the sword, and he scatters a third to the winds (Ezek 5:1-13). By this surprising drama he presents to his fellow countrymen the fate of the city of Jerusalem threatened by Nebuchadnezzar. The message proclaimed 150 years earlier by the prophet Isaiah is rendered visible by means of a corporeal act and thus made into the message for his day.

Thus, despite the archaic elements that bind him with preliterary prophecy, Ezekiel also stands in the line of the literary prophecy that preceded him, and is certainly not to be understood apart from it. A particular problem in this connection is posed by the remarkable closeness of many of the statements in his book to those of Jeremiah, who was, in part, his contemporary.[15] Ezekiel shares with him, among other things, a basic political proclamation; the call for unconditional submission to the Babylonian king, Nebuchadnezzar. For Ezekiel, as for Jeremiah, Nebuchadnezzar is God's instrument of punishment against the sinful people of Judah and the world beyond. Ezekiel 17 charges that Zedekiah (the successor of, or perhaps only the regent for, the deported Jehoiachin,[16] who had once again broken away from the dominion of the Babylonians) has broken his oath, not only to the human authority, but also to Yahweh the Lord, the real protector of Jerusalem.

SPECIAL ELEMENTS IN EZEKIEL

Leaving these preliminary considerations on the Book of Ezekiel and its ties with the older prophetic tradition, we must now turn to the special elements in Ezekiel's proclamation.

The introduction of the book, which reports the call of the prophet to his office, shows as clearly as one might wish that Ezekiel understands himself not only as the successor and disciple of earlier prophets, but also as the recipient of a quite personal call.

In the fifth year of his exile,[17] near the exilic colony Tel Abib on the Chebar River (most probably the *nar kabari*, the great canal near ancient Nippur), the divine majesty appeared to Ezekiel. Did the colony of Tel Abib perhaps have its place of prayer near the rivers where the necessary washings could take place, as did the Jewish community in Philippi (Acts 16:13; compare the description in Ps 137)? Then Ezekiel, like Isaiah, would have encountered the living presence of God at the community's place of worship.

The prophet is confronted in this meeting with the manifestation of the majestic royal glory of Yahweh that proceeds from a storm advancing from the north, recalling Isaiah 6. That description in the present text includes an abundance of additional details, which indicate the intense interest of the "school" in the mystery of the appearing God. Thus, the combining of the manifestation of God's throne, borne by four creatures, with the conception of a wheeled chariot in Ezek 1:15-21 may well be the result of such an expanded interpretation.

More significant, however, is the observation that here, far away in exile, God's glory in its full majesty now confronted the prophet. As a priest, he well knew that God's dwelling place was in Jerusalem, the chosen place of his presence,[18] and that here at the place of worship in exile, Yahweh had been "a sanctuary to them only in small measure" (Ezek 11:16). Is the appearance in full majesty also an archaism? In earlier times Israel had experienced Yahweh's appearance from his distant dwelling place on the holy mountain to help them in situations of need (see Judg 5:4-5; 2 Sam 5:24). But Ezekiel's description is clearly more than a simple archaism. It is the miracle of Yahweh's faithfulness that (contrary to correct dogmatics) he now unexpectedly confronts the prophet in a distant land in his full, royal glory. To those far away who seem to have lost every close relation to temple and home, God can also appear quite surprisingly as the living, majestic One.

To be sure, the commission to which the prophet is called is first of all extremely harsh. The scroll handed to him containing God's message with which he is entrusted, "had writing on the front and on the back, and there were written on it words of lamentation and mourning and woe" (Ezek 2:10). Under strict orders to swallow the scroll, the prophet finds that the words become sweet as honey in his mouth. But the sweetness does not refer to the content Ezekiel has to deliver; rather, as in Jer 15:16, it is the knowledge that it is grace and sweetness when God's word is given to people at all. Misery and blessedness in tension with each other are mirrored here, as in the confession of Jer 15:15-21.

In Yahweh's summons to Ezekiel there echoes an understanding that the messenger will experience opposition. So he is commanded not to be rebellious himself (Ezek 2:8). Does this indicate acquaintance with the rebellious words of Jeremiah who, under the burden of his office, curses the day of his birth, hurls charges in God's face, and seeks to escape his burden by simply keeping silent (Jer 20:7-17)? God admonishes Ezekiel, as he admonished Jeremiah (Jer 1:8, 17-19), to be fearless, and he equips him with the necessary temper for his office. "Behold, I have made your face hard against their faces, and your forehead hard against their foreheads. Like adamant harder than flint have I made your forehead" (Ezek 3:8-9). And it seems precisely this temper that characterizes Ezekiel's further proclamation.

Unique to the Book of Ezekiel is a second call in 3:17-21 (see also 33:1-9) that follows the great narrative of the initial call. This second call charges him specifically with the office of lookout (watchman). We shall return to the significance of this second calling in a later context.

SYMBOLIC ACTIONS

The report of his call does not yet reveal any of the actual content of Ezekiel's harsh proclamation. This content is given in the subsequent chapters of the first half of the book.[19] They also show that Ezekiel delivered his proclamation in two ways, as Yahweh ordered. Accompanying the proclamation of the word is a proclamation by deeds, particular symbolic acts that he is commissioned to perform. These acts present most graphically the real content of the

prophetic proclamation. They are not like sermon illustrations; they anticipate in a physical way what will occur soon after God's announcement.

Already in prophecy prior to Ezekiel, symbolic actions occur, and not just
in a limited way.[20] For they are found in preclassical, preliterary prophecy and
in the great literary prophets, Hosea (1 and 3); Isaiah (20:1-6; compare also the
sons' names in 7:3; 8:1-4; and perhaps 7:10-14); and Jeremiah (13:19; 27–28; 43:8-
13; 51:59-64). In Ezekiel they become particularly numerous.

A short, formally complete composition of three symbolic actions concerning the siege and subsequent fall of Jerusalem may well have been the origin of the present passage Ezek 4:1—5:3. The beginning of the siege of
Jerusalem is announced by a figurative siege that Ezekiel conducts against a
brick on which a map of Jerusalem is drawn. The increasing famine in the
besieged city is anticipated by Ezekiel's partaking of rationed food and drink
(4:9a, 10-11). And through the strange act of cutting off and destroying his hair,
which is to be understood on the basis of Isa 7:20, the prophet proclaims the
destruction of Jerusalem's population after the fall of the city. Two further
symbolic actions have been inserted into the present context. Ezekiel 4:4-8, a
later expansion, makes clear by the prophet's lying in fetters the burden of
guilt that lies on the house of Israel.[21] In 4:12-15, a passage also expanded later,
the unclean food the prophet is to eat proclaims the situation of exile where
one is compelled to live in an unclean territory as a situation of spiritual
homelessness. What the prophet is commanded to do in 12:1-2 symbolizes the
fall of Jerusalem and the subsequent deportation of its people. He is to pack
his small exile's baggage in bright daylight in the view of the people and then
in the evening load it on his shoulders for his departure.[22] The present text is
daubed over with references to the catastrophe of the fugitive King Zedekiah
as reported in 2 Kgs 25:4-7. According to Ezek 12:17-20 and 21:11-12, the quaking
with which Ezekiel eats his bread and his sighing are symbols anticipating the
agony that will come to the people. In the foreground of 21:23-29 is the tension
surrounding the final threat to Jerusalem by Nebuchadnezzar's army: the
prophet is commanded to draw two roads and a signpost before the people:
Nebuchadnezzar stands there and decides to take the road to Jerusalem and
not that to the Ammonite capital. The sudden death of Ezekiel's wife when he
is unable to carry out the normal customs of mourning also points to the coming catastrophe. So shattered will the people be by the fall of Yahweh's holy
place, "Israel's stronghold . . . the delight of your eyes and desire of your soul"
(24:15-27).

These symbolic actions make very clear how the prophet's whole person is
possessed by his proclamation. He becomes totally the servant of the acts that
he intentionally undertakes, such as the three symbolic acts in the composition in Ezekiel 4–5. But he is also the servant of what befalls him, so that he is

affected simply as one who suffers; his numbness after his wife's sudden death is an example.[23] Further, the sequence of the symbolic acts in the first half of the book makes clear that the prophet's proclamation is concerned first of all with the fate of the still-existing city of Jerusalem and its temple.

His proclamation in words alone, not symbolized with actions, also points toward Jerusalem's end. This reference may not be too clear in the judgment pronounced against the "mountain of Israel" in Ezekiel 6 and in the proclamation of the coming "end" and "day of Yahweh" in chapter 7, which are stated very broadly. But it is directly indicated in the judgment on Jerusalem in the sword passage of 21:1-12 and in the image of the furnace in 22:17-22. Judgment against the oath-breaking King Zedekiah who sinned against Yahweh himself, before whom he had sworn his oath, is expressed in chapter 17. The lamentation over the kings of Judah in chapter 19 may have been directly attached at an earlier time to chapter 17. Above all, however, the great vision in rapture, chapters 8–11, reveals to the prophet the coming judgment on Jerusalem. Here he sees not only (in chapter 8) the abomination that vaunts and boasts in the temple and its immediate vicinity, but also (in chapter 9) he sees the coming of God's terrible agents of judgment who at Yahweh's behest break forth in the city with their instruments of murder to kill all except the small remnant who sigh over the abominations and whom a priestly figure had previously identified by a protective sign.[24] It is then precisely this priestly figure, however, who receives the commission to cast fire from God's sanctuary on the city and to spread the judgment that begins in the sanctuary itself (9:6) throughout the city. This process of judgment reaches its climax, however, when the prophet sees Yahweh's glory withdraw from the sanctuary and desert the land. Into this context, the later school has inserted in chapter 10 once again a full description of the glory of God's throne, which is in many respects a more extensive reflection than the description in chapter 1. Thus, for example, the four creatures that bear the throne are here expressly identified as cherubim. In the description of their four faces, 10:13-14 deviates from 1:10. The interpolation of the two passages 11:1-13 and 14-21 is also to be attributed to later editing.

The scroll that Ezekiel swallowed when he was sent out from Yahweh to prophesy contained "lamentation, mourning, and woe." The exile Ezekiel is sent out to pronounce in God's name an unconditional "No" to all hopes of restitution of the former life in Jerusalem and thereby also to all hopes of those who had lived in its surroundings. God is on the move, the prophet announces, to execute his judgment to the bitter end. Yahweh has disposed himself to forsake Jerusalem, the holy center of the "house of Israel."

In all this, Ezekiel radicalizes to the last degree the announcement of disaster that had already been heard from the mouths of the earlier literary prophets.

PROCLAMATION OF JUDGMENT

In all this is God not unjust, and has he not become a demon of destruction? At this point we must speak of the second element of Ezekiel's prophecy in which the radicalizing of the older prophetic message is still more uncompromisingly driven forward.

The older literary prophecy also spoke of the sinfulness of Israel and Jerusalem. Hosea sharply attacked the faithlessness of Israel, who in the beginning in the wilderness and in her youth before her entrance into Canaan, had belonged completely to her God. So also in Jeremiah, God recalls: "I remember the devotion of your youth, your love as a bride, how you followed me in the wilderness, in land not sown" (Jer 2:2). Similar statements appear in Isaiah about the earlier history of Jerusalem as a city "that was full of justice." Righteousness lodged in her." To this the promise then says: "I will restore your judges as at the first, and your counselors as at the beginning (Isa 1:21, 26). Even though Jeremiah in despair confirms that Judah is as little capable of good as an Ethiopian is of changing his skin or a leopard his spots (Jer 13:23), the memory of a glorious past is not extinguished among the older prophets.

With Ezekiel this is radically altered. Jeremiah's terrible statement on the impossibility of change is here carried to its logical consequences in comprehensive historical-theological contours. It is made clear that Jerusalem and Israel fell hopelessly into evil. Ezekiel takes up images of the earlier prophets, but with terrifying rigor forms them in a message that the people of Yahweh are radically corrupt, in the literal sense of "radical," that is, from the roots. Ezekiel is the great prophetic proclaimer of "radical evil;" one is almost tempted to introduce the term "original sin."

Thus Ezekiel 16 tells the story of Jerusalem as the unfaithful wife. Here the prophet takes up a motif from Hosea and Jeremiah, but formulates it in his own way. His introduction, "Your origin and your birth are of the land of the Canaanites; your father was an Amorite and your mother a Hittite," contains historical elements of tradition. For a particularly long time, Jerusalem was a non-Israelite, Canaanite city.[25] But it is the prophet, not the historian, who speaks here. The entire sinful propensity of Jerusalem is already contained in this Canaanite origin. It is a hereditary condition. The elaboration in 16:44-52 begins with a proverb: "Like mother, like daughter." As a modern proverb puts it: "The apple does not fall far from the tree." The description continues how Yahweh raises this child who had been turned out by her parents, as a foundling,[26] gives her fine jewelry, even takes her in marriage, but receives nothing from her but thanklessness and faithlessness. The judgment that she will be treated "according to the law concerning adulteresses and murderesses" is the only possibility left.[27]

The same motif is taken up again in Ezekiel 23. Although clearly starting with Jer 3:6-10, the writer here speaks of two women representing the two kingdoms of Israel. He adds the ancient creedal statement of Israel's exodus from Egypt,[28] and traces the paths of both women from Egypt. But here also, even beyond the beginnings of the Exodus, the theme of the original depravity of these two women is included:

> Son of man, there were two women, the daughters of one mother; they played the harlot in Egypt; they played the harlot in their youth; there their breasts were pressed and their virgin bosoms handled. (23:2)

Then follows the story of Yahweh, who married them: "They became mine, and they bore sons and daughter" (23:4). But the history quickly turns toward evil. If chapter 16 considered primarily, as in Hosea 2, the *religious* digression into the cults of Baal and the high places, chapter 23, taking up ideas from Hosea (and Isaiah),[29] considers the *political* adultery with foreign powers—the Assyrians and the Neo-Babylonians. Precisely as in chapter 16, here also the original depravity of the women gains the upper hand. The sinfulness of the beginning leads with an inner compulsion to the later faithlessness. That is the nature of the house of Israel, in both kingdoms.

There is also a third elaborated presentation. In Ezck 20:1-31, the school's later work expanded the text, especially with vv. 27-29. Here without symbolic coverings, Israel's beginnings in Egypt and the Exodus are related, as also in the creedal tradition.[30] But what is said here of these beginnings? Immediately at the election of the people when Yahweh promised to be their God and to bring them out of Egypt,[31] God commanded the people to turn away from the idols of Egypt. But already at this beginning, when the people were still in Egypt, they showed their evil nature. They rebelled against Yahweh and did not listen to his command,[32] so that even in Egypt, before he had led them out, he had to threaten the people with destruction. In the wilderness the same thing happened again, so that in his anger God condemned the first wilderness generation to death. The story was repeated with the second wilderness generation. Thus, even before the people were led into the land, Yahweh decided on their later dispersion among the peoples—the exile of Ezekiel's day. It can be shown that in this historical presentation there are traces of the spy story of Numbers 13–14 and perhaps of the story of the golden calf.[33] The overall view is uniquely Ezekiel's, however, and lies within the perspective of Ezekiel 16 and 21. Here in a powerful reformulation of the ancient tradition the radical sinfulness of the house of Israel from its beginnings and the unresisting decline to God's judgment are expressed.

In this context, the prophet makes a statement that, as far as I can tell, is unique in the Old Testament and that candidly approximates Pauline statements. In view of the sinfulness of the second wilderness generation, Yahweh decides not only that he will disperse Israel among the peoples, but over and beyond that he gives them "statutes that were not good and ordinances by which they could not have life; and I defiled them by their very gifts by making them offer by fire all their firstborn" (20:25-26). Here the puzzle is pondered, that Israel finds in its law the commandment to bring its firstborn to Yahweh.[34] Second Kings reports that Ahaz and Manasseh burned their sons as offerings (2 Kgs 16:3; 21:6) and recognizes in this the height of sinfulness against Yahweh and the cause of Judah's decline (2 Kgs 17:17). Ezekiel had to face the riddle of "statutes that were not good," which came from Yahweh, that no more led to life as good laws were intended (Ezek 20:11-13), but to death. Ezekiel could understand it only out of the dark mystery of God's will for a judgment of hardening that breaks forth where sinfulness reaches its peak. In another way, the same idea is intimated also in Ezek 3:20 and 14:9—an idea of last resort that emerges when human thought encounters impossible excesses of opposition to God and yet attempts to come to terms with the reality disclosed by such events.

Jerusalem's excess of guilt is expressed in another way in Ezek 22:1-16 by the catchword "bloody city." In vv. 6-12 in his presentation of the sinful city, the prophet proceeds through lists of legal prescriptions in the style of the Decalog or the lists in Leviticus 18–20 and accuses the city of every single sin. Such a legal "accusation of sin" was already introduced in Ezek 16:2 and 20:4 with similar introductory words: "And you, son of man, will you not judge, will you judge the bloody city? Then declare to her all her abominable deeds." The stereotyped repetition of this introductory formula leads one to think that we have here a genre (*Gattung*) of judicial accusation (perhaps only from Ezekiel's school).

Finally, we must not overlook in this connection the allegory of Ezekiel 15. The images of the vineyard and the vine are not foreign to Israel's cultic language. They like to use them to express the nobility of the people chosen by Yahweh.[35] Ezekiel does something shocking with this image, however; he employs it in the form of a debate into which he has woven historical parables. In his introductory question he simply bypasses what constitutes the nobility of the vine. He does not ask about the sweet fruit, but about the usefulness of the wood of the vine, and inserts throughout features of contemporary historical experience. What can one do with a piece of wood that has already been charred? The question refers to the events of 597. Out of the internal logic, the answer can only be that this wood cannot serve any purpose but to be thrown into the fire and burned up. Thus the noble image of the vine is destroyed internally. But there is no joy in such negation and destruction. It certainly has to do, however, with the destruction of all the self-glorification of the people and of their holy city of Jerusalem. With the people and the city nothing is praised, nothing. Everything is evil, depraved, useless, and ready for the fire. All "glory" is here destroyed. Man, even now the man within Yahweh's chosen people (Ezek 20:5), can only confess before God that god is just and that God's people are full of injustice and sin.

GOD'S REVELATION

Here a most decisive point is introduced. We might formulate the question: How did Ezekiel come to this proclamation? Do we find in him a person with an especially developed ethical conscience? Is it the anger of the prophet over the corruption and ungodly life of his people that moves his hand and forces his mouth to speak?

To explain Ezekiel in this way would be to misunderstand him. Here we must point to a form of address that occurs with particular frequency in his language and that cannot be overlooked in any interpretation of his proclamation. This is the so-called proof-saying (*Erweiswort*).[36] Ezekiel's announcement of an approaching action by Yahweh repeatedly leads to proclamation: "and you [or they] shall know that I am Yahweh." There are certain variations: "and they shall know that I, Yahweh, have spoken in my jealousy" (Ezek 5:13), or "that I am Yahweh who smites" (7:9). Ezekiel in no way invented this form or used it for the first time. A particularly elegant double example of this short formula is to be found in the older prophetic histories in 1 Kgs 20:13 and 28. In v. 28 a man of God tells the king of Israel, prior to the battle against the Syrians: "Because the Syrians have said, 'Yahweh is a god of the hills but he is not a god of the valleys,' therefore I will give all this great multitude into your hands and you shall know that I am Yahweh." In this text we see anew something of the archaic character of Ezekiel's proclamation. In this element of speech, which he employs often, he stands in the tradition of the earlier, preliterary prophecy (see pp. 77–78).[37]

A more detailed form-critical analysis of this language reveals that two different elements are combined in the final formulation.[38] The formula "and you shall know" or "thus you will know" derives from the legal language of a process of proof. For example, Pharaoh says to the brothers whom he suspects of being spies, but who in defense of their innocence have told him about their younger brother Benjamin: "Bring your youngest brother to me; and then I shall know that you are not spies but honest men" (Gen 42:34). Bringing the youngest brother is the proof by which the Pharaoh will recognize the truth of the brothers' statements.

Combined with this way of speaking, in the recognition formula of Ezekiel and 2 Kings 20 is the element "that I am Yahweh." In Hebrew this is a short objective clause (in the form of a predicate nominative) introduced by "that." This form, "I am Yahweh," has a clear setting in life (*Sitz im Leben*).[39] It is the form of self-presentation by which in an encounter an unknown person introduces himself. Thus in the great scene at Sinai, Yahweh in the first sentence of the Decalog emerges from his mystery and reveals himself to his people with "I am Yahweh your God, who brought you out of the land of Egypt, out of the house of bondage" (Exod 20:2).[40] Thus, here, according to the full recognition formula, the one to be recognized is Yahweh, who comes forth in revelation.

Closer examination shows that the recognition formula always precedes a statement about Yahweh's actions; in our context, his judgmental action toward his people. This formula seeks to say that the ultimate meaning of God's action toward his people is to recognize God's revelation in this action. He presents himself to his people in his action as the one he is. By his deeds he wants to be recognized as the Lord with whom Israel has to deal.

Here the real purpose of God's action and judgment is expressed. It is not ethical anger that moves the hand of the prophet in his writing and opens his mouth in speaking. Rather, he knows that through everything that he proclaims, Yahweh, the God of Israel, is underway to reveal himself to his people. Where people bow their knees before this God and acknowledge that in his just action he is on the move, there Ezekiel's proclamation achieves its proper goal. The man affected by God's action properly answers God's address to him through the prophet's word and the deed of judgment by recognizing God, by acknowledging him, and submitting to him.

Here it would perhaps be helpful to glance at the general style of the entire book.[41] The order and uniformity of the general structure of the book are striking. That explains the long delay in critical work and makes understandable Smend's judgment cited earlier. The framework for the various sections of the book is a first-person report by the prophet. This form might at first indicate a strong biographical character. Closer examination shows, however, that Yahweh's action and speech are the thoroughgoing content of the prophet's first-person report. The great visionary intrusions into his life open his eyes for God's appearance and action (Ezek 1:1—3:15; 3:22—5:17; 8–11; 37:1-14; 40–48). Almost all the other pericopes include the formula "and the word of Yahweh came to me." It speaks of the inbreaking of the divine word into Ezekiel's life; God's word is the principal experience reported.[42]

This reference to the word of God as the true event leads to remarkable consequences. Even the words the prophet hears from his environment and with which he must contend come to him, not simply as commonly accessible knowledge, but by way of the word of Yahweh. Repeatedly Yahweh informs the prophet that people in Israel are saying certain things, are answering him in certain ways or with certain questions.[43]

Thus we cannot overlook that all of Ezekiel's reporting is full of Yahweh's action and seeks to point to the deeds of the God of Israel and to lead people to submission to this God and his majesty. "They shall know that I am Yahweh."

PROPHETIC SILENCE

The only dated pericope does not seem to fit this characterization. It is the short passage in Ezek 33:21-22.[44] There is neither the intrusion of the divine vision nor the event of the divine word. The passage simply says that an escapee from Jerusalem reports to the prophet, "The city has fallen." This information, however, releases the prophet's tongue, which the hand of Yahweh had bound the evening before.

To the statement that the prophet's mouth is opened is added, "and I was no longer dumb." This alludes to an event of broader importance for the prophet's proclamation.[45] Ezekiel 3:26-27, which is certainly editorial, leaves the impression that the prophet's inability to speak began seven days after his calling.[46] The expansion in Ezek 24:25-27, which once may have been the direct transition to 33:21-22, foretells his renewed ability to speak when the escapee will have arrived. But everything handed down in 4–24 about the preaching between the time of the prophet's call and the fall of Jerusalem speaks against such an extended time of dumbness;[47] it must have been for a shorter period. With the sensitivity of the prophet, which is to be observed elsewhere, we must not rule out that such periods of dumbness could have happened before. These would account for the school expansions in chapters 3 and 24.

When, however, Ezek 33:21-22 speaks of a freeing for proclamation for an unlimited period, it contains more than a short biographical note. It is to be understood within the framework of the prophet's entire proclamation. The school expansion of the word of the prophet in Ezek 16:63 says that after she is pardoned, the unfaithful wife will not be able to open her mouth. On the other hand, the late passage, 29:21, says that when the salvation promised to Israel has fully come, the prophet will be given full freedom to open his mouth. When compared with these passages, it must not be overlooked that 33:21-22 also intends to point to Yahweh's mighty action. Through the message of the eyewitness who comes from Jerusalem,[48] the prophet is informed how Yahweh has proved himself in his act of judgment. This opens the prophet's mouth in a deeper sense and gives him freedom (*parrhēsia*) to speak this word anew.

JUDGMENT AGAINST ISRAEL'S NEIGHBORS

Before we turn to the new speaking of the prophet after God proves himself in judgment, we should also consider briefly the extent to which Yahweh's intrusion in judgment affects Israel's neighbors.

In the general editing of the book, statements in Ezekiel 25–32 against seven peoples or cities and their leaders were inserted between the immediate announcement of the city's fall and the eyewitness report of this event in 33:21-22.[49]

Here the words against Egypt and Pharaoh (Ezekiel 29–32) again stand out. At one time they must have formed a complete, chronologically well-ordered, little book. The Tyre passage in 26–28, with its incomplete chronology at the beginning, may also have once been independent.[50]

From the dates, the Egyptian passage can certainly be placed around the time of the fall of Jerusalem.[51] From Jer 37:3 we learn that during this final period of fighting, after the beginning of the Babylonian siege of Jerusalem, Pharaoh marched out to support Judah. This entanglement of Egypt in the fate of Judah called for the prophetic proclamation of Pharaoh's judgment also at the hand of Nebuchadnezzar since, according to Ezekiel 17, Egypt had earlier been Judah's tempter, demanding its secession from Nebuchadnezzar (Ezek 20:20ff.; 32:11; see also 29:17-20).[52] Yet it is striking that only in 29:6b-9a is Egypt's relationship to Judah given as a reason for the judgment. The country's internal weakness is pictured by the image of the staff that breaks where one leans on it, as in Isa 36:6. Only at the beginning of the Tyre passage in Ezek 26:2 is there a certain malicious delight by the commercial city of Tyre in the destruction of its rival Jerusalem. Otherwise the words of judgment against these two neighboring powers follow different rules. Insofar as reasons are given for their fall, the points of attack are the great power's hubris and ostentatious display. With the picture of the fall of the mighty into hell,[53] the impending judgment is depicted in an especially impressive way. Mythical material from the environment is drawn in to skillfully increase the imagery of the language. Thus in Ezek 28:11-19, the myth of the expulsion of the original man from paradise; in chapter 31 the myth of the world-tree. Further, there is the understandable symbolizing of Tyre in chapter 27 as a glorious luxury ship[54] and Pharaoh in 29:1-16 and 32:16 as a crocodile of the Nile.

The announcement of judgment against Ammon, Moab, Edom, and the Philistines in Ezekiel 25, formed throughout as proof-sayings (*Erweiswörte*), has a quite different character. Here malicious delight at an enmity against the judged people of Yahweh and Jerusalem are the cause of the divine sentence. Thereby, however, a new zeal of God for his people is proclaimed in which he will prove himself as the Lord. The thought of Yahweh's self-glorification entirely dominates the short word against Sidon (28:21-23). It was possibly added late so that the number of powers addressed would be seven.

It may be surprising that there is no word of judgment against Babylon. Doubtless this is to be understood from the prophet's clear proclamation, following Jeremiah. For the prophet, King Nebuchadnezzar is God's ordained instrument of judgment against whom no prophetic word is to be directed. In contrast to the Book of Jeremiah, no threat against Babylon later forced its way into the Book of Ezekiel.[55] This counsels against going too far in reconstructing the final editing of the book. How differently Deutero-Isaiah, the prophet of the end of the Exile, speaks on this matter! In other places, though, he clearly takes up themes from Ezekiel.

HOPE FOR THE FUTURE

In the judgment in Ezekiel 25 against the Palestinian neighbors of the house of Israel, a new zeal of Yahweh for the house of Israel destroyed by his judgment is proclaimed. This zeal for his people, which quite surprisingly becomes the announcement of complete salvation for the house of Israel, is to be recognized fully in chapters 34ff. In the first part of the book, however, it also determines particular expansions of original words of judgment made somewhat later by Ezekiel himself or by his school. Thus Ezek 11:14-21; 16:42, 53-63; 17:22-24; 20:32-44.

The time depicted in Ezek 33:21-22 when the prophet opened his mouth anew suggests itself immediately as the beginning of this new proclamation. But 11:14-21, which seems to have been spoken at a time when Jerusalem and the temple still stood, keeps alive the question whether, in view of the deportees, the prophet may not have been empowered to speak a word that opened up a renewed future for the people.

The vision in Ezek 37:1-14, doubtless to be dated after 587, quite clearly allows us to see how the image quite unexpectedly becomes a dramatically experienced reality for the prophet. In 37:11 we hear the deep sighing of the people, shattered by the judgment: "Our bones are dried up, and our hope is lost; we are clean cut off." The divine judgment has performed its work to the bitter end. From these sighs arise the first of three lamentations, employing imagery used, for example, in Ps 31:11 [MT v. 12] and Prov 17:22. Seized by the "hand of Yahweh," the prophet is introduced "in the spirit of Yahweh" to a vision where people's laments acquire corporeal reality. The prophet is led through a huge field of dry bones that proclaim death at every turn. Here, however, he receives the commission of speaking to these dead bones with a prophetically empowered word. And during his prophecy he experiences how the bones come together, how sinews, flesh, and skin grow; and at his second word the dead bodies rise to life through the invoked "spirit." This vision he is to interpret to the house of Israel as the promise of a new homecoming into the land of Israel.[56] Here again is the recognition formula of the "proof-saying" (*Erweiswort*): "and you shall know that I, Yahweh, have spoken and I have done it."

From this we can derive two things: First, it is clear that for the people who experienced the judgment on their sins of the year 587, one can, in my opinion, speak only of the future with the category of awakening from the dead. Thus, as in the original creation (Gen 2:7), when humanity was first formed into a body and then created as a living being with God's own breath, so "the spirit" whom the prophet called in by his word awakens to life again those bodies that had assembled from the dead bones under the prophet's word. There is, however, nothing viable from Israel's old existence that is drawn upon here. The judgment has been dispensed up to the end. But by virtue of his absolute creative authority, Yahweh creates new life out of this utter lostness.

Second, what is announced here cannot afterward be evaluated to honor anyone. It takes place so that Yahweh will be acknowledged insofar as in his new act of creation he reveals himself to his people. God is the one who speaks here through his prophet's word; God's word is what happens.

But why this new beginning? Ezekiel 36:16-21 reveals the reasons. It repeats once more the sorry history of Yahweh with his people that necessarily ended in exile. During the Exile, however, Yahweh's name, which is bound up with his own people, is ridiculed among the foreign countries. "These are Yahweh's people and they had to leave their land." It is now God's unique logic, however, that he does not disassociate his name from this people, but in an inexplicable faithfulness allows it to remain bound to them. Because of this connection, he begins to be jealous of his name. Ezekiel 36:21 says that he concerned himself about his holy name. Therefore he acts. "It is not for your sake, O house of Israel, that I am about to act, but for the sake of my holy name . . . and I will vindicate the holiness of my great name." It is remarkable how closely Ezekiel here approaches the formulation of Deutero-Isaiah (Isa 43:25).

This connection also occurs in other places. We hear in Ezek 20:33 the despairing self-abandonment of the dispersed people. "Let us be like the nations, like the tribes of the countries, and worship wood and stone." Here the only possibility that the house of Israel thinks it can see is the assimilation of the exiles into their heathen environment. Against this, however, the prophet is summoned to proclaim a new event of exodus that God will accomplish as formerly when he led them out of Egypt "with a mighty hand and an outstretched arm" (Deut 26:8). As God then met his people in the wilderness of Egypt" as the Holy One and held judgment, so will he meet his own people face to face "in the wilderness of the nations" and separate them in judgment as one allows a flock to "pass under the rod." Those thus pruned out will march to "the high mountain of Israel" in order properly to offer sacrifice to God. Here is the proclamation of the new Exodus, already formed in Hos 2:14-15 [MT vv. 16-17] and rejoicingly developed in the proclamation of Deutero-Isaiah.[57]

Furthermore, the prospect arises here of a new, peaceful life in the land under a new David who as the *one* shepherd will make the house of Israel, torn in the past into two states, again one people (Ezek 37:15-28) and will replace the evil shepherds of the past (34:1-31).

Two aspects of the new time of the future salvation are depicted. It will be the time when Yahweh will heal the people's old disobedience by giving them a new heart and a new spirit and by replacing their stony hearts with hearts of flesh (Ezek 36:26; see 11:19). And Yahweh will also in that time once again dwell in the midst of his people and will be their God in a new, saving covenant. The double covenant formula appears in this connection (37:37; see also 11:20; 14:11).[58] All this is not to be understood in just a spiritual sense, however. This great concluding vision (40–48), powerfully elaborated, describes the pure symmetry of the future temple where, according to 43:1-12, Yahweh's glory will enter in anew. Here we can clearly recognize the work of the school as it planned and considered the order of a pure worship in the sanctuary and the proper course of the princes in the service of the sanctuary. In 40–48 the plans of the generation following the Exile, which realistically thought and planned toward an imminent day of the return, are ever more clearly expressed.[59]

Cynicism and Hope

One final aspect hitherto left aside in the proclamation of the prophet himself must still be considered. It witnesses to the realism and concrete responsibility in which the prophet understood his mission to his people after their great collapse. The sublime proclamation of impending return and new creation of the people must have left open a question in the concrete, everyday life of the exiles: What shall we do today? Ezekiel did not sidestep this question.

He did not deal with it in meaningless generalities, but in lively discussion with the voices of resignation and cynical nihilism that threatened to spread among the people after the catastrophe. Ezekiel 33:24 shows that among those who still remained in the country in 587 were some who sought to bypass the seriousness of the judgment with pious self-consolation: "Abraham was only one man, yet he got possession of the land; we are many; the land is surely given to us to possess." Toward such a position Ezekiel had only new judgment to pronounce (33:25-29).

Even stronger are the voices of those who have rejected hope. On the one hand there are cynical nihilists who reject any righteousness of God: "The fathers have eaten sour grapes, and the children's teeth are set on edge" (Ezek 18:2); and with this the open provocation of God: "The way of Yahweh is not just" (18:25, 29; 33:17, 20). On the other hand there are the voices of pious despair that likewise believe no more in a future: "Our transgressions and our sins are upon us, and we waste away because of them; how then can we live?" (33:10).

The teaching in Ezek 18:4-20 concerns that resignation that believes that guilt is firmly anchored in the sequence of generations. Against this, the prophet passionately proclaims that each generation is responsible for its own action and receives life or death accordingly. Ezekiel 18:21-32, however, has to do with the fatalistic cowardice of those who think themselves ultimately bound in their fate by their yesterdays. To them he proclaims that today the freedom to turn around stands open. Behind this call for conversion emerges the face of a God who is not simply a dispassionate judge casting lots with equanimity. "Have I any pleasure in the death of the wicked, says the LORD Yahweh, and not rather that he should turn from his way and live?" (18:23). God is a partisan on the side of life.

One further thing in this exposition must be recognized. A general call to conversion is not enough. In the first passage, which seeks to release people from the fate of a guilt transmitted through the generations, the prophet describes in a sequence of three generations—a just person, an unjust person, and a just person. In the introductory description of the just person, we can recognize a formula that enumerates the individual traits of the just person and probably comes from the liturgy of entrance at the temple gates. Here these traits might have been specified: One who "does not eat on the mountains or lift up his eyes to the idols of the house of Israel . . . does not oppress any one, but restores to the debtor his pledge, commits no robbery. . ." (18:5-9). A characteristic form of a declaratory judgment of righteousness was pronounced at the temple gate over the one who measured up to all this: "He is just,"[60] and he was allowed entrance into the sanctuary where life was promised under God's blessing: "He shall live, says the LORD Yahweh."[61] Here is made visible in individual examples what conversion must mean. Using the temple formula in a time when the temple in Jerusalem lay in ruins and the exiles had to worship in an unclean land in which God had become "a sanctuary to them in small measure" (11:16), Ezekiel, as it were, calls individuals anew to the temple gate and promises them even in exile entrance into life that was once proclaimed in the sanctuary.

Is this not, however, precisely that second aspect of the office entrusted to him in Ezek 3:17-21—a formulation presupposed both by 33:1-9 and chapter 18? Here Ezekiel is called by God to be a lookout (watchman) and is taken into this service with full responsibility.

> So you, son of man, I have made a watchman for the house of Israel. . . .
> If I say to the wicked, O wicked man, you shall surely die, and you do not
> speak to the wicked man to turn from his way, that wicked man shall die

in his iniquity, but his blood I will require at your hand. But if you warn the wicked to turn from his way, and he does not turn from his way; he shall die in his iniquity, but you will have saved your life. (Ezek 33:7-9)

The harsh proclaimer of the judgment that is inexorably breaking in over a deeply guilty people, the proclaimer of God's promise to call to new life his people dying in exile and to give them again his presence in his sanctuary, has become, as well, the admonisher and warner of the individual. He admonishes him to set out toward his God in obedience. He stands there as the admonisher who knows himself to be responsible for the individual's salvation.

Ezekiel is the Old Testament prophet who proclaims more radically than any other that no righteousness of the people called by God can stand up before God. After the collapse, however, he proclaims a new future to those who have been destroyed by the judgment. In expectation of such a future, he calls to obedience today.

All of this is not yet the message of the Son of God who, for the world's sins, himself went to death in order that man through faith in this death would turn toward the life given to him. But who would deny that Ezekiel is a messenger on the way to the Son?

6

The Word of God in the Book of Ezekiel

According to the book bearing his name, Ezekiel was a priest exiled to the east in the year 598 B.C.E., eleven years before the final catastrophe of Judah, along with other members of the upper class. There he lived with a Jewish group in Tel-Abib, on the Chebar canal near the Babylonian city Nippur, and by a vision of God was commissioned to be a prophet to his fellow exiles. He is not one of the most easily understood figures of Old Testament prophecy.

In the last two generations of research the enigma of Ezekiel has taken a new form. Can the man who wrote the colorful figures of the central part of the book also be the author of the monotonous casuistry that discusses the question of just retribution (Ezekiel 18)? Hölscher tried to save the poet Ezekiel by giving up more than half of the Book of Ezekiel.[1] Can the words that appear to be addressed directly to the situation in Jerusalem, and the action of Ezekiel in killing a man in Jerusalem by his prophetic word (11:13)—can these things be understood as the word of someone who is residing in Babylon? By means of critical emendations some have tried to posit a figure who worked solely in Jerusalem and was only exiled in 587.[2] It is not necessary to discuss here the fantastic criticism that tries to understand the whole book as a pseudepigraph.[3] But even if these methods are rejected, must we not at least regard Ezekiel as a pathological phenomenon, as does Karl Jaspers in a pathological study of Ezekiel as a schizophrenic?[4]

Literary-critical, biographical, and psychological attempts to understand Ezekiel are confronted with a mystery that is still unsolved. It may thus be worthwhile to raise the question whether or not the traditio-historical method, which has been applied with admirable results to the Pentateuch, can give us some information about the uniqueness of this mysterious, strange prophet and the nature of his message. The following remarks are an attempt to apply this method. They purposefully proceed from passages that even the most radical critics regard as essential parts of the book.

THE VINE—EZEKIEL 15

We may begin with Ezekiel 15. This chapter contains a parable about the vine. The vine-stock plays a role in the poetry of Israel at a very early date. In the story of the spies (Num 13:23), its noble fruit is a sign of the luxury of Canaan. And in Jotham's fable the vine-stock appears along with the cedar and the olive tree as a royal planting, in contrast to the thorn bush (Judg 9:8-15). In the Judah saying of the Blessing of Jacob, it is a characteristic of the paradisiacal time of fulfillment that the coming ruler from Judah will bind his ass to the vine, and the foal of his ass to the vine-stock; he will wash his clothes in wine and his mantle in the blood of the grapes (Gen 49:11). The vineyard occupies a prominent place in the symbolism of the love song, and therefore it can appear in a prophetic oracle such as Isaiah's daring use of the love song for expressing a word of judgment (Isa 5:1-7). In this connection it is important to note that in the figurative language of the cult, the vine clearly becomes an image of the nobility of the elect people, Israel.

> You did bring a vine out of Egypt;
>> you did drive out the nations and plant it.
> You did clear the ground for it;
>> it took deep root and filled the land.
> The mountains were covered with its shade,
>> the mighty cedars with its branches;
> it sent out its branches to the sea,
>> and its shoots to the River. (Ps 80:8-11 [MT vv. 9-12])

A glance at Hos 10:1 shows that the idea of Israel as the noble vine must have been well known in the figurative language of the liturgy of the eighth century: "Israel is a luxuriant vine, bearing [much] fruit."

What does Ezekiel do with this figure for the nobility of the people of God, hallowed by ancient liturgical tradition? "Son of man, how does the wood of the vine surpass any wood, the vine branch, which is among the trees of the forest? Is wood taken from it to make anything? Do men take a peg from it to hang any vessel on?" (Ezek 15:2-3). Is the point not evident? Note the violent and provocative manner in which the liturgical image, which is supposed to characterize the nobility of Israel's election, is disfigured. The central element of the figure, namely the valuable fruit, is simply ignored, and with brusque indifference God asks about the wood of the vine. By forcing the figure into this unsuitable perspective, its nobility is completely destroyed. It is just as if someone should look at a beautiful medieval altar painting and notice only that the wood is full of worm holes and, with this observation, pass judgment on the picture as a whole. But this is not enough. In a curious dual movement, which is to be found elsewhere in Ezekiel, the prophet analyzes the situation even more intensely. He speaks to Jerusalem, which had only recently suffered the catastrophe of the year 598 B.C.E., and continues the comparison with a reference to this event: "Lo, it is given to the fire for fuel; the fire has consumed both ends of it, and the middle of it is charred—is it useful for anything?" (15:4). With strange, stubborn thoroughness the prophet spells out the result of all of this for the people dwelling in Jerusalem: "Lo, when it was whole, it could not be used for anything; how much less, when the fire has consumed it and it is charred, can it then be used for anything?" (15:5). The purpose is clear: the figure that once described the nobility of the chosen people Israel is destroyed at its very center and has now become a derogatory image for something that is basically useless. The fire that finally destroys the vine becomes, in terms of the context of the figure, a logical necessity. The vine is now useless in itself, but it can still serve as fuel.

UNFAITHFUL JERUSALEM—EZEKIEL 16 AND 23

We may choose two further examples. In chapters 16 and 23 the people of God appear as the bride of Yahweh. The ultimate source of this figure may be Canaanite. The cultic festival of the divine "sacred marriage" (*hieros gamos*) includes a wedding of the god of the heavens to the earth, which, by means of fructifying rain, is once again awakened and bears new fruit. We may observe that Hosea, who is the first prophet clearly to apply the figure of marriage to the relationship between Yahweh and Israel, calls not the people, but the land, the partner of Yahweh (Hos 1:2). This may reveal something of the Canaanite background of the idea. Naturally Hosea, and then Jeremiah following him, uses the figure only as a saying about broken marriage, with reference to the present situation of Israel.[5] Isaiah applies the expression to the city of Jerusalem.

A further examination of the use of this figure by Ezekiel's predecessors—Hosea, Isaiah, and Jeremiah—shows that these earlier prophets were working with the antithesis: pure beginning over against corrupt present, of Israel or of Jerusalem. For Hosea the moment when Israel entered the fruitful land of Canaan was the occasion for her fall. Accordingly, at the end of time Yahweh will once again lead his people into the wilderness and there speak to her heart; in other words, the end of the time is described as a time of betrothal.[6] Jeremiah, in somewhat milder language, surveys the past in his lament, "I remember the devotion of your youth, your love as a bride, how you followed me in the wilderness, in a land not sown" (Jer 2:2).

What happens to the content of this figure when it is taken over by Ezekiel? The sketch of the history of the unfaithful wife of Yahweh in Ezekiel 16 differs from the earlier use of the same theme in Isaiah, Hosea, and Jeremiah, not only in the broad scope of the portrayal, which pictures the contrary character of Jerusalem's whoredom in shocking frankness, but also, in respect to the material itself, by the introduction of the figure of a foundling child. The use of this motif enables the prophet to strengthen the emphasis upon the grace of Yahweh, who not only marries the wife, as in Hosea, but also makes her very life as such possible. Without the saving intervention of Yahweh in the life of this foundling child, who had been wallowing in its own blood and cast forth into the wilderness, the child would have lost its life.

But Ezekiel's language also provides for the introduction of information about the real parents, and thus about the actual significance of the child. And here we once again find material characteristic of the prophet. "By origin and birth you are of the land of the Canaanites. Your father was an Amorite, and your mother a Hittite" (Ezek 16:3). In the first place, there is reliable historical memory in this statement. Jerusalem was an old Canaanite city with a Hittite ruling class. Abdi-Hepa of the Amarna letters, who ruled in Jerusalem in the fourteenth century, is known by his name to have been a servant of Hepa, the great Hittite and Hurrian goddess whose picture is to be seen on the relief of Yazilikaya.[7] Among the followers of David in Jerusalem was Uriah the Hittite (2 Sam 11:3, 6, 17, 21, 24; 12:9-10). Jerusalem became an Israelite city only under David. But Ezekiel's statement is not intended to be primarily a historical datum, but rather a religious value judgment. When, in another context later in the chapter, we find the proverb "Like mother, like daughter" applied to Jerusalem, the real meaning of the prophet becomes clear (Ezek 16:44).[8] Jerusalem is corrupt because even her parents were corrupt. It is no wonder that the whole story of her marriage with Yahweh is one of unfaithfulness.

In Ezekiel 23 the motif of the unfaithful wife appears twice, applied to both parts of the divided kingdom, Israel and Judah. And here it is connected with another tradition complex. The basic element of the credo, by means of which Israel understands and describes her particular connection with Yahweh, is the statement about the Exodus from Egypt.[9] It is Israel's primal *evangelium*, and became, as we now see clearly, the kernel around which the whole tradition of the Pentateuch crystallized. Chapter 23 shows how Ezekiel takes up even this sacred element of Israel's confession of faith and subordinates it to the motif of the unfaithful wife, now carried to its extreme:

> Son of man, there were two women, the daughters of one mother. They played the harlot in Egypt; even in their youth they played the harlot. There their breasts were pressed and their virgin bosoms handled . . . . They became mine, and they bore sons and daughters. (23:2, 4)

In the following verses Ezekiel completely ignores the whole saving history of grace and utterly rejects any tradition of a glorious past. Rather he goes on to tell of Israel's prostitution to Egypt, Assyria, and Babylonia, and by this he means primarily political, and, as a result, religious subservience. The intercourse with Egypt is portrayed in particularly crass terms. The point cannot be missed: Even in Egypt, Israel ordinarily finds the beginnings of the history of grace, even at the roots of the faith there is the indelible stain of the corruption of Israel, both north and south.

I Would Pour Out My Wrath—Ezekiel 20

Chapter 20 also belongs in this context; in spite of its prosaic language, it is one of Ezekiel's most unique and unprecedented statements.[10] What happens to the noble Israelite credo here? At first the main lines of the original form are entirely discernible. In a formulation that is surprisingly close to that of the latest source of the Pentateuch, the priestly credo, the passage begins,

> On the day when I chose Israel, I raised my hand (to swear) over the seed of the house of Jacob, and I revealed myself to them in the land of Egypt. And I raised my hand to them: "I am Yahweh your God." On that day I raised my hand to them that I would bring them out of the land of Egypt into a land that I had told them about, a land flowing with milk and honey, the most glorious of all lands. (Ezek 20:5-6)

Up to this point Ezekiel is still within the framework of the ancient traditions, here transmitted with theological precision. But then the passage turns clearly in the direction of Ezekiel's particular theme:

> And I said to them, Cast away the detestable things your eyes feast on, every one of you, and do not defile yourselves with the idols of Egypt. I am Yahweh, your God. But they rebelled against me and would not listen to me; they did not every man cast away the detestable things their eyes feasted on, nor did they forsake the idols of Egypt. Then I thought I would pour out my wrath upon them and spend my anger against them in the midst of the land of Egypt. But I acted for the sake of my name, that it should not be profaned in the sight of the nations among whom they dwelt, in whose sight I made myself known (in the promise) to them in bringing them out of the land of Egypt. So I led them out of the land of Egypt and brought them into the wilderness. (20:7-10)

This, according to Ezekiel 20, is the history of the Exodus.

Then follows the story of the subsequent period, written in strange, stereotyped language full of parallel formulas like that of a casuistic document. It is divided into three phases: the sojourn in Egypt, the first generation in the wilderness, and the second generation in the wilderness. A similar series of events takes place in each of the three phases, but every time there is a heightening of the dark and foreboding language—like a storm coming nearer and nearer. Each phase begins with Yahweh's act of grace, combined with a particular legal demand. In Egypt the people receive the promise of the land along with the demand to put away their idols. The first generation in the wilderness experiences the Exodus from Egypt and receives from Yahweh the law "by which man lives, if he performs it." In spite of the sins of their fathers, the members of the second generation are preserved and hear again the demand to turn to Yahweh (vv. 6-7, 10-11, 18). But in that generation the people are again obstinate (vv. 8, 13, 21). In each of the three phases we have Yahweh's threatening decision that he will destroy Israel (vv. 8b, 13b, 21b). But three times this is replaced by the decision that Yahweh will not profane his name in the eyes of the people (vv. 9, 14, 22). Yet the threats become more and more ominous. Although there are none at the end of the first phase, in the second phase (the first generation in the wilderness) the people are denied entrance into the promised land (v. 15). And in the third phase there is a unique double expression of Yahweh's anger (vv. 23-24, 25-26): First we have a curse containing an anticipation of the future: "Then I raised my hand over them in the wilderness, that I would scatter them among the nations and disperse them through the countries." Second, there is an expression unparalleled in the Old Testament: "I gave them statutes that were not good and ordinances by which they could not have life." Here Ezekiel is thinking of the sacrifice of the first-born and its sinister ambiguity.[11] It is difficult to measure how much brusque disregard of the piety of Israel is contained in this summary of history. Israel's whole history of decision is compressed into the events in Egypt and the wilderness. All the following centuries of history in Canaan—Jerusalem, the temple, David, and Josiah—are simply passed over.[12] Possibly this is to be explained in terms of the conviction that the roots of Israel's salvation lie in this early period, as other passages indicate.[13] But this is impossible for Ezekiel, since his accent is exactly the reverse: that early history is the history that determines Israel's judgment. These early phases of Israel's history have already forced Yahweh to make the decision to scatter them among the nations and send them into exile.[14] And so speaks an exile among the exiles.

Ezekiel destroys all trust in the self-righteousness of Yahweh's people, no matter how well-hidden it may be. He attacks the very period that gave rise to romantic and heroic notions of Israel's history, since even the great prophets of the earlier generations had spoken of it as a golden age. With reckless abandon, he is capable of turning even the most sacred traditions into an accusation against Israel herself.

As for the origins of this harsh message, it is to be noted that here Ezekiel is the natural fulfillment of the message of the pre-exilic prophets about the sin of Israel. But the judgments of Amos, Hosea, Micah, and Isaiah were derived from actual encounters with gluttony, social injustice, insolent hubris, and religious self-certainty, and were only occasionally grounded in the history of Israel.[15] Here, however, the scope of the message is extended to the whole of Israel's history in an almost catechetical way. But a reference to Ezekiel's fulfillment of the prophetic tradition does not suffice. He himself would refer to a more recent encounter. He knows the destructive will of his God. "I am Yahweh, your God!" This is the formula with which Ezekiel conceives the original revelation of Yahweh, reduced to its bare essentials (20:5, 7).[16] It is the formula that appears at every point as the source of each particular command in the legal material of the so-called Holiness Code (Leviticus 17–26) and it has long been noted that there is a close relationship between this code and the Book of Ezekiel.[17] Against this holy will of the sovereign God, who, in his mercy, gives life to the foundling child and the honor of marriage to the adolescent virgin, who—now without images—calls Israel out of Egypt and thus grants her existence itself against this sovereign will, "I am Yahweh," Israel is shattered.

Ezekiel's proclamation of sin is so formally inflexible that we are justified in asking the question whether there could be any meaningful response other than fatalistic suffering.[18] But Ezekiel came to terms with this fatalistic, almost cynical acceptance of judgment. In the image of the sour grapes that leave behind an unpleasant taste in the mouth or "set the teeth on edge," as it is put, we have the mocking words "The fathers have eaten sour grapes, and the children's teeth are set on edge" (Ezek 18:2).[19] In chapter 18 Ezekiel answers this complaint with a discussion that reveals the same casuistic, variegated thought as the story of the generations in chapter 20, and therefore cannot be separated from the latter and attributed to another hand. Does this casuistic method of discussion and determining an issue come from the official function of the priest, so that, in considering the origin of Ezekiel's material, we find the priest-prophet going about his original priestly business? In the development of the theme, Ezekiel first sets forth a statute of the divine law: "As I live, says Yahweh . . . all souls are mine; the soul of the father as well as the soul of the son is mine: the soul that sins shall die" (18:3-4). Then this thesis is developed in terms of three generations, reminding us of the three historical phases of chapter 20: the righteous man, the unrighteous son of a righteous man, and the righteous son of an unrighteous man. Each of these cases is measured by the norm of the divine law, and then for each there is a brief sentence like the priestly mediation of the decision of God: He is righteous; he shall surely live. He shall surely die.[20] He shall surely live. This is the first breach in the wall of fatalism: No, not the son for the father! Each separate generation suffers for its sin and deserves its own reward. But then we have still another casuistic series: a discussion of the theoretical case in which the godless man turns back to the law, and that of the righteous man who turns away from his righteousness. Once again, and in an even more decisive way, the wall of fatalism is pierced: not only is the freedom of a new beginning given to each generation, but this freedom continues into the present in the life of the individual. Your yesterday is not your fate; take your today from your God.

> Repent and turn away from all your transgressions. . . . Cast away from you all the transgressions which you have committed against me. Create for yourselves a new heart and a new spirit. Why will you die, O house of Israel? (18:30b-31)

And behind these words there appears a view of God that has nothing more to do with the image of a stern judge coolly deciding cases with blindfolded eyes. "I have no pleasure in the death of the person worthy of death; return, that you may live!" (18:32).

These expressions throw new light on the prophet's strict reckoning with the history of Israel. To be sure there is no chance of escape. There can be no appeal to the golden days of Israel's early history. But at the same time this reckoning does not block the way forward, the way from today to tomorrow. It is intended to be a warning, a call for right decision today, and therefore it clearly knows something of tomorrow's possibilities—possibilities before Yahweh.

Once again chapter 20, which, in my opinion, is the key to Ezekiel's prophecy, can help us to find the proper approach. This hard saying about the corrupt history of Israel is an answer to the people who try to bring a conclusion to the history of judgment. "We want to be like the nations,[21] like the tribes of the countries, and worship wood and stone" (20:32). Are the exiles here resigning from and abandoning their own further existence: We have suffered so much; let us, therefore, be absorbed into the nations? Or, shall we accept another suggestion and see here the expression of a tentative claim of independence by the exiles; was there a desire to institute sacrifice in the exile, against all the ordinances of the law, in order to maintain religion at least at this level?[22] At any rate, this word of the people is strongly opposed by Yahweh's own claim, which has a very different intent: "As I live, says Yahweh, with a mighty hand and an outstretched arm, and with wrath poured out, I will be king over you" (20:33). It is a strange, intense word full of the most radical tension. Elsewhere in Ezekiel we have no reference to the idea of the kingship of Yahweh, which is so extensively developed in other Old Testament passages, and which certainly had strong cultic roots in the New Year's festival of Israel.[23] So we must be all the more discerning in our interpretation of the single passage in which the prophet does use these terms. Over against stricken Israel's discouraged resignations, these words proclaim that Yahweh's royal power has not been shaken, and that it will once again be established over his people. But now the words have a surprising double meaning. "With a mighty hand and an outstretched arm"—there are the ancient formulas for God's saving act in the Exodus from Egypt.[24] They express freedom, escape from bondage, new life. But connected with them we have "with wrath poured out"—the formula used three times in the first half of the chapter to express the threatening, but then withheld, anger of Yahweh (vv. 8, 13, 21).[25] Will the storm now break in full force? The continuation of the passage shows the wonderful way in which the old salvation history is given new reality in this forthcoming act of Yahweh, while at the same time the refinement of his judgment is carried out to its conclusion.

> I will bring you out from the peoples where you are scattered, with a mighty hand and an outstretched arm, and with wrath poured out. And I will bring you into the wilderness of the peoples, and there I will enter into judgment with you face to face, as I entered into judgment with your fathers in the wilderness of the land of Egypt. I will enter into judgment with you and I will make you pass under the rod, and I will make you go in by number. (20:35-37)[26]

But after this refining judgment there follows the new future of the people, their new dwelling with the holy mountain as the center.

THE VALLEY OF DRY BONES—EZEKIEL 37

The examination of one last passage may help us to interpret the ultimate depth of meaning in the possible tomorrow clearly envisioned by the prophet. Ezekiel 37 records a bizarre vision of the prophet.

> The hand of Yahweh was upon me, and he brought me out by the Spirit of Yahweh, and set me down in the midst of the plain [RSV: valley]; it was full of bones. And he led me round among them; and behold, there were very many in the plain [upon the valley]; and lo, they were very dry. (vv. 1-2)[27]

Where does this unbelievable image come from? The immediate background of the material can be determined with a relative degree of certainty. The sequel shows that in this speech the prophet is replying to a word of discouragement from the Israelites. "Our bones are dried up, and our hope is lost; we are clean cut off" (v. 11). The people express their doubt in a threefold statement: the plain word about lack of hope, then the two images of the dry bones and the cut flower(?). And in the context of these expressions it happened that one of the two images suddenly struck the prophet and was transformed into the reality of visionary experience.

It seems to me that such a process, which is clearly characteristic of Ezekiel's experience and helpful in interpreting the genesis of his material, can be traced in other passages as well. Two examples may serve to clarify the point. In one of his confessions, Jeremiah complains, "Your words were found, and I ate them, and your words became to me a joy" (Jer 15:16a). In Ezekiel's visionary experience of his call, this image, which may have come to Ezekiel along with other words of Jeremiah, became visionary reality: a scroll with the words of Yahweh is given to Ezekiel to eat (3:1-3). Among Isaiah's threatening words from the year 733 we have, "In that day the LORD will shave with a razor which is hired beyond the River . . . the head and the hair of the feet, and it will sweep away the beard also" (Isa 7:20). In Ezekiel this image is transformed into the dramatic reality of a symbolic action. He publicly cuts off the hair of his head and beard with a sword, and then (note once again that the action occurs in two stages), as a sign of judgment, he takes some hairs from the three piles he has made and burn them in the fire, cuts them with the sword, and strews them to the wind (Ezek 5:1-12). In an analogous process of "incarnation" that reveals something of the unique inner structure of the prophet's thought, we have in Ezekiel 37 the spectacle of the field full of dry bones, representing the dead people in the Exile.

The prophet receives the commission to speak a prophetic word over this field of the dead and by means of this word of God to call the spirit of life from all four directions of the wind. Again we may note a dual movement in the event, already known to us from other passages. After the first speech of the prophet there is a rattling in the field full of bones; they join each other, sinews begin to grow on the bones, flesh comes upon them, and finally skin covers the whole. This precise description derives from the anatomical knowledge of the priest. But then the prophet is given another commission, and after this second speech, life comes into the dead bodies. They raise themselves up, and finally they stand on their feet, "an exceedingly great host." Thereupon follows the interpretation, in which the word of Yahweh casts off its cloak of imagery: "Behold, I will open your graves, and raise you from your graves, O my people; and I will bring you home into the land of Israel. And you shall know that I am Yahweh, when I open your graves . . ." (37:12-13).

In Ezekiel 20 we have the entrance to the new life embodied in the figure of a shepherd separating the sheep, and here, at the ultimate extreme of the prophet's thought, the subject is the awakening of the dead to life. At this point we cannot survey the extensive material on the new temple, the new presence of Yahweh, and the consequent revival of Israel—ideas particularly appropriate to Ezekiel the priest (20:40; 40–48). But even for chapters 20 and 37 we can maintain that this revival is not a goal in itself, but is rather related to a final act of knowledge: "You shall know that I am Yahweh." This formula has already appeared in the context of judgment passages.[28] There the judgment makes known Yahweh's nature. But here it becomes clear that full knowledge of Yahweh's nature can only be reached when the desire to save is seen behind the act of judgment. Or, stated more precisely, when one knows Yahweh himself, both in his judging and in his rising up in majesty, which contains within itself both the blessing of his holiness and his utter faithfulness to the work that he has begun. For this is the center around which all of Ezekiel's words revolve: Yahweh's glory is revealed in Israel, and beyond Israel to all the world. Therefore, even when his word announces the revival of the slain, it can still remain a curious rejection of the very ones who are to be revived. "It is not for your sake that I will act, says the LORD Yahweh; let that be known to you. Be ashamed and confounded for your ways, O house of Israel" (36:32). But what is the purpose of all of this emotional activity on Yahweh's part? "For the sake of my name"—thus runs the divine answer in Ezekiel's mouth.

In Ezekiel we hear a curious and strange formulation of "grace alone" (*sola gratia*). But who could fail to see that all of his prophecy is extremely close to that kerygma that experiences in Jesus Christ the final divine proclamation and its extension beyond the historical people of Israel? Who could fail to see that even in our own broken time, which suffers from the loss of its righteousness and its true life, Ezekiel's words are full of breathtaking actuality?

7

Form and Tradition in the Book of Ezekiel

In spite of all the work that has been done on the prophet Ezekiel, his prophecy still remains difficult to comprehend. I do not presume to illuminate all of those difficulties here. Rather, I will take up the more modest task of presenting certain facts about the form and material of Ezekiel's message, and on the basis of these, draw several conclusions about the personal character of this prophet and the background of his traditions. We will proceed in this task from the opinion that even though a complex redactional work can be recognized in the Book of Ezekiel, it preserves for us on the whole the peculiar characteristics of the prophet. Thus, the critical work of Hölscher, Messel, Torrey, Irwin, and others appears to me not to do proper justice to the text.

FIRST-PERSON SPEECH

When one considers the Book of Ezekiel according to its form, one is immediately struck by the consistent recurrence of speeches by the prophet in the first person. Only the superscription in 1:3a, which has been secondarily inserted into the text, is in the third person. Von Rabenau has shown how deeply this structure has penetrated into the substance of the book,[1] so that it can by no means be stripped away as a secondary redactional veil. Of the fifty-two units that I find in the book, only one can be considered strictly a narrative without a word of proclamation. This is Ezek 33:21-22, the account of the arrival of the news that Jerusalem had fallen. Because of the peculiarity of this form, the news of the fall of Jerusalem receives unusually strong emphasis. Five of the units then are accounts of visions (Ezek 1:1—3:15; 3:22—5:17; 8–11; 37:1-14; 40–48). All of the remaining forty-six units, with the single exception of the lament (*qinah*) in Ezekiel 19,[2] are introduced with the sentence "The word of Yahweh came to me."

This sentence is formally an element of narrative. In many texts in Samuel and Kings we find it in a narrative context,[3] reporting in the third person that the word of Yahweh had confronted a prophet. Apart from secondary superscriptions, the formula does not appear in the earlier classical prophets down to Jeremiah. In Jeremiah it appears again in narrative texts (Jer 1:2; 14:1; 28:12; et al.). It can be seen here, however, that this short sentence, formulated in the third person, is a simple introduction formula of a prophetic speech. This recalls the fact that the prophetic word does not express a timeless knowledge of Yahweh, but is, in fact, an event, an intrusion of divine reality into the prophet's life. Along with the narrative formula in the third person, the first-person formulation of the sentence is also found in Jeremiah (Jer 1:4, 11, 13; 2:1; et al.). And this is the form that appears exclusively in Ezekiel. By means of this personal account, Ezekiel subordinates everything else to the intrusion of the divine word and vision. And in light of this, all else recedes into the background. Thus we learn nothing of a circle of disciples such as we do in Isaiah, although the Book of Ezekiel clearly betrays the work of a group of students who were responsible for handing his prophecy down to subsequent generations. Neither do we know of a figure that would correspond to Jeremiah's Baruch. The message in this prophet is dominated completely by the event of the divine word to which he refers in the first person.

This strong accent of personal encounter with the word of Yahweh might well allow us to presume that Ezekiel goes his own original way and finds original forms for his proclamation. But such is not the case. In reality, his proclamation shows a completely different picture.

Yahweh's Hand and Spirit

We discover first a clear line that leads back from Ezekiel to the manner of expression and the world of ideas of preclassical prophecy. This is best shown in the visions. All five are introduced by the stereotyped expression "the hand of Yahweh came (*hyh*) or fell (*nfl*) over me." The phrase "the hand of Yahweh" appears only once in Isaiah (8:11) and once in Jeremiah (15:17). But the most common place for it is in the stories of the earlier preclassical prophets. Second Kings 3:15 reports that after music had been played, the hand of Yahweh came over the prophet Elisha so that he could deliver an oracle. According to 1 Kgs 18:46, the hand of Yahweh came over Elijah after the divine judgment on Mount Carmel so that he could run to Jezreel alongside the chariot of Ahab, an inconceivable feat of strength.

This leads us next to the expression that the "spirit of Yahweh" seizes the prophet and transplants him into some different state, indeed, translocates him from one place to another. In 2 Kgs 2:16, after Elijah had made his ascen-

sion, the prophetic disciples express the apprehension that the spirit of Yahweh might have lifted up Elijah and tossed him into some mountain or into
some valley. On the other hand, we find in 2 Kgs 5:26 an inner translocation
that allows the prophet to see things that occur at a great distance. Elisha perceives from his remote vantage point the fact that Gahazi had accepted a gift
from Naaman against his command. He describes this with these words: "Did
my heart not go along when a man descended from his chariot and met you?"
It is even more conspicuous that the classical prophets before Ezekiel avoided
the expression of the prophetic spirit (*ruah*). It seems that these prophets
wanted consciously to disassociate themselves from the spirit character of the
older prophets that could be so readily incited to extreme manifestations. In
Hos 9:7 we hear the people say: "The man of the spirit is mad." But in Ezekiel
this aversion is completely missing. He stands unconditionally in the old
prophetic tradition when he says at the end of his call vision that the spirit
lifted him up and took him away, or when in Ezek 8:3 he says concerning his
translocation to Jerusalem that a figure seized him by the hair, and the spirit
lifted him up between heaven and earth and brought him in a divine apparition to Jerusalem. Thus, just as Elisha looked into the distance to see Gahazi
accept a gift from Naaman, Ezekiel saw what was happening in the temple.
According to 11:24, the spirit lifted him up again and brought him back to
Jerusalem. Also 37:1 reports his translocation "by the spirit of Yahweh" into a
field full of dead bones.

Still a further minor feature should be discussed in this context. According
to Ezek 8:1ff., the vision of his translocation suddenly falls on the prophet as he
sits in his house while the elders of Judah are sitting before him. This stereotyped situation is to be found also in 14:1-11 and 20:1-44 (see also 33:31). We seek
in vain for this situation in the Books of Amos, Hosea, Isaiah, Micah, and Jeremiah. But its exact equivalent is found in 2 Kgs 6:32, where Elisha is "sitting in
his house" and the elders are "sitting with him." We may conclude, therefore,
that we have discovered here a typical scene from the prophetic "school"
(*Lehrhaus*). Its relationship to similar typical scenes in the Egyptian royal
novella needs further clarification.[4]

At this point, we have established nothing more than a connection
between the tradition of Ezekiel and the earlier prophetic spirit-theology. This
leads us next to the essential question of the relationship in content. The phenomenon of dramatic incitation plays an incomparably stronger role in the
visions of this prophet than in the earlier classical prophets. Whereas the
visions of most of the others show one single picture (locusts, a basket of fruit,
an almond rod), the visions of Ezekiel are much more strongly dramatized.
The prophet not only feels himself bodily removed and led around in his
visions. He himself initiates a part of the action that comprises the visions.

Under his prophecy, Pelatiah collapses dead (11:1-13). According to the vision in 37:7, the dead bones come together again and receive new life at his word. Ezekiel's visions contain, to use Lindblom's terminology, a strong autodramatic element that does not appear in the other major classical prophets.[5]

PROPHETIC SIGN ACTS

This observation leads us to another group of words that are characteristic for Ezekiel. The older preclassical prophets already knew the prophetic sign acts. Ahijah of Shiloh tore his mantle apart and gave Jeroboam ten of the twelve pieces—the ten tribes that Jeroboam would receive as the future king (1 Kgs 11:29-39). Elijah threw his mantle on Elisha, and by this act invested Elisha with the office of prophecy (1 Kgs 19:19-21). Georg Fohrer has carefully collected all of the material relevant to a study of these acts under the title *Die symbolischen Handlungen der Propheten* (The Symbolic Acts of the Prophets). Yet it seems to me that the designation "symbolic act" is nevertheless unsatisfactory because it does not make it clear enough that the prophet wants these acts to represent something more than the symbolic. In his sign (thus, the Old Testament itself speaks of this act), he initiates the beginning of a future event. The coming event is in fact already present in the sign act. This form of proclamation that anticipates future events is also found in the other major prophets: Isaiah goes around for three years naked and barefoot (Isa 20:1-6), and Jeremiah carries a yoke around his neck (Jeremiah 27–28). Fohrer counts three such acts in Isaiah. In Jeremiah there are seven (Jer 13:1-11; 16:1-9; 19:1-15; 27–28; 32:1-15; 40:8-13; 51:59-64). But in Ezekiel there are twelve, far more than in any of the other prophets (Ezek 3:22-27; 4:1-3; 4:4-8; 4:9-11; 4:12-15; 5:1-3; 12:1-16; 12:17-20; 21:11-12; 21:23-29; 24:15-24; 37:15-28). If one examines the formal structure of the accounts of the sign acts in Ezekiel, the most conspicuous aspect that strikes his attention is how rarely the completion of the sign act is expressly narrated. As a rule, only the divine word that calls forth the act is reported. Thus, the accounts of the sign acts often stand in units that are introduced by the formula "The word of Yahweh came to me." This shows once again the concentration on the word-event that was established above.

These units also illuminate the especially strong autodramatic character of Ezekiel's proclamation that marked his visions. The proclamation shows again and again the strong personal participation of the prophet in that which he proclaims. Or to formulate it the other way around: The event that is proclaimed by the prophet seizes him again and again and makes him a part of the event itself. His person—even his body—participates in the event that his word proclaims. With regard to the content, it is surprising how often Ezekiel's sign acts revolve around the fall of Jerusalem. The supposition that this event has special emphasis because it is reported in the only purely narrative unit in Ezekiel is thus confirmed from another angle. The three sign acts that form the literary basis for Ezekiel 4–5 describe the event of the siege and fall of the city. The prophet besieges a city that has been drawn on a brick—this is the beginning of the siege of Jerusalem. He eats a rationed amount of food and drinks a rationed portion of water. This is the hunger of the besieged city. He cuts off his hair with his sword, burns a third in fire, cuts up a third with his sword, and scatters a third to the four winds. This is the end of the inhabitants of Jerusalem. He marks two roads with signposts (Ezek 21:18-23). This points to the time before the beginning of the siege when Nebuchadnezzar was in the midst of finding his way to Jerusalem. He leaves his house by night with only a small bundle of goods that could be carried by an exile (12:1-16)—this is the deportation of the inhabitants of Jerusalem. The sighing of the prophet in 12:17-20 gives voice to anxiety over the devastation of the land. According to 21:6-7 [MT vv. 11-12], the groaning of the exiles is attested. And according to 24:15-27, the dumb grief of the prophet over the sudden death of his wife represents the dumb grief of the exiles over the news of the fall of the city and the temple, a grief that is no longer capable of the normal process of mourning. All of these texts show how the prophet saw himself participating in the event of the siege and fall of Jerusalem and the deportation of its inhabitants through acts that were in part consciously executed and in part unconsciously experienced (such as trembling or mute mourning).

With the autodramatic characteristics that recall the phenomenon of rapture associated with the spirit in the older prophets belongs that which is suggested by the introductory formula in Ezek 6:11: "Clap your hands and stamp your feet and say . . ."; or in 21:14 [MT v. 19]: "Prophesy, therefore, son of man; clap your hands. . . ." With these fomenting gestures, Ezekiel proclaims his word. Also the formula that calls for a type of *qibla* in the prophetic announcement must be discussed here, a formula that is found eight times in Ezekiel. According to 6:2-3, the prophet should set his face against the mountains of Israel; in 21:3 [MT 20:47], against the forest in the south (the Negeb; which in 21:2 [MT v. 7] is interpreted as "Jerusalem"); 25:2, against Ammon; 27:21, against Sidon; 35:2, against the mountains of Seir. He is also required to do the same against persons: in 13:17, against the false prophetesses; in 32:2, against Pharaoh; and 38:2, against Gog. In the other classical prophets, this formula is completely missing. But we are reminded here of the Balaam stories, where the seer Balaam must first set his face toward the valley where the people of Israel are encamped before he could speak (Num 22:41; 23:13; 24:1-2). The visual contact of the seer with the addressee of his words is necessary in order for his word to be effective. Thus, we can establish an archaic tendency here that fits into the strong autodramatic character of Ezekiel's proclamation.

From still another side, we may show that this tendency toward dramatic animation that recalls the spirit-theology of the older prophets represents an essential characteristic of Ezekiel. In one of the confessions of Jeremiah, we hear the affirmation of the prophet before God: "As often as your word appeared, I swallowed it, and it became a joy to me" (Jer 15:16). Doubtlessly this is a figure of speech in Jeremiah. That God's word is sweeter than honey is also affirmed in Ps 19:10 [MT v. 11] as well as Ps 119:103. But in the story of the call of Ezekiel, this figure develops into a dramatic reality. The prophet sees the word set before him in the form of a scroll, and he receives the commission to eat it. "So I ate it, and it became in my mouth sweet as honey" (Ezek 3:3b). In Isa 7:20, one hears in the form of a prophetic threat that Yahweh will shave Judah—the head, the hair of the feet, and the beard—with a razor that had been hired in the East. Again we are dealing with a figurative expression. Again Ezekiel develops this figurative expression into a dramatic reality, this time in a sign act. For Yahweh commands the prophet to take a sword at that very moment, cut off his hair, and execute judgment on it (Ezek 5:1). In 37:11 we can hear the sigh of the exiles: "Our bones are dried up. Our hope is gone. We are lost." The first sentence of this threefold complaint employs a figurative expression. Prov 17:22 says: "A cheerful heart is a good medicine, but a downcast spirit dries up the bones." For the third time this surprising process is seen in Ezekiel. A figure of speech develops into a dramatic event (here in the form of a vision). In his vision (37:1-14) the prophet sees himself transplanted into a large field of dried bones, and he receives the command to awaken them through a prophetic word. This process of developing a figure of speech into reality that without doubt appears at least three times shows the dramatic sensitivity of this prophet with great clarity.

THEMATIC DEVELOPMENT

We may move on here to a further trait that is characteristic for the form of Ezekiel's proclamation. It is striking how often we find lengthy units in Ezekiel that completely exhaust one particular theme, while no such phenomenon is to be found in the earlier classical prophets. Yet many of the themes that Ezekiel so expounds are borrowed from his predecessors. Thus the message "the end has come" (ba' ha-qeṣ) appears in Amos 8:2 by association from the vision of "summer fruit" (kelub qayiṣ). This ba' ha-qeṣ then forms the text for an exhaustive portrayal of the last days in Ezekiel 7. It is cited and modified several times in 7:2-4, 6-9. In Hosea we find the comparison of Israel with an unfaithful wife. Ezekiel 16 paints this figure of the unfaithful wife in great breadth for application to Jerusalem, making use of various memories from Jerusalem's history and religion. Jeremiah modifies the theme in Jer 3:6-14, in which he applies it to both kingdoms of Israel, addressing Israel with a type of personal name, "Faithless One" (*mešubah*), and Judah with "False One" (*bagôdah*). Along these same lines, Ezekiel 23 develops the figure of the two faithless sisters, who now receive the names Oholah and Oholibah, and especially emphasizes their Egyptian origin. The principal difference is that here again Ezekiel paints his picture with greater breadth and more drastic fantasy. Compare further the oracles against the nations, especially against the ship of Tyre and the world tree of Egypt. This broad painting of figures with stark impressions belongs to the peculiar character of Ezekiel's speech. And once again, behind this peculiarity of form, the definite face of the man appears.

DISPUTATIONS

This picture of the dramatically stimulated sensitivity, of the power of experience, and the capacity for fantastical visions must not mislead us to suppose that we can see in Ezekiel an introverted mystic who is sunk in the world of his own experiences. In order to guard against this mistake, we must consider a further form of speech that is rather common to Ezekiel—the form of the discussion or disputation. Ezekiel's words often begin with citations from his peers that are quite valuable for our knowledge of his environment. We hear the words of people who cast aside the prophetic word as a word that will not come to pass at all (Ezek 12:22), or that can be expected only in the far distant future (12:27). We hear of cynical mockery (18:2), and open accusation against Yahweh (18:25, 29; 33:17, 20). After the catastrophe, we hear words of self-righteousness from the inhabitants who were left in the land after 597 B.C.E. (11:15) and then after 587 (33:24), as well as the arrogance of the neighboring peoples (25:3; 26:2) and the deep doubt (33:10; 37:11) and resignation (20:3) of the exiles. The prophet takes up the discussion with all of these voices, and thereby develops a style of discussion that later becomes dominant in the Book of Malachi. But here again we see a characteristic tendency to set both the complaint of the people and the answer of the prophet formally in the oracle of Yahweh. Yahweh himself tells the prophet what the men will think about him and how he should answer them. The citations almost always form a part of the word-event that confronts the prophet.

PRIESTLY TRADITION

An especially common form of speech is formed in this context by the speeches of accusation in which the prophet is required by Yahweh to judge the people (*špṭ*; 16:38; 20:4; 22:2; 23:36), and to make their abominations known to them (*hôda'*... *'et-tô'eboteha*; 16:2; 20:4; 22:2). The stereotyped manner of formulation creates the impression that a fixed form of technical accusation, perhaps having its background in the priestly sphere (*da'at* — *hôda'*) lies before us. This is worth still further form-critical investigation.

This leads, however, to a further broad area of tradition in Ezekiel. In Hos 4:1 and Jer 7:9 one sees that a prophet can formulate an accusation against his people by enumerating a series of commandments that his people have transgressed. It is widely recognized that the classical Decalog may be seen in the background of the texts from Hosea and Jeremiah. This phenomenon is also found in Ezekiel, but here the series of laws that are set before the people carries a strong priestly color and has a certain resemblance to the formulation of the Holiness Code (Leviticus 17–26). Thus the bloody city of Jerusalem is characterized in Ezek 22:6-12 by an enumeration of the commandments that it has transgressed. In Ezek 18:5-9 and 14-17 the pattern of the righteous and in vv. 10-13 that of the wicked are marked by a series of enumerations that give the impression of formulas. A fragment of such a series is also found in 33:15. Ezekiel 18:5-9 allows us to go a step further, for here the righteous is characterized by a series of sentences that are then concluded with a completely superfluous "he is righteous" (*ṣaddiq hû'*). One can recognize here, according to the research of Rendtorff and von Rad, a "declaratory formula" that is particularly characteristic in priestly terminology.[6] It probably has its setting in life in the priestly declaration at the temple gate. By means of this formula, the priest expresses his decision at the threshold of the temple whether a temple visitor will be allowed to enter the sanctuary or not. In Ezek 18:17 we have the formula "he shall surely live" (*ḥayoh yiḥyeh*), which certainly reflects the speech of the temple, for whoever enters into the temple enters into the sphere of life.[7] The priestly torah that is cited polemically by Amos suggests a priestly invitation: "Seek Bethel, and thus you will live" (compare Amos 5:4-7). We are therefore within the tradition that is reflected by the entrance torah, best known to us from Psalms 15 and 24. Thus Ezekiel develops what he has to say about the new life in the language of the temple liturgy.

LEGAL TRADITIONS

In the context of this priestly speech we may move on to the form of the casuistic sections in the Book of Ezekiel. In the Book of the Covenant (Exod 20:22—23:33) we have a casuistic style in which a conditional sentence is introduced with "when/if" (*kî*). In the style of the priestly casuistic, as we know it in the Book of Leviticus, the *kî* appears regularly in the second position of the sentence, immediately behind the subject (see Lev 1:2, "If a human," *'adam kî*; 2:1, "If a person," *nefeš kî*). This very form appears in Ezekiel not only in the description of a righteous man in 18:5 ("If a man is righteous"; *'iš kî yihyeh ṣaddiq*), but also in the casuistic development in the picture of the watchman in 3:19—"If a man" (*'iš kî*); in 33:2 and 14:13—"If [on] a land" (*'ereṣ kî*); 33:6—"If the watchman" (*haṣṣofeh kî*). In Leviticus 17 (vv. 3, 8, 10, 13) one finds a more complete style in a series of four regulations. Here the individual command-ments are introduced with the heavily accented:

> If a man from the house of Israel (or from the strangers that sojourn among them) . . .

> *'iš 'iš mibêth yiśra'el (umin ha-ger hagar betôkam) 'ašer*

Exactly this same style can be found twice in the unit of Ezek 14:1-11, which has grown formally out of sacral law.

These observations show that Ezekiel was strongly influenced both for-mally as well as traditionally by priestly language and the traditions of the sanctuary. And they confirm the information given to us in Ezek 1:3 that he was a priest.

EPIC TRADITIONS

We must pose still another question in our study of the traditions behind the prophecy of Ezekiel. Recent research has shown very clearly that a strong line of Jerusalem–David traditions stands alongside the "all Israel" perspective of the Exodus traditions.[8] This duality of traditions is especially apparent in the prophets. While the prophet of the northern kingdom, Hosea, stands exclu-sively in the former group of traditions, the proclamation of the Jerusalemite Isaiah is determined decisively by the latter. But when one examines Ezekiel for these traditions it very readily appears that here the question of alternatives does not apply. Ezekiel 20 shows the full use of the tradition of the election of Israel in the exodus, even though this tradition in Ezekiel is recast in the dark light of a history of sin. Also in the story of the two unfaithful wives in Ezekiel 23, the Egyptian origin of both Israelite kingdoms is strongly emphasized. According to Robert Bach, there is an old tradition that can be recognized behind the motif of the foundling in Ezekiel 16 that maintains that Yahweh "found" Israel in the wilderness (see Hos 9:10; Deut 32:10).[9] This story in Ezekiel 16, however, is about Jerusalem, whose father was an Amorite and mother a Hittite (16:3). Thus it appears here polemically in a prophetic accusation. In Ezekiel 40–48, however, the new Jerusalem stands at the center of the hope for salvation, the place to which the new exodus would lead according to 20:32-38. There on the high mountain of Israel (20:40), the new pure sacrifice will be offered. The anticipation of a new David is mentioned in 34:23-24, and in 37:25. Ezekiel appears, therefore, to be a latecomer for whom the ancient salvation traditions are thoroughly entwined. He is also clearly a latecomer among the prophets, for his work presupposes the earlier classical prophets. The phrase "the end has come" in Ezekiel 7 stems from Amos, shaving his head from Isaiah, the proclamation about the adulterous wife from Hosea, the story of the two adulterous wives from Jeremiah, which, as J. W. Miller has shown, has influenced Ezekiel in an especially strong measure.[10]

But this poses the peculiar problem of tradition in Ezekiel. Ezekiel shows traditio-historical influence from various sides. He lives on the one hand in an archaic world of elements from preclassical prophecy. Along with this, his themes are strongly influenced by the earlier classical prophets. Seen from this aspect, he seems to be an unoriginal follower, the heir of earlier prophetic proclamation. But then on the other hand, there is a sharp distinction between Ezekiel and the earlier prophets who influenced him. This can be seen more clearly in the field of his theological peculiarity with its unprecedented sharp attack on the sin of his people. Unfortunately time prevents our saying more about the theological character of his message here.[11] The peculiarity of Ezekiel's message can also be demonstrated in his vocabulary, for important terms from the proclamation of his predecessors are missing. Thus this Jerusalemite priest never speaks of Yahweh Sabaoth (also missing in the Priestly [P] narrative).[12] He never mentions the love of Yahweh (the verb *'ahab* appears in Ezekiel 16 and 23 only as a participle that refers to the lovers that Israel, or Jerusalem, takes). The term *ḥesed*, which is so important in Hosea and Jeremiah, never appears in Ezekiel. Nothing is said in any form about the fear of God (*yir'at Yhwh*). Never does he speak of trust in Yahweh. The verb *bṭḥ* appears only twice (Ezek 16:15; 33:13), and both times are colored by negative accents (false coincidence). The only text in which we meet the accusative formulation, to know God, which is so dominant in Hosea and Jeremiah, is critically suspect (Ezek 38:16). Ezekiel never speaks of a "plan" (*'ṣh*) or "work" (*m'śh*) of Yahweh. Neither do we find a verb, adjective, or substantive from the stem *ṣdq* applied to Yahweh.

On the other hand, completely new forms of speech come into the foreground and give his proclamation an unmistakable individuality. So finally, we must briefly sketch out one of these: the so-called "proof-saying" (German: *Erweiswort*) that Ezekiel uses in a particularly characteristic way to speak about the knowledge of Yahweh.[13] With this peculiar form of proclamation, the prophet not only announces a future act of Yahweh but formulates this announcement in a manner that expresses the hidden intention of Yahweh's act. In Ezek 37:12 we hear: "Behold, I will open your graves, and raise you from your graves, O my people." Yahweh acts, and the goal of that action is the creation of knowledge, the knowledge that he is Yahweh. But this is always formulated in the first person. The content of this knowledge is the sentence "I am Yahweh" (*'anî Yhwh*). We have in this a formula of self-revelation by which Yahweh steps out of his incognito,[14] just as we find it in the preamble of the Decalog or the postscript of the Holiness Code.

This form of speech is found in 1 Kgs 20:13, 28 in a narrative about the old northern prophets of the ninth century. So once again we meet a relationship in the tradition of Ezekiel to the preclassical prophets. This formulation, which again is completely missing in the classical prophets before Ezekiel, has central meaning for Ezekiel. I cannot speak further here about the prehistory of this form of speech.[15] It is enough simply to have presented something of the peculiar stamp that Ezekiel receives from this formulation, a stamp that is of decisive importance for our understanding of this prophet. Ezekiel, this prophet of sensitivity, of dramatic personal involvement who is seized by the sudden intrusion of the word of Yahweh, who paints his pictures with the glaring color of extreme fantasy but nevertheless stands in a passion-filled dialogue with his peers, who speaks out of a rich priestly heritage and takes up many themes that have reached him through the earlier traditions of Israel and her prophets, this prophet Ezekiel with all of his characteristics recedes into the background when one asks about the goal of his proclamation. And in his place appears the *one* who is revealed by his intrusion, who desires to make the mystery of his person known to the world.

We must look back to our beginning. The whole book of Ezekiel is stylized as a report in the first person, not because the prophet wants to emphasize his own experience but because he has been invaded by one who is greater than himself. The prophet is the son of man, the creature. "The word of Yahweh came over me." The whole accent in Ezekiel lies on the word of Yahweh. This word he has experienced as a fomenting assault from the Lord that he must then make known to his people and the world—I am Yahweh. All else is entwined with and recedes behind this Yahweh who is revealed in both judgment and grace.

8

Biblical Theology

INTRODUCTION

The question concerning a "biblical theology" is a specifically Christian question.[1] It presupposes the duality of the testaments of the Christian Bible that are separated by time and by language. It has become a problem to more recent times that, through their awareness of history, received a keener vision for the differences of periods in history. On the other hand, the fundamental faith of the Christian community necessitates a thoughtful correlation of individual biblical statements in view of the whole because it contends that the two testaments do not witness to two different gods, but to one single Lord. After a period that had devoted, in increasingly more subtle and specialized research, all attention to the recognition of the ever moving character of history and that had by this method attained insights that must not be given up, we are now confronted with more intense urgency by the question about the validity and appropriateness of the language concerning the *one* God toward whom Scripture points in all stages of its way.

The question demands attention because of the situation of Christian preaching. If texts from both parts of the Bible are read and expounded in the Christian pulpit, how can this be possible unless the preacher renders an account about a "speaking of God" that is nurtured by both testaments, in other words about "biblical theology"? For what is theology if not the critically clarified speaking of God? Valid preaching lives by hearing that word that is attested by the whole Bible.

Does this amount, however, to the continuation of "that huge philological farce" that Nietzsche ridiculed and whose victim the preacher is if he claims to open his ears equally wide to the Old as to the New Testament?[2] Nietzsche describes this farce as the "attempt to tear the Old Testament from the hands of the Jews under the pretext that it contained only Christian doctrines and belonged to the Christians as the true people of Israel." And that puts us before the other dimension of the question that arose in our present situation with new vigor. Christian faith has become newly aware of the reality of a living Judaism that draws its identity from the soil of the Old Testament in which it is rooted. In spite of all its evolutions over the centuries, Judaism cannot be dismissed as a reality that is basically no longer alive out of its Old Testament ground. With what right, then, can the Christian preacher reach out for the word of the Old Testament? Does that preacher not indeed tear it from the hands of the Jews, as Nietzsche says? Does it not amount to the confiscation of a property by pretending a title to which there is no lawful claim? Does it not also amount to a renewed murder of Judaism that is robbed of its ground of existence if it is denied the Old Testament? There is no shortage of voices (including Christian voices) that make these affirmations.

This raises the question anew concerning the possibility and concrete form of a biblical theology. It is subjected to questioning from two sides. On the one side, in the wake of the Enlightenment, from a critically sharpened consciousness of history that, after the removal of biblical theology from doctrine, led quickly also to the differentiation between an Old and a New Testament theology.[3] And on the other side, from a Judaism that appeals to the first part of the Christian Bible and lives from it.

THE TWO TESTAMENTS AND CHRISTOLOGY

Theology speaks of God. Biblical theology perceives, coming from both testaments, the statement that the human being cannot appropriate this speaking, but rather that God gives himself in speaking to us as humans.[4] Theology is possible only on the basis of this self-giving of God in speaking, who addressed himself to us in the two testaments not as a dual God, but as one and the same God. Faith in the identity of the one God is to the Christian church the basis of which cannot be surrendered for all reflection about biblical statements. At no point can this be subjected to questioning in the way of Marcion.

Simultaneously, however, Christian language of God confesses that "In many and various ways God spoke of old to our fathers by the prophets; but in these last days he has spoken to us by a Son" (Heb 1:1). Biblical theology will not be able to deviate from the two statements "of old to the fathers" and "in these last days by a Son." It is prevented, therefore, from speaking of God in timeless absolutes that level that which is "of old." At the same time it is certain that it is one and the same God who has spoken once "of old" and then in the fullness of time in "the Son." Again, in speaking of "the Son" it cannot disregard the mature Johannine formulation "I and the Father are one" (John

10:30). According to Christian faith, it cannot be expressed who the Father is, of whom Christian theology will in every instance have to speak, if it bypasses the Son in its speaking.

Consequently, even confronted by the duality of the testaments, biblical theology will have to search with all intensity for the meaning of "the Son" through whom, for Christian faith, God gave himself in his speaking to his community "when the time had fully come" (Gal 4:44) and through which it was called to faith in him.

In order to answer this question, an external witness may be placed at the beginning. The four Gospels report that the Roman procurator, Pontius Pilate, had a *titulus* placed on that cross on which was to be eliminated the who had become suspect to the Romans: "Jesus of Nazareth, the King of the Jews."[5] By this inscription Pilate, the Roman, meant to draw the conclusion from that which this executed man had claimed to be. The adamant consistency of this tradition about the *titulus* on the cross from the Synoptics down to John expresses with sufficient clarity that, even according to the faith of the earliest Christian community, Pilate had not been mistaken in his inscription. Consequently, when the Christian community in Greek-speaking areas from its beginnings called this Jesus the anointed one (*Christos*)—which is nothing but the Greek rendition of Messiah or king-title that was found in the earliest Palestinian community—and when subsequently this title becomes but a proper name beside which the name Jesus can in many instances be neglected, then this process confirms, through the language of the community, the designation of Jesus of Nazareth as the anointed one, as the king. Pilate had ordered "King of the Jews" to be written on the cross. The early Christian community also accepts the title of Messiah so important to the religious life of Israel. In so doing, the community indicates that not only Pilate but the Christian community as well can speak of Jesus in no other way but as king, more specifically as the Lord expected by the Jews, as the Israel of their day, who establishes his royal claim in and on behalf of this Israel.

The Hellenistic Christian community, whether of pagan or Jewish-Christian origin, confirmed this claim to Lordship in its own way and with a new expression by calling on Jesus as the *kyrios* (lord). First Corinthians 12:3 demonstrates how the basic confession of the community is stated in the phrase *kyrios Iē sous*. Taking into consideration that in the Bible known to Greek-speaking Judaism, the Septuagint, *kyrios* is the translation with which the divine name "Yahweh" is rendered, one can fathom how much emphasis is placed on Jesus' claim to royal power through the *kyrios* title. The bearer of this title has an authority far beyond that of a scribe that, looking at the Old Testament, entitled him to say: "You have heard that it was said to the men of old . . . . But I say to you . . ." (Matt 5:21-22).

By this process, however, is not Judaism robbed of the Old Testament and the "farce" continued that declares the Old Testament to be a book belonging to Christianity and not the Jews? I am of the opinion that one needs to listen to that very intently. Jesus of Nazareth, king of the Jews, Christ, *kyrios,* in the Greek Old Testament the rendition of Yahweh in the Hebrew Scriptures—this entire movement does not evidence an intent on the part of the Christian community to commit an act of thievery against the people and the community of the Old Testament. Rather, the Lord who is called "king of the Jews" is allowed to stay where he belongs. He does not step out of Israel, or out of Judaism, but he asserts his sovereignty precisely within it; and they, therefore, remain his people. He is the king of that people that in the first part of the Bible finds its establishment and description. This, however, he does now as the Christ, the anointed, the king, the Lord (*kyrios*) in view of whom his people are meant to be defined, as of the Son in whom the God witnessed to by the Old Testament has made himself heard in ultimate form. But it belongs to this new definition of his kingship that now all those people who had at first remained outside the door find themselves, to their surprise, called into the sphere of sovereignty of this Lord. Later children, they are beside this first-born, but sons as much as the others and no longer slaves and aliens (Gal 4:7). Paul has put this surprise in the form of a parable, which is offensive to the natural thought of a gardener, by speaking of a wild shoot grafted into a tree (Rom 11:17-24). A normal human gardener grafts a cultured shoot onto a wild tree.

But this talk of the Lord, the king, is to be supplemented immediately by a second sentence so that it not be misunderstood and lead in the end to the image of the church triumphant over the synagogue as it is portrayed in the statues of the Strasbourg cathedral.

It is again Paul who, in another passage in the same letter to the Romans, expresses in yet another way the surprise of a sovereignty reaching out to invite a people far away from it, when he writes: "For I tell you that Christ became a servant to the circumcised to show God's truthfulness, in order to confirm the promises given to the patriarchs, and in order that the Gentiles might glorify God for his mercy" (Rom 15:8-9a). Side by side with the "king of the Jews" is placed unmistakably the "servant of the Jews" who, in these verses, are simply called "the circumcised" in view of the sign of circumcision that singles them out. And behind the word "servant" appears the fact, undeniable to any historian, that it was a cross, driven into the earth of Jerusalem, on which the inscription was placed "king of the Jews." This, then, is the stumbling block: his kingship was service unto the depth of death.

Everything that will yet be said about the Lordship of Jesus of Nazareth, whom the Christian community knows as the Christ, its Lord, is wrongly construed from the bottom up if it is not understood as service, as a service for his people Israel down to the giving up of his life on the cross. The sovereignty of the Lord is a sovereignty that, in service, bestows gifts on the people of the circumcision, no matter how often Christianity has denied this in its questionable history of relations with Israel. A biblical theology, nurtured by the word of the two testaments, that speaks of God and attempts thus to put into words what it has first heard God say himself—this biblical theology has to deal, consequently, with the wide sphere of God's sovereignty that reaches back into that "of old" in which the Old Testament speaks of Yahweh, the God of Israel, who eventually utters his unabridged word through the royal service of his Son.[6]

SPEECH OVERARCHING BOTH TESTAMENTS

After these summary introductory remarks it cannot be our task in what follows to develop a biblical theology—even in a nutshell. An essay like the one offered here is not appropriate for this aim. We have to admit soberly, moreover, that at the present moment, in spite of some beginnings, we are only starting to grope from afar toward a phenomenon that has become largely unaccustomed to us, namely a speech that overarches the two testaments and points to the one God who is attested in both. It will not do to leap thoughtlessly over ditches that are still opening up before us, but it is necessary rather to clear some passable roads in the territory along which the exploration of a biblical theology will have to move in further work.

In all this exploration it remains solidly established that biblical theology starts from the faith in the identity of God in both testaments that provide a witness to the One, each from its own time: the times "of old" and "now." It is the God who has created heaven and earth, who keeps faith with his creature to whom he has uttered his "yes" in creation—even beyond the crisis of the great flood. It is the God who, within creation, turns to humanity in a special way, distinguishing it through special gifts from the other creatures to which humanity remains bound and indebted. To this humanity, God has given the power to rule, as a privilege on loan from God, and also instruction that means both help and limit for its life. It is the God whom it had pleased "of old" in his selective freedom to speak and act with Israel in a special way. In gifts and commands this God had to deal with his people Israel, reaching over times of crisis and even of destruction and judgment, down to that day when the creator of the world gave himself and manifested himself in his work through the Son, the servant King of the Jews.

In that crisis of all that is human—be it Israel or the Gentiles, the Jews or the Greeks—condemned by the exemplary people of legislation (the Romans), handed over to them by his own people (the nation of election), deserted by his most intimate disciples whom he had personally called into discipleship, he dies on the cross outside the gates of the holy city.[7] Through God's affirmation of the crucified on Easter day, the free and novel dedication of God becomes manifest beyond crisis and the disaster of all that is human.[8] He fashions out of the firstborn, Israel, and of the world of the nations a humanity that is given gifts out of the pure gracious freedom of God. In this event, hope is established for a world in its ever renewed alienation from God, a hope that allows a vision of the new heaven and earth transcending human nature. In the event of the Son the creature is guaranteed this hope for the world in a fashion arousing joy far beyond Jerusalem (Rev 21:1) and which had already been seen from afar in the expectation of the Old Testament (Isa 65:17—66:22).

CREATION

In the preceding section some general directions were sketched in which biblical theology will have to move. What follows now is meant to clarify this by more concrete biblical statements.

The creation accounts of Genesis 1 and 2 speak in retrospect of the events in the beginning about the creator who, even in the affirmation of his creation, remains its Lord. The first of these accounts has been clearly appropriated at the beginning of the Gospel of John in a new form that is shaped by the knowledge of the revelation of God in the Son. In his saying about the indissolubility of marriage (Matt 19:5-6), Jesus refers back to the creation of man and woman and the will of God that establishes their communion (Gen 2:21-25). The knowledge of this unambiguous origin of the world and humanity binds the two testaments together.

A closer look reveals already within the Old Testament how great the freedom is with which individual formulations can shape the narrative in very different ways. The juxtaposition of Genesis 1 and 2 manifests different ways of theological formulation. The Priestly writer of Genesis 1:1—2:4a knows that the origin of the world reaches far behind the special encounter of Israel with God in the name of Yahweh. It speaks of the creator, therefore, with the more general word 'Elohim in order to reserve for the time of Moses the extraordinary manifestation of the name Yahweh (Exod 6:2-8). In the movement of the days of creation toward the seventh day as the day of God's rest, it reveals the hidden presence of that God who much later will impart to his people, Israel, of its own rest on the Sabbath (Exod 31:12-17). Eventually, Hebrews 4 dares to reformulate this movement of the ways of God toward a great promise in the light of God's self-revelation in his Son. The narration of the Yahwist uses the name of Yahweh, from Gen 2:4b onwards, without hesitation already for the event of creation in which no other God can be at work but the one who is later invoked in Israel by the name of Yahweh. In the same way, the Fourth Evangelist sees in creation none other at work but the one who has expressed himself in the Son. At the same time, John adopts the manner of speech of the Priestly writer in a new way when he confesses the Son as the primal light of the world (John 1:4-5; 8:12; 12:46). While different from Genesis 1, it resides uncreated within the Father. In a different way, the Pauline formulation in 2 Cor 4:6 comes close to this statement.

In both parts of the Bible, however, the creator is more than a *deus otiosus* (disengaged god) from the beginning of all history. He is the Lord who completely encompasses every now, and who wants to be adored in the miraculous works of the created and blessed world that even now the eye is able to discern. The psalms of creation speak of that (Psalms 8, 19, 104, and others). The divine speeches in the Book of Job (38–41) are permeated by the wonder caused by the presence of the visible miracle of the created world or by the sentences of the wise man who thoughtfully contemplates the world in the enumeration of the marvels of the world in some of the sayings in Proverbs 30. The same is true in the words of Jesus concerning the lilies of the field (Matt 6:28) and the birds of the air (Matt 6:26). The same sentiment finds strong expression in Psalm 139 in view of the miraculous work of the creation of the individual human. Within the prophetic words of the Old Testament these insights of the Psalms have been incorporated most powerfully in Deutero-Isaiah. In him the future dimension is fully recognizable, side by side with the dimension of the past and the present. The God who brings about salvation is "the first and the last" (Isa 44:6; 48:12). In the Revelation of John, this finds its echo again when God is praised in the style of Psalms in the revelation of the Son who has given himself as the lamb of God (Rev 4:11; 11:15; 15:3).

Throughout, the creator remains the Lord who never abandons himself to his creature and never enables the human partner to possess him in a formula—even if it is ever so correctly derived from God's giving himself in his word within the human world. The mysterious character of the creator, who in the history of the world holds in his hands the disposition over "fallen time," finds its most extreme expression in staggering onesidedness in the Book of Ecclesiastes, which stands at the fringe of the Old Testament. The enigma of the wisdom of God is expressed in this book in extreme acuity, a wisdom of God that cannot be comprehended by any worldly wisdom and that finally renders all human wisdom impotent in the cross of Christ and yet pronounces the hidden wisdom of God in the foolishness of the cross. Whatever is given by God to the human is in each case the gift of the creator (Eccl 2:24; 3:13; 5:17-18; 8:15). This is in no way different even when a human being dares to believe, in the face of the creator, in the Son.

GOD REMEMBERS

It would be completely erroneous, however, if we were now to speak of the creator and preserver of the world as a "fate." This is true even of Ecclesiastes, in spite of all assertions to the contrary. Fate enslaves humanity. The creator of whom the Bible speaks comes close to humans, gives them gifts, addresses them, demands of them, loves them in judgment and in grace.[9]

The creator is demanding of humans because he "remembers" them. The Old Testament employs this phrase when God remembers Noah in the great primal crisis of the flood by preserving him in judgment in the midst of the storms of destruction (Gen 8:1). It is found in places where the human creature faces with astonishment the rich inheritance that the one whose name is majestic in all the earth has granted to lowly humanity by providing it with the power of dominion (Ps 8:6). In the night of blackest despair, Job risks the audacious thought that he offers up as his wish to his God that God would hide him in the world of the dead and would remember him when God's wrath be passed so that God would call him and would, in reply to Job's answers, turn again with longing compassion to the work of his hands (Job 14:13-15).

Those who pray the Psalms call out for this remembering, appealing to the gracious love of God for them (Ps 25:6-7) and for their people (Ps 74:2).[10] They call out because they know that this remembrance of God for his people stands at the beginning of Israel's history when it sat in Egypt in the dismal situation of slavery. The Priestly narrator, who uses the verb in Exod 2:24, says that "God remembered his covenant with Abraham, with Isaac, and with Jacob" (see Lev 26:42).[11] The reference back to God's acts with the patriarchs, at a time when no people of Israel existed, expresses the word of the Old Testament that God's loving approach to his people has its origin at a time long before Israel itself could be actively involved.

In this context, deuteronomic language dares to adopt the full expression in which God, in the New Testament, gives of himself in his act through the Son. In an unambiguous rejection of all pride on Israel's part, Moses says to his people:

> It was not because you were more in number than any other people that Yahweh set his love upon you and chose you, for you were the fewest of all people; but it is because Yahweh loves you and is keeping the oath that he swore to your fathers, that Yahweh has brought you out with a mighty hand . . . . from the house of bondage, from the hand of Pharaoh, king of Egypt. (Deut 7:7-8)

Love chooses in free selection, which cannot be second-guessed nor called to give account for its reasons. Such "election" separates. Old Testament language witnesses to this kind of free approach toward Israel through which it is made into God's special possession (Deut 7:6; 14:2).[12]

Biblical theology will not conceal the priority of God's election; but it will allow it to stand up clearly, even if it knows that in the election God has reached out through the Son into the world of the nations beyond the confines of Israel, and elected for himself a community of "saints" out of all people (*klētoi hagioi* ["those called to be saints"]—Rom 1:7; 1 Cor 1:2; *hagioi* ["saints"] alone—2 Cor 1:1, etc.; alongside the *'am qadoš* ["holy people"]—Deut 7:6; 14:2). They are called through the Son into the realm of the same love of God. The firstborn of Israel are joined side by side with the brothers from the world of the nations. The dividing wall between Israel and the pagans is broken down where the word of God's love in Jesus Christ is received, the word in which God gives himself to the world (Eph 2:14). "There is neither Jew nor Greek . . . for you are all one in Christ Jesus" (Gal 3:28).

THE DIVINE IMPERATIVE

The one who loves with that intensity puts a demand on the loved one. To a biblical theology this opens up the wide area of biblical instruction. The statement of Heb 1:1 "in many and various ways God spoke of old to our fathers" becomes particularly manifest in this area. In the Old Testament precise individual instructions regulate broad sectors of life. The phenomenon of Israel's "nationhood" determines many details but we recognize already in the Old Testament the quest after the unitary behind the manifold. The Decalog is an attempt to collate the essential out of the manifold in a composition of ten sentences. In Deuteronomy 5, the framework of a parenetic introduction, the Decalog is placed as a hermeneutical key before the multitude of individual deuteronomic instructions. This fact represents the will to coordinate that which is manifold, and to coordinate it with a concisely worded rule that covers the whole. Even within the Decalog one may find a further element of this accentuation in the way in which the first two commandments are placed first, formulated in direct speech by Yahweh in distinction from the other commandments.

The concentration on that which provides unity can be seen even more clearly in Deut 6:4-9, which became significantly enough the central prayer of Israel and which is heard from the mouth of Jesus as the primary commandment in the statement of the double commandment of love in Mark 12:29-30 (also vv. 32-33). The "primary commandment" that stands at the head of the Decalog calls for love of Yahweh with all the heart and all the soul. This has achieved a formulation that aims at God's prevenient love to the fathers and to the people elected in them in an even more concentrated and determined form.[13] In a different way the core element of the Holiness Code attempts to find a summary for Yahweh's demand and to coordinate it even in its linguistic form with Yahweh's nature by the wording that is set at the beginning in Lev 19:2: "You shall be holy; for I Yahweh your God am holy."

Again, in the New Testament the appropriation of the Old Testament's language about God's instruction to his "holy ones" occurs in the Son, the "holy one of God (Mark 1:24; Luke 4:34; John 6:69). The distinctive freedom in the New Testament is disclosed issuing from this center in which the multiple commandments are focused into the One, although this freedom knows that the one thing that matters has to work itself out in the manifoldness of all relationships in life. The Old Testament continues to have abiding importance for this extension of the instruction into the manifoldness of relations to God, to the neighbor, and to all co-created creatures. It preserves the divine instruction in the concreteness of life relationships, in the responsibility for the orders of a life together in justice, and in the proper disposition of property. It avoids the slide into a vague principle of love and sympathy that lacks concreteness. The Old Testament points to the "here and now" of the answer of love that is born of faith (Gal 5:6).

At the same time, something even more radical is happening. When the servant Son enters into the world of the divine imperative that is made visible in the Old Testament, it becomes visible in him who is the only truly righteous and holy one and in whom God's love is completely present. Confronted with the law of God, the human is again and again demonstrated to be a sinner. This is true particularly when he strives to realize God's will in an outstanding performance. The sober warning of the preacher "be not righteous overmuch," who, for the sake of security, has immediately added the counternotion "be not wicked overmuch," does not lead to a middle way that one might safely walk or to a jolly compromise of realism, in spite of the further statement, "It is good that you should take hold of this, and from that withhold not your hand" (Eccl 7:16-18)—although this has on occasion been suggested to be Qoheleth's meaning.[14] Rather, Ecclesiastes retains the human in the embattled existence between good and evil, about which one should have no illusions.

Weightier yet than the speech of Qoheleth, which is moving in the practice-oriented sphere of wisdom, is the word of the pre-exilic representatives of prophecy. Everything is now coordinated to the reality of Israel's experienced national history with which God had to deal under his name Yahweh. In proximity to the historical events of the destruction first of northern Israel and then of southern Judah, prophetic speech experiences an increasingly sharper focusing. In God's approach to his people, it becomes ever more starkly manifest how little this people is able to correspond to the will of God.

Israel was no worse than the people around it, but it is the people that have experienced like no other the nearness of the holy God and in this nearness the power of human incapacity to correspond to God's will. "You only have I known (elected) of all the families of the earth; therefore I will punish you for all your iniquities" (Amos 3:2). The verdict that is expressed in Amos's fourth vision (8:2) is based on the statement of this incapacity: "the end has come." This appropriated in Ezekiel 7 as a text in a broad elaboration on the day of Yahweh that leads to the end, even though it is couched in Ezekiel's completely different style, and also in the Priestly Code. It has entered, in cosmic dimensions, into the preamble of the cosmic catastrophe of the great flood (Gen 6:13).[15]

In Micah the event of the "end" is concentrated on the place at which Yahweh's people believe to be particularly close to its God: "Therefore . . . Zion shall be plowed as a field; Jerusalem shall become a heap of ruins, and the mountain of the house a wooded height" (Mic 3:2). In the proclamation of Micah's contemporary, Isaiah, the announcement of the day of judgment in the approaching day of Yahweh is occasionally punctured by the historical proclamation of a holding back of the Holy One of Israel in his judgment on his people (Isa 2:11). In the Syro-Ephraimite War, the prophet calls for fearless and quiet confidence in the divine help in the face of the approach of the two enemies of northern Israel (Ephraim) and the Arameans toward Jerusalem: "It shall not stand, and it shall not come to pass" (7:7). But in Isaiah the announcement of God also comes to the fore again and again—which had been stated in the report of his call—that because of the people's hardness of heart everything would have to end in the desolation of the entire country in God's judgment (6:9-11).[16] In Hosea, the contemporary of Micah and Isaiah, the sentiment has found its most passionate expression that God himself will, like a beast, have to be the destroyer of his people (Hos 5:12, 14) in spite of God's compassion, which stands in the way of the annihilation of the people (11:8-9).

In the late period of Judah, at the time of the Neo-Babylonian empire, it is Jeremiah who speaks of God's suffering with his people, whom he has to destroy because of its sins (Jer 12:7-8; 45:4). He who in his confessions curses his office and the day of his birth for the task of a messenger of judgment is the one who poses the desperate question in view of a people incapable of doing the good: "Can the Ethiopian change his skin or the leopard his spots?" (13:23a). The last of these prophets, Ezekiel, who toward the final phase of the "end" of Jerusalem had already been deported to Babylon, states—without Jeremiah's desperate and personal lament—the incapacity of Israel and Jerusalem to be obedient, which had become apparent from the origins of the people and the inescapability of its failure in the judgment of God. Ezekiel's statements are found in the broadly developed theological retrospects on Israel's history in Ezekiel 16 and 20:1-31; and 23. In the parable of the useless wood of the vine (chapter 15), he comes dangerously close to an ontologically based statement about the inability of Jerusalem to live up to its election.

And yet it is precisely Israel's policy that far below in the darkness of Israel's demise has to announce a new future and the raising from the dead on behalf on Israel's God (Ezek 37:1-14). Not only the unity of a dispersed people will be reestablished by God (37:15-28), he will even give it a new heart (36:26). God promises a new covenant to it, which will unite the people's heart wholly with the divine command (37:26; see Jer 31:31-34) and in Deutero-Isaiah can be heard the cry of joy over the immediate restitution to life and the renewed reciting of God at the place of Jerusalem's ruins (Isa 52:7-10).

In the message of the New Testament, the Son enters into this knowledge of Israel's failure and of God's faithfulness in spite of the failure—both confirming in a new way that which is old and ascertaining it in a royal manner. Biblical theology will embrace the particular priority of prophetic preaching and historical experience of an Israel condemned to live in exile and restored from it. It will have to insist on the identity of God, which stands over this full proclamation, and which does not only develop "doctrine" intellectually, but points (in both testaments) to an event.

The knowledge of the holy will of God finds its ultimate and final form through the Son. Here the impossibility becomes manifest to the whole world that the human being can stand the test of the holy will of God. What was to be heard, in Jeremiah 23, from the mouth of the prophet about his people receives validity far beyond the boundaries of the people addressed by Jeremiah. The history told about Jerusalem in Ezekiel 16 and about Israel (or the two parts of Israel) in Ezek 20:1-31 and 23 tends in its evolution toward the divine judgment in the direction of a history of humanity even outside Israel, as it is most fully developed in Rom 1:18—3:20. Israel and the nations merge together in dark solidarity. The judgment over all humanity that comes from Adam is pronounced and enacted in the death of the King of the Jews, who dies on the cross for the sins of the many. The statement about the just and suffering servant of God in Isaiah 53, who gives his life as a ransom for the many and thereby has "born our iniquity," receives its surprising validation in the event of the cross. Paul can understand the act of baptism in Christian community (Rom 6:1-14) in no other way than as the event of being incorporated into the Christ who was delivered to death.

The proclamation of the exilic prophets—which had announced the rejuvenation of the dead, the new beginning, and "the pardoning of iniquity" (Isa 40:2)—receives precisely in this way its new validation in the Easter proclamation of the New Testament. The condemned is called to a hope of new life in faith in the Son of God. "But if we have died with Christ, we believe that we shall also live with him. For we know that Christ being raised from the dead will never die again" (Rom 6:8-9). This also puts into the light of a new validity those promises of the Old Testament that speak of future and new life after the condemnation to death in the exile. Once more the solidarity is fully observable between those who are called into the kingdom of Christ from all the ends of the earth and the firstborn people of the King of the Jews. The "new creation" that believes that in Christ "the old has passed away" becomes the new reality of life for everyone who knows to be called in faith to Christ, either Jew or Greek. This hope for the first-called people of Israel is explicitly retained in Romans 11. In this faith the hope has a pledge of a new heaven and earth that spans the world.

A SINGLE GOD

Paul's preaching of the gospel is distinguished by the sharp antithesis between "works of the law" and "faith in Christ." This antithesis impressed itself upon him when he encountered the living Christ and he maintains in it that the new future toward which faith is moving owes itself altogether to the free grace of God, which calls the dead to life independent of any prior human achievement. The radicality of Deutero-Isaiah's phrase "I and no other" (Isa 45:5-6, 18, 21-22, etc.) is expanded here into a worldwide implementation.

The priestly prophet Ezekiel had stated in a soaring proclamation: "It is not for your sake, O house of Israel, that I am about to act, but for the sake of my holy name" (Ezek 36:22, see v. 32), and it is no different in the gospel of Deutero-Isaiah, which is addressed to move the heart of Israel: "I, I am he who blots out your transgressions for my own sake, and I will not remember your sins" (Isa 43:25). The Pauline antithesis of faith and "works of the law" is intended to safeguard this "I, I." Paul's antithesis cannot yet be heard in the Old Testament even though the statements in Deutero-Isaiah and in Ezekiel that have just been quoted are intended to run in this direction. In these prophets the exclusive activity of God is intended when they announce, in the depth of judgment, Israel's new beginning through the return to the country and the new presence of God in the midst of his community (Isa 52:7-10; Ezek 43:7, 9). This insight is intensified to the antithesis "faith" and "works of the law" when the proclamation of the gospel envisages the service of the Son in his suffering and death, forsaken by all those who were his own, including the pious ones, and his new life-giving presence at Easter in its worldwide validity.

No new God is here proclaimed, but the great freedom is announced that is reality when faith knows about the perfection of the love of God in the giving of the Son (John 3:16). A biblical theology will not be allowed to avoid the acuteness of this antithesis as it had presented itself to Paul "the old has passed away, behold the new has come" (2 Cor 5:17). The validity of this statement that makes recede any prerogative to salvation on the part of Israel, which was the firstborn and which dares to speak of the "end of the law" (Rom 10:4) also places Jeremiah's saying in 31:31-34 about the old and new covenant into the context of the act of service of the king of Israel, which is valid for the whole world. It casts its light also on Deutero-Isaiah's call: "Remember not the former things, nor consider the things of old. Behold, I am doing a new thing" (Isa 43:18-19a). The event of the cross and of Easter is more than the liberation of exiled Israel through the anointed of the Lord, Cyrus, which Deutero-Isaiah had announced (Isa 45:1).

This is the place at which not only the historian but also the theologian who asks about the speech and act of God faces the stumbling block of a new step in the act of God. To Marcion, the super-Paulinist, the unity of the testaments broke in pieces here. The God of the law and the God of works cannot be the same as the God of the gospel in Jesus Christ. In the Old Testament, Marcion sees the creator God at work and not the God of redemption who performs his act in his son.

The historical-critical investigation of the Bible that begins in the eighteenth century has not started at this point. It has, however, impressed itself again more acutely on the sharper theological reflection of our century. By way of his studies on Marcion, Adolf Harnack arrived at his demand for the elimination of the Old Testament in the Christian church.[17] Emmanuel Hirsch concludes a deep searching investigation with the judgment that the Old Testament as a whole could be retained in the church only as the classic form of a faith in the law as an "antipode" of the gospel of Christ.[18] In a different way, Rudolf Bultmann found described in the whole Old Testament the way of the law that leads humanity into failure.[19] He continued to say that the Old Testament retains its validity for the church in preparing a "preunderstanding" for Christian faith in the experience of failure because only the human being who has experienced failure is able to understand the gospel of faith. A middle way has been attempted by Friedrich Baumgärtel, who thought to be able to recognize in the Old Testament a "primary promise" that is, however, encumbered throughout the whole Old Testament by its connection with historical events and the historical nation of Israel.[20] A biblical theology would have to dedicate itself to the tracing of a promise stated in terms of a promise free of historical shackles (although the term biblical theology is not found in Baumgärtel, nor with Hirsch and Bultmann). Read in its historical and literal context, Baumgärtel called the Old Testament the witness to an "alien religion."

What is to be said about these theological proposals, each of which contains in its way a "biblical theology," even though they do not use the term? Does one have to retain, as Gunneweg does, the minimal requirement that the Old Testament witnesses, on the one hand, to the same creator who is known also in the New Testament, and on the other hand, that the terminology of the Old Testament prepares "the language" in which the New Testament witnesses speak of the Christ-event when they talk of sin, grace, forgiveness, etc.?[21] Does the phenomenon of the historical priority have to recede into the background as unimportant to Christian faith, as A. H. J. Gunneweg claims? For the Old Testament speaks, he says, in its historical narratives about the destruction of the Canaanites, of revenge, of the wars of Yahweh, and of similar things that can no longer be considered valid for faith in the Son. This view of the matter goes clearly a step beyond Baumgärtel in that he does not only filter out of the Old Testament word a historical "primary promise," but the temporal priority in the Old Testament's witness of God's act with Israel is deprived of its significance to point toward the previously occurring act and speaking of God. A piece of doctrinal instruction (creation, linguistic form) is extracted from the Old Testament like a garment that can be stripped off one person and put on by another. In this proposal it no longer plays a vital role that the doctrines of creation, sin, and redemption are connected indissolubly in the Old Testament with a specific divine act and that transgression and judgment are historically experienced events in the Old Testament. One may notice the reluctance to fall victim to an ideology of "salvation history" that became beholden, in the nineteenth century, to an idealistic philosophy of history, thereby falsifying it—a reluctance that functions like a trauma from which one cannot extricate oneself.[22]

As it stands, it is impossible to miss the unabashed reference in the New Testament witness to that which has happened before and was reported in the Old Testament (although unquestionably transformed with charismatic intentions). Jesus, in healing a crippled woman, opposes the ruler of the synagogue with the statement: "And ought not this woman, a daughter of Abraham . . . be loosed from this bond on the sabbath day?" (Luke 13:16). In recent times, considerations by New Testament scholars have moved the historical Jesus again out of the corner of theological insignificance, and this Jesus has limited his earthly activity to his own people Israel and replied, at first, to the Canaanite woman with the frighteningly negative answer: "It is not right to take the children's bread and throw it to the dogs" (Matt 15:26 // Mark 7:27).[23] And the same Paul who phrased the most radical formulation of the antithesis "justification by faith—justification by works of the law" prefaces his thought about the mystery of his people, which refuses its "anointed," and about the question of what might be the validity of the divine promise to Israel, with the words: "They are Israelites, and to them belong the sonship, the glory, the covenant, the giving of the law, the worship, and the promises; to them belong the patriarchs, and of their race, according to the flesh, is the Christ" (Rom 9:4). These statements cannot be pushed onto the sidetrack of a sentimental dependency of Paul on his traditions. These formulations belong to the context of a central reflection on the question whether the promises of God are valid or not, a question that was heard already in Rom 3:1-2 in a different formulation. Precisely because it is a matter of faith that attaches exclusively to the promise, the question of the validity of the prior promises retains its significance for Paul, which cannot be surrendered.

The question is again connected to what we considered before: Is it negligible for the recognition, i.e., for the tracing of the way in which God has ultimately expressed himself in the Son, that Jesus of Nazareth is the King of the Jews, the Christ of Israel for whom to wait the Old Testament word appeals? Can his people be simply separated from him whose service was dedicated to this people down to the giving up of life on the cross, a people that has retained life across the centuries by its cleaving to the Old Testament? Can one neglect that the Christ-event is at first entirely an event in Israel, a coming to power through the lowly "service of the circumcision" (Rom 15:8), even though precisely through it comes the crisis of Israel and then also beyond it the crisis of all of Adam's progeny and the announcement of a dominion over the entire world, both Jews and Greeks. Even John risks the daring statement: "salvation is from the Jews" (John 4:22).[24]

Is "promise" still promise if the temporal gap is simply eliminated between that which went before and that which is to come after (which is in itself again an event full of promise for the future as is the case in Christ)? Or if this gap is at least erased by turning it into an event that describes existence merely at the point of decision? Can genuine hope for humanity then still be expressed that, after all, lives in a history with its yesterday and its tomorrow?

Torah and the Law of Christ

We return, however, to the fundamental question concerning the antithesis of law and faith, justification by works or justification by faith in Christ alone. It was already stated that the Old Testament does not yet know of this antithesis in its sharpest form.[25] But it is still illegitimate to reduce it for that reason to the common denominator *nomos* (in Pauline understanding), even if it has been designated in the context by the word *torah*, "instruction," and to reject the fact that its proclamation remains connected with a national history as evidence of its essentially legalistic nature.[26] Rather, the Old Testament witness in its historical priority continues to live in a largely unreflected correlation of gracious promise and demanding command. The danger, therefore, always lies close by to understand in the commandment the genuine way to salvation: "If you keep the commandments . . . you will live" (Deut 30:16). Deuteronomic as well as priestly-Ezekielian phrases can lead to this danger of a misunderstanding. In the history of the Son, the seriousness of the demand of the law becomes fully manifest, expressed in the sentence: "For the wages of sin is death" (Rom 6:23), but in the light of this proclamation it is equally manifest that the Son has taken upon himself "the wages of sin" and that every call to obedience that demands the human "spiritual worship" (*logikē latreia*; Rom 12:1) happens on the background of this history. In the Old Testament this was expressed in advance with particular clarity in the time of catastrophe in which God's killing judgment does not imply the "end." In Deutero-Isaiah's message of redemption founded exclusively on God's act we can hear: "I have swept away your transgressions like a cloud, and your sins like mist; return to me, for I have redeemed you (or: I am redeeming you)" (Isa 44:22). "Only from the word of salvation does the theme of 'return' enter into the oracle of admonition."[27]

Throughout, the royal power of the Son manifests itself precisely in the form of his lowliest service. His authority extends, however, in this way over the entire content of his command. He abolishes the saying "an eye for an eye, a tooth for a tooth" as something that was said to the generation of old. Israel's holy wars no longer retain any place before this king in that God himself has waged holy war against all sin and Satan fell from heaven like lightning (Luke 10:18). Every Old Testament law will have to pass through the manifestation of love in the Son in whom the perfect fulfillment of the commandment has taken place. That implies by no means the abolition of the zeal for the will of God and his righteousness. But the boundary line between that which belongs to God and to the "enemy," which seems to run so clearly between two different groups of people in the Psalms, will have to be drawn within the individual who appears before God as sinner but who is accepted into his righteousness through the Son. The sacrifice, of which we find a wealth of instruction in the Priestly legislation of the books of Moses, is collected into the sacrifice of the Son. The Epistle to the Hebrews has reflected on this question in its own way, but so also has Paul, for example in Rom 12:1 and other passages.

Consequently, a biblical theology that strives to be more than the tracing of individual instructions in the religious history of Israel will have to reflect not only on the basic problem of the law, but also on the individual admonitions in light of the "law of Christ (Gal 5:18)—a enormous task that could only be hinted at here in outline.

CANON WITHIN THE CANON

I have attempted up to this point to show some basic lines that have to be taken into account in the design of a biblical theology. Its concrete shape is thereby, however, not yet determined. It must be emphasized again that we are today still a long way off from a concrete design and that we are still in need of several preparatory steps.

It should be evident, however, in the proposals that I have made that according to the view advocated here, it will not suffice to make an attempt to summarize a biblical theology under the comprehensive idea of order that is derived from a theology of creation, as has been proposed in several works by H. H. Schmid, taking wisdom as their starting point.[28] The nature of address that distinguishes the biblical witness of both testaments is not sufficiently recognized in these attempts. The biblical theology of creation must also be thought through from this character of address on which wisdom literature, with its quest for the order of nature and human life, is largely dependent. Job's questions that are allocated in wisdom theology are answered in chapters 38–41, not through the neutral observation of exalted orders of creation, but through the divine address.

Stimulated by Gerhard von Rad's theology, Hartmut Gese (partially dependent upon Peter Stuhlmacher) has attempted to demonstrate a continuous approximation of the two testaments.[29] He does this by adopting a traditio-historical mode of investigation that seeks the elements of tradition that were adopted by Jesus and the New Testament (including the intertestamental writings of the Alexandrian canon). In spite of a number of valuable traditio-historical insights, this approach also seems to fail to give all that is due to the character of address in which God elects Israel and in which he grants himself, in giving himself through his addressing word, fully to the world in the Son.[30]

In a different way, Samuel Terrien attempts to find the connecting bond between the testaments by starting with the statements about the presence of God that remain forever elusive.[31] The self-revelation of God in his word becomes, without a doubt, more cogently discernible when he discusses in this book theophanies (which never happen without words); prayers in the Psalms that answer divine addresses; the word, name, and glory of God. Much preparatory theological work has yet to be done in both testaments. This is true for the New Testament scholar: the witness of the event in the Son experiences a variety of refractions in the New Testament. The factor cannot be missed that the witness of the Christ-event brought with it continuous new formation and internal reflection. Is it possible, under these circumstances, to write *one* New Testament theology? The *one* gospel with which the New Testament witness is concerned breaks up for the historical view into the different aspects of its temporal development: from the historical Jesus to the earliest congregation in Jerusalem, the Hellenistic community of Stephen to Paul, to the deutero-Paulines, to the Letter to the Hebrews, to the Johannine writings, and to James. A "New Testament theology" is faced with the task of being more than a diachronically organized addition of theologies of Mark, Matthew, of Paul, and John, and the individual Catholic Epistles. "Is Christ divided?" (1 Cor 1:13). The task is put before us to make visible the *one* Christ in the multitude of refractions of the one light in the words of the various witnesses.[32] The task will by no means be to erase recognized differences and even tensions within this witness. Rather, it is expected that the unity—or more properly "the One"—be made intelligible in the manifoldness of its attestations.

Since the goal is not a leveling out of the individual formations of the witness to Christ, it cannot be overlooked that the question is placed before us regarding the "canon (that is the criterion of judgment) within the canon."[33] But this must not be allowed to lead to a Marcion-like reduction of a part of the witness to Christ. It is to be insisted, rather, that the unity of Christ comes to the fore in the various witnesses of him in view of the broad area that the church has marked off as the relevant witness to Christ. That this cannot be done without an internal process of evaluation is not to be denied. But the quest for the "whole Christ" must not be relinquished in which equal attention is granted to the Matthean message of the teacher of the new Torah as part of the witness to that Christ who is more than a formula, and to the Pauline "end of the law," and the Johannine speeches of revelation in which elements of the reality of Christ manifest themselves with a particular clarity that must not be abandoned.[34]

The development of an Old Testament theology faces the same question. It may be that the phrase is open to misunderstanding that speaks of a "center of the Old Testament."[35] One may dismiss the phrase if one is able to find a better one for the undeniable fact that the Old Testament's language of God is determined by Yahweh's self-revelation in word and deed in which the diachronic element plays an even more obvious part than in the New Testament because of the long historical extension of the Old Testament record. This is valid even at the edges of the practical instruction of wisdom literature. Here Ecclesiastes—which has rightly been received into the canon—passionately and one-sidedly holds on to the fact that "God" can never be possessed but can only manifest himself in his "giving," which is accompanied by his denying as its counterpole (see above).

Consequently, in the area of the Old Testament also, the task is not at all adequately performed if the historical way of the manifestation of Israel's God is hidden. But the concentration on the *One* who from the creation of the world on remains one and the same must remain the guiding principle, whether this be developed in the statements of Genesis 1 or of Genesis 2. This is so even if God's acts assume different forms at different times and the witnesses speak with different images of history.[36]

At this point Old and New Testament language must coalesce into a "biblical" language, into the formation of a biblical theology. It will not be enough to bring out general structural similarities between the testaments, even though they may often enough be obvious. It will also not be sufficient to talk about linguistic correlation in terminology on either side, even if this is also frequently a unifying element. Rather, the task will be to make discernible in all these similarities and correlations—which, for the most part, were properly noted—the One who is addressed in the Old Testament with the name Yahweh, the God of Israel, who is also the Father of the son who reveals his face "once and for all" (*ephapax*; Rom 6:10; Heb 7:27; 9:12; 10:10) in Jesus Christ, the incarnate "King of the Jews" and "servant of the circumcision."

CONCLUSION

In closing we insist, once more with emphasis, that a genuine biblical theology must not allow the relinquishing of what the phrase "of old" stands for together with the phrase "when the time had fully come," which through the Holy Spirit becomes the "today" for faith. In so doing we by no means wish to save a piece of historicism or to snatch the log of a philosophical element of "salvation history" out of the fire. The biblical message of the "faithfulness of God" is meant to be retained in the insistence on the line of demarcation that is anchored in human history and that prevents the loss of the yesterday, today, and tomorrow that constitutes our real historical life. Beyond all vicissitudes of time and in all extensions of his kingdom, which has its testimony in the real history of the Son, God remains dedicated to his own intention and does not deny his yesterday in his present. This alone can also provide the certain hope for the promised tomorrow that is given in the Son to our world infected by death.

Also, this alone can lead to a promised fraternal dialogue with Israel that cleaves to the Old Testament and that is not to be deprived either of the Old Testament or of the God who calls Israel, through a "huge philological farce." Christian faith is by no means a Christian know-it-all attitude that is certain of its own possession. It could be that in the dialogue with an Israel taking seriously its Old Testament the Christian partner may be confronted with very serious questions.[37] At the same time, however, an Israel cleaving to its Old Testament must not be deprived of the glory of its own king that is shown in the New Testament. The Christ on whose cross was placed the inscription "King of the Jews" is a figure that cannot be eliminated from the history of Israel.

Notes

1. Prophetic Proclamation and Reinterpretation

1. As in Ernst Würthwein, "Amos-Studien," *ZAW* 62 (1950) 10–52, reprinted in *Wort und Existenz: Studien zum Alten Testament* (Göttingen: Vandenhoeck & Ruprecht, 1970) 68–110. More distinctly this is addressed in Henning Graf Reventlow, *Das Amt des Propheten bei Amos*, FRLANT 80 (Göttingen: Vandenhoeck & Ruprecht, 1962).

2. Rudolf Smend, "Das Nein des Amos," *EvTh* 23 (1963) 404–23.

3. Compare, for example, Edzard Rohland, "Die Bedutung der Erwählungstraditionen Israels für die Eschatologie der alttestamentlichen Propheten" (Ph.D. diss., University of Heidelberg, 1956), 119–208; Hanns-Martin Lutz, *Jahwe, Jerusalem und die Völker*, WMANT 27 (Neukirchen-Vluyn: Neukirchener, 1968). Differently, Gunther Wanke, *Die Zionstheologie der Korachiten in ihrem traditionsgeschichtlichen Zusammenhang*, BZAW 97 (Berlin: de Gruyter, 1966).

4. Exodus 3:14 attempts to "decode" the name and its etymological meaning; yet it is striking how in this passage itself the expression "I am who I am" defies any possibility of grasping who the Lord is. Hans Walter Wolff's suggestion of finding in Hos 1:9 a reference to Exod 3:14 is questionable; see his *Hosea*, trans. Gary Stansell, Hermeneia (Philadelphia: Fortress Press, 1974) 21–22.

5. Zimmerli, "The Word of Divine Self-Manifestation (Proof-Saying): A Prophetic Genre," in *I Am Yahweh*, ed. Walter Brueggemann, trans. Douglas W. Stott (Atlanta: John Knox, 1982) 99–110.

6. This assertion remains valid even in light of the fact that the "recognition formula" (*Erkenntnisformel*) can later be subject to expansions. I have gathered this material in Zimmerli, "Knowledge of God according to the Book of Ezekiel," in *I Am Yahweh*, 29–98.

7. Against, for example, Hans Werner Hoffmann, *Die Intention der Verkündigung Jesajas*, BZAW 136 (Berlin: de Gruyter, 1974).

8. Hugo Gressmann, *Der Ursprung der israelitisch-jüdischen Eschatologie*, FRLANT 6 (Göttingen: Vandenhoeck & Ruprecht, 1905).

9. Sigmund Mowinckel, *Psalmenstudien II: Das Thronbesteigungsfest Jahwäs und der Ursprung der Eschatologie* (Kristiania: Dybwad, 1922). In this same direction, though also with reference to Ugaritic texts, see now John Gray, "The Day of Yahweh in Cultic Experience and Eschatological Prospect," *SEÅ* 39 (1974) 5–37. The latter also contains recent literature on this subject.

10. Gerhard von Rad, "The Origin of the Concept of the Day of Yahweh," *JSS* 4 (1959) 97–108.

11. Reinhard Fey, *Amos und Jesaja: Abhängigkeit und Eigenständigkeit des Jesaja,* WMANT 12 (Neukirchen-Vluyn: Neukirchener, 1963).

12. K. Gross, *Die literarische Verwandtschft Jeremias mit Hosea* (Borna-Leipzig: Noske, 1930); idem, "Hoseas Einfluss auf Jeremias Anschauungen," *NKZ* 42 (1931) 241–56, 327–43.

13. John Wolf Miller, *Das Verhältnis Jeremias und Hesekiels sprachlich und theologisch Untersucht: Mit besonderer Berücksichtigung der Prosareden Jeremias,* VGTB 28 (Assen: Van Gorcum, 1955).

14. Dieter Baltzer, *Ezechiel und Deuterojesaja: Berührungen in der Heilserwartung der beiden grossen Exilpropheten,* BZAW 121 (Berlin: de Gruyter, 1971).

15. Gerhard von Rad, "The Form-Critical Problem of the Hexateuch," in *The Problem of the Hexateuch and Other Essays,* trans. E. W. Trueman Dicken (London: Oliver & Boyd, 1966) 1–78.

16. Martin Noth, *A History of Pentateuchal Traditions,* trans. Bernhard W. Anderson (Englewood Cliffs, N.J.: Prentice-Hall, 1972).

17. This "knowing" includes on the one hand intimacy, but beyond this also election. Jeremiah 1:5 uses it parallel to the one who "consecrates" whomever he will.

18. However, there may be some question whether this statement, which has a parallel in Jer 7:22 with its explicit reference to burnt offerings and sacrifices, belongs to the original text of Amos. On this, compare Jochen Vollmer, *Geschichtliche Rückblicke und Motive in der Prophetie des Amos, Hosea and Jesaja,* BZAW 119 (Berlin: de Gruyter, 1971), who links Amos 5:25 with 5:26 and thus considers it only as a polemic against burnt offerings and sacrifices that are connected with idolatry. Compare also Hans Walter Wolff, *Joel and Amos,* trans. Waldemar Janzen et al., Hermeneia (Philadelphia: Fortress Press, 1976) 258–68.

19. Compare Vollmer, *Geschichtliche Rückblicke.*

20. George W. Coats, *Rebellion in the Wilderness: The Murmuring Motif in the Wilderness Traditions of the Old Testament* (Nashville: Abingdon, 1968).

21. Nevertheless, Hosea was not at all unfamiliar with the positive element of tradition, "Yahweh's gift of land"; compare Hos 2:7-15 [MT 2:9-17].

22. "When Israel was young, I became fond of him; out of Egypt I called my son" (Hos 11:1). Alongside this and rather incongruously, 9:10 states that Yahweh found Israel in the wilderness. It is perhaps too extreme to suggest, as does Robert Bach ("Die Erwählung Israel in der Wüste," [Ph.D. diss., Univ. of Bonn, 1951]), that this and a few other passages give evidence of a separate discovery-tradition.

23. The MT reading in Hos 11:11 of "cause to dwell" (*wehoshabtim*) is probably a scribal error for "and I will cause them to return" (*wehashibotam*). [Ed.] See Rolf Knierim, "'I Will Cause It to Return' in Amos 1 and 2" in *Canon and Authority: Essays in Old Testament Religion and Theology,* ed. George W. Coats and Burke O. Long (Philadelphia: Fortress Press, 1977) 163–75.

24. There is a strong threat similar to this in Hos 2:3 [MT 2:5].

25. For more details on this stream of tradition, see Odil Hannes Steck, "Theological Streams of Tradition," in *Tradition and Theology in the Old Testament*, ed. Douglas A. Knight (Philadelphia: Fortress Press, 1977) 183–214, esp. 193, 199–202.

26. This image, referring here not to the people but to the city of Jerusalem, shows clearly how close—yet with differences as well—Isaiah is to Hosea.

27. Compare Rohland, "Die Bedeutung"; Lutz, *Jahwe*; as well as Fritz Stolz, *Strukturen und Figuren im Kult von Jerusalem*, BZAW 118 (Berlin: de Gruyter, 1970); and Jörg Jeremias, "Lade und Zion: Zur Entstehung der Ziontradition," in *Probleme biblischer Theologie: Gerhard von Rad zum 70. Geburtstag*, ed. Hans Walter Wolff (Munich: Kaiser, 1971) 183–98. [Ed.] See also J. J. M. Roberts, "The Davidic Origin of the Zion Tradition," *JBL* 92 (1973) 329–44.

28. Ernst Würthwein, "Jes. 7,1-9: Ein Beitrag zu dem Thema: Prophetie und Politik," in *Theologie als Glaubenswagnis: Festschrift für Karl Heim zum 80. Geburtstag*, Furche-Studien 23 (Hamburg: Furche, 1954) 47–63; reprinted in Würthwein, *Wort und Existenz: Studien zum Alten Testament* (Göttingen: Vandenhoeck & Ruprecht, 1970) 127–43.

29. For the present discussion it is unimportant whether this second scene was connected immediately with the first or separated from it by time.

30. Zimmerli, "Verkündigung und Sprache der Botschaft Jesajas," in *Fides et communicatio: Festschrift für Martin Doerne zum 70. Geburtstag*, ed. Dietrich Rössler et al. (Göttingen: Vandenhoeck & Ruprecht, 1970), 441–54; reprinted in Zimmerli, *Studien zur alttestamentlichen Theologie und Prophetie: Gesammelte Aufsätze II*, ThBü 51 (Munich: Kaiser, 1974) 73–87.

31. Micah 5:2-6 [MT 5:1-5] has the messianic king stemming from Bethlehem and not from Jerusalem. It may be asked whether this utterance presupposes judgment on Jerusalem and Yahweh's return to the origins of the Davidic dynasty in Bethlehem.

32. Both Ezek 28:25 and 37:25, referring to Yahweh's land given "to my servant Jacob," surely do not stem from the hand of the prophet himself but from a later editor. Compare Zimmerli, *Ezekiel 2*, trans. James D. Martin, Hermeneia (Philadelphia: Fortress Press, 1983) 100, 276.

33. Here we can recognize the transformed tradition about the reconnaissance of the land in Numbers 13–14.

34. The reference is to child sacrifice. On this problem, compare Zimmerli, "Erstgeborene und Leviten: Ein Beitrag zur exilisch-nachexilischen Theologie," in *Near Eastern Studies in Honor of W. F. Albright*, ed. Hans Goedicke (Baltimore: John Hopkins Univ. Press, 1971) 459–69; reprinted in Zimmerli, *Studien zur alttestamentlichen Theologie und Prophetie*, 235–46.

35. Verses 27-29 were added later when one missed any reference to the conquest or to life in the land; compare Zimmerli, *Ezekiel 1*, trans. Ronald E. Clements, Hermeneia (Philadelphia: Fortress Press, 1977) 412–14.

36. This election to be the "city at the center" results from the *omphalos* (navel) notion (explicit in Ezek 38:12). This notion is transformed here into a new adoption statement.

37. The same promise is found in Ezek 37:25 immediately following the promise of reunification of the two kingdoms.

38. Compare, for example, Aage Bentzen, *King and Messiah*, trans. G. W. Anderson (Oxford: Blackwell, 1970) 64–67.

39. It is especially evident that the speech about the two faithless women in Ezekiel 23 is dependent on Jer 3:6-11.

40. On Trito-Isaiah's dependence on Deutero-Isaiah, compare Zimmerli, "Zur Sprache Tritojesajas," *STU* 20 (1950) 110–22; reprinted in Zimmerli, *Gottes Offenbarung: Gesammelte Aufsätze zum Alten Testament*, ThBü 19 (Munich: Kaiser, 1969) 217–33.

41. This inner-prophetic transmission can be considered in terms of two further, different aspects. We have been treating above the way one prophet's proclamation may be dependent on that of another, but in addition to this there is also a path from a prophet's utterances to the prophetic book itself. We must consider that prophetic utterances were transmitted, in part along school lines, within circles of traditionists who in turn sought to affect the "thrust" of a prophet's message by the way they collected his utterances together into a whole and added further elements to them—such as in the addition of the salvation prophecy at the end of Amos's words in 9:11-15. Redaction-critical analyses attempt especially to trace such later stylizations of an entire prophetic collection. Such an interpretative post-history, however, can be discerned even for individual prophetic utterances. An example is the way in which the original symbolic act in Ezek 12:1-16 was later reinterpreted in light of the historical fate of King Zedekiah (compare 2 Kgs 25:1-7). Such "interpretative post-history" can occasionally lead to extensive overpainting of the original texts (compare, for example, my *Ezekiel* 1 on chap. 1 of Ezekiel. This phenomenon has not been treated in the above discussion and is therefore not considered in this summary. For an example, compare the analysis of the Book of Nahum in Jörg Jeremias, *Kultprophetie und Gerichtsverkündigung in der späten Königzeit Israel*, WMANT 35 (Neukirchen-Vluyn: Neukirchener, 1970) 11–55. [Ed.] On fundamental matters, compare Sigmund Mowinckel, *The Spirit and the Word*, ed. K. C. Hanson, FCBS (Minneapolis: Fortress Press, 2002) 3–80; and discussions in Douglas A. Knight, *Rediscovering the Traditions of Israel*, rev. ed., SBLDS 9 (Missoula, Mont.: Society of Biblical Literature, 1975) 215–399.

42. For the most pronounced position on this, compare Reventlow, *Das Amt.*

43. Martin Noth, "The Re-Presentation of the Old Testament in Proclamation," in *Essays on Old Testament Hermeneutics,* ed. Claus Westermann and James Luther Mays (Richmond: John Knox, 1963) 76–88.

44. Compare Zimmerli, "Alttestamentliche Traditionsgeschichte und Theologie," in *Probleme biblischer Theologie,* 632–47; reprinted in *Studien zur alttestamentlichen Theologie und Prophetie,* 9–26.

2. FROM PROPHETIC WORD
TO PROPHETIC BOOK

1. Compare, for instance, the harshness of the announcement of judgment in the early days of the prophet, typified by Isaiah 6, with the exhortation to rest and confidence that is anchored in the apodictic promise of the crisis of 733: "It shall not stand, and it shall not come to pass" (Isa 7:7).

2. For the lively discussion about oral tradition, especially during the decades between 1930 and 1950, see the introduction and critique by Antonius H. J. Gunneweg, *Mündliche und schriftliche Tradition der vorexilischen Prophetenbücher als Problem der neueren*

Prophetenforschung, FRLANT 73 (Göttingen: Vandenhoeck & Ruprecht, 1959). [Ed.] See Ehud Ben Zvi and Michael H. Floyd, eds., *Writings and Speech in Israelite and Ancient Near Eastern Prophecy,* SBLSymSer 10 (Atlanta: Society of Biblical Literature, 2000).

3. Hans Wildberger, *Isaiah 1–12,* trans. T. H. Trapp, CC (Minneapolis: Augsburg, 1991) note b on Isa 8:1.

4. Siegfried Morenz, "Eilebeute," *TLZ* 74 (1949) 697–99; reprinted in *Religion und Geschichte des alten Ägypten: Gesammelte Aufsätze,* edited by Elke Blumenthal and Siegfried Herrmann (Colone: Böhlau, 1975) 395–400.

5. These terms refer to the first babbling words: Papa, Mama.

6. We seem to have encountered here an almost institutionalized form of questioning Yahweh and of the announcement of prophetic information, which should then also have a retrospective effect on the evaluation of the position of Isaiah.

7. See, for example, Otto Kaiser, *Isaiah 13–39,* trans. R. A. Wilson, 2d ed., OTL (Philadelphia: Westminster, 1980) on Isa 30:8.

8. The problem of the expansion of the subsection beyond the "final word" of 8:16 cannot be discussed here.

9. The translation suggested in KBL (and also, for example, by Wildberger), "I must remain silent," hardly reflects the depth of the prophet's cry of terror.

10. This change of form that becomes visible in the texts has not, in my view, been adequately considered in the whole discussion regarding oral tradition.

11. Siegmund Böhmer, *Heimkehr und Bund: Studien zu Jeremia* 30–31, Göttinger Theologische Arbeiten 5 (Göttingen: Vandenhoeck & Ruprecht, 1976).

12. On this phenomenon, which appears elsewhere in Ezekiel as well, see Zimmerli, *Ezekiel 1,* trans. R. E. Clements, Hermeneia (Philadelphia: Fortress Press, 1979) 68–74.

13. See, for example, H. Eberhard von Waldow, "Anlass und Hintergrund der Verkündigung des Deuterojesajas" (Ph.D. diss., Univ. of Bonn, 1953).

14. Christian Jeremias, *Die Nachtgesichte des Sacharja,* FRLANT 117 (Göttingen: Vandenhoeck & Ruprecht, 1977).

15. See, for example, Hans Walter Wolff, *Joel and Amos,* trans. Waldemar Janzen et al., Hermeneia (Philadelphia: Fortress Press, 1977) 106–13.

16. Here also belong the words of the unnamed prophet or man of God from 1 Kgs 20:13, 28, which have the form of a "proof-saying," a form especially common in Ezekiel; see Zimmerli, *Ezekiel 1,* 36–40. [Ed.] See also Zimmerli, "The Word of Divine Self-Manifestation (Proof-Saying): A Prophetic Genre," in idem, *I Am Yahweh,* ed. Walter Brueggemann, trans. Douglas W. Stott (Atlanta: John Knox, 1982) 99–110.

17. The attempt of Rudolph to consider only Amos 2:5bβ as later expansion is unconvincing; Wilhelm Rudolph, *Joel, Amos, Obadja, Jona,* KAT 13/2 (Gütersloh: Gütersloher, 1971) 120.

18. Friedrich Horst, "Die Doxologien im Amosbuch," *ZAW* 47 (1929) 45–54; reprinted in idem, *Gottes Recht,* ThBü 12 (Munich: Kaiser, 1961) 155–66.

19. Wolff, *Joel and Amos,* 111–12.

20. Werner H. Schmidt, "Die deuteronomistische Redaktion des Amosbuches," *ZAW* 77 (1965) 168–93; Ulrich Kellermann, "Der Amosschluss als Stimme deuteronomistischer Heilshoffnung," *EvTh* 29 (1969) 169–83.

21. Regarding the sequence "destruction for the nations / salvation for Israel," we may recall the structure of the message to the foreign nations in pre-classical prophecy, which has been discussed above.

22. Sigmund Mowinckel, *Zur Komposition des Buches Jeremia*, SNVAO (Kristiania: Dybwad, 1914).

23. Wilhelm Rudolph, *Jeremia*, 3d ed., HAT 12 (Tübingen: Mohr/Siebeck, 1968).

24. Winfried Thiel, *Die deuteronomistische Redaktion von Jeremia 1–25*, WMANT 41 (Neukirchen-Vluyn: Neukirchener, 1973).

25. Zimmerli, "Deutero-Ezechiel?" *ZAW* 84 (1972) 501–16.

26. Kaiser, *Isaiah* 13–39, 234–36.

27. Kaiser, *Isaiah* 13–39.

28. Paul D. Hanson, *The Dawn of Apocalyptic* (Philadelphia: Fortress Press, 1975).

29. Zimmerli, "Alttestamentliche Prophetie und Apokalyptik auf dem Wege zur 'Rechtfertigung des Gottlosen,'" in *Rechtfertigung: Festschrift für Ernst Käsemann zum 70. Geburtstag*, ed. Johannes Friedrich et al. (Göttingen: Vandenhoeck & Ruprecht, 1976) 575–92.

3. The "Land" in the Prophets

1. Gerhard von Rad, "The Promised Land and Yahweh's Land in the Hexateuch," in *The Problem of the Hexateuch and Other Essays*, trans. E. W. Trueman Dicken (New York: McGraw-Hill, 1966) 79–93.

2. On the relation of cult and life see von Rad, "'Righteousness' and 'Life' in the Cultic Language of the Psalms," in *The Problem of the Hexateuch and Other Essays*, 243–66.

3. For the basis of Amos's proclamation see Walther Zimmerli, "Das Gottesrecht bei den Propheten Amos, Hosea und Jesaja," in *Wesen und Wirken des Alten Testament: Festschrift für Claus Westermann*, ed. Rainer Albertz (Göttingen: Vandenhoeck & Ruprecht, 1980) 216–35. See also Richard Bach, "Gottesrecht und weltliches Recht in der Verkündigung des Propheten Amos," in *Festschrift für Günther Dehn*, ed. Wilhelm Schneemelcher (Neukirchen-Vluyn: Neukirchener, 1957) 23–34.

4. Isaiah 10:24, 26; and 17:9 are not authentic words of Isaiah and are later in origin.

5. Hans H. Schmid, *Gerechtigkeit als Weltordnung*, BHT 40 (Tübingen: Mohr/Siebeck, 1968) 74–77. [Ed.] See Bernard F. Batto, "Zedeq," in *DDD²*, 929–34.

6. The "and removes far away" (*weriḥaq*) of Isa 6:12 belongs to a subsequent expansion and may represent a "relecture" under the impact of the event of 587 B.C.E. See J. Vermeylen, *Du prophèt Isaïe à l'apocalyptique I: Isaïe, I-XXXV, miroir d'un demi-millénaire d'expérience religieuse en Israël*, EBib (Paris: Gabalada, 1977) 195–96. Compare also Walter Dietrich, *Jesaja und die Politik*, BEvT 74 (Munich: Kaiser, 1976) 178; Dietrich also wants to transpose vv. 12-13 before v. 11 and to see in vv. 12-13 an original textual element, which—under the impact of the event of 701 B.C.E.—would have been added to vv. 9b-10 changing the original sequence of verses. That, however, is hardly convincing.

7. Dietrich, *Jesaja und die Politik*, sees as a later composition the whole of Isa 14:28-32. Jochen Vollmer, *Geschichtliche Rückblicke und Motive in der Prophetie des Amos, Hosea und Jesaja*, BZAW 115 (Berlin: de Gruyter, 1971), finds in the answer to the messengers an awkward imitation of Isa 28:16. Vermeylen concludes that a "remaniement" of a post-exilic redactor can be recognized behind the original Isaianic text by the exclusion of the "poor" (*Du prophèt Isaïe à l'apocalyptique I*, 301–2).

8. Vermeylen (*Du prophèt Isaïe à l'apocalyptique I*, 392–95) finds in 28:16aβb-17a an addition that stems from the circle of pious Jews of the second temple period (a view

followed in many commentaries); Dietrich, on the other hand, wants to retain at least v. 17a as original (*Jesaja und die Politik*, 164–68). Compare, however, Hans Wildberger, *Isaiah 28–39*, trans. Thomas H. Trapp, CC (Minneapolis: Fortress Press, 2002) 31–32, 40–42.

9. With Wildberger (*Isaiah 28–39*, 63–79), I wish to find in Isa 29:1-7 the original Isaianic text, against Vermeylen, who confines it to Isa 29:1-4 (*Du prophèt Isaïe à l'apocalyptique I*, 401–3), and against Dietrich, who, along with most radical research opinion, confines it to Isa 29:1-4a (*Jesaja und die Politik*, 188).

10. Herbert Donner, thinks along the lines of Alt of a negative result of the feudal system; and Hans Bardtke thinks of a surplus of money that fugitives from the catastrophe of the northern empire brought to Judah and invested in property. Donner, "Die soziale Botschaft der Propheten im Lichte der Gesellschaftsordnung Israels," *OrAnt* 2 (1963) 229–45; Albrecht Alt, "Der Anteil des Königtums an der sozialen Entwicklung in den Reichen Israel und Juda," in idem, *Kleine Schriften* (Munich: Beck, 1959) 3.348–72; and Bardtke, "Die Latifundien in Juda während der 2. Hälfte des 8. Jahr.," in *Hommage à A. Dupont-Sommer* (Paris: Adrien-Maisonneuve, 1971) 235–54.

11. Albrecht Alt, "Micha 2,1-5: ΤΗΣ ΑΝΑΔΑΣΜΟΣ in Juda," in *Interpretationes ad Vetus Testamentum pertinentes Sigmundo Mowinckel septuagenario* (Oslo: Lund og Kirche, 1955) 13–23; reprinted in idem, *Kleine Schriften*, 3.373–81.

12. Hans Walter Wolff, *Micah*, trans. Gary Stansell, CC (Minneapolis: Augsburg, 1990) 80.

13. Wolff translates "as in the days of meeting"; *Hosea*, trans. Gary Stansell, Hermeneia (Philadelphia: Fortress Press, 1974) 207. Hans-Joachim Kraus postulates a "tent festival" that lived on in the Feast of Tabernacles; *Worship in Israel: A Cultic History of the Old Testament*, trans. Geoffrey Buswell (Richmond: John Knox, 1966) 32.

14. Leonhard Rost, *Israel bei den Propheten*, BWANT 4 (Stuttgart: Kohlhammer, 1937). Zimmerli, "Israel im Buche Ezechiel," *VT* 8 (1958) 75–90.

15. Peter Diepold, *Israels Land*, BWANT 5 (Stuttgart: Kohlhammer, 1972).

16. Winfried Thiel, *Die deuteronomistische Redaktion von Jeremia 1–25*, WMANT 41 (Neukirchen-Vluyn: Neukirchener, 1970); idem, *Die deuteronomistische Redaktion von Jeremia 26–45*, WMANT 52 (Neukirchen-Vluyn: Neukirchener, 1981).

17. Bernard Keller, "La terre dans le livre d'Ezekiel," *RHPR* 55 (1975) 481–90.

18. Keller, "La terre," 490.

19. All three examples for *'ereṣ yiśra'el* occur in the second half of the book. Ezekiel 27:17, however, is part of the context of a prosaic list of trading partners and wares, originating perhaps from a trading post of Tyre, which has been inserted only later into the song of lament in the *qinah*-meter of Ezekiel. Ezekiel 40:2 stands in a context in which the return of the glory of God is for the first time imminent. And Ezek 47:18 stands in a record of the boundary of the land to be newly apportioned, which has a remarkably close parallel in Num 34:3-12 and may on no account be interpreted apart from it if the specific theological position of Ezekiel is to be understood. Compare, for the particulars, Zimmerli, *Ezekiel 2*, trans. James D. Martin, Hermeneia (Minneapolis: Fortress Press, 1983) 66–67, 347, 531–32. On the other hand, the seventeen examples for *'admat yiśra'el* are spread freely over both parts of the book without the special connotation maintained by Keller having been brought to expression in them.

20. The use of the image of the opened graves for the interpretation of the figure of the revived bones of the dead does not justify the separation of 37:11-14 from 37:1-10 as in

Dieter Baltzer, *Ezechiel und Deuterojesaja*, BZAW 121 (Berlin: de Gruyter, 1971) 100–118; and in Peter Höffken, "Beobachtungen zu Ez 37,1-10," *VT* 31 (1981) 305–17.

21. Against Brownlee, who sees in Ezekiel a person who, like Jeremiah, remained chiefly in the land in 587 B.C.E. He maintains that Ezek 11:14-21 is contemporaneous with 33:24-26 and judges the present arrangement of the book as a result of a complicated process of redaction. See William H. Brownlee, "The Aftermath of the Fall of Judah according to Ezekiel," *JBL* 89 (1970) 393–404; and idem, "Ezekiel's Parable of the Watchman," *VT* 28 (1978) 392–408. [Ed.] See also Brownlee, *Ezekiel* 1–19, WBC 28 (Waco: Word, 1986).

22. If my suspicion that the striking predominance of the number 25 in the description of the new temple is connected with the twenty-fifth year as the mid-point of the year of release in which, according to Leviticus 25, not only slaves obtained their freedom but also alienated land reverted to its previous owner, then "the land" plays an important, unnoticed role in connection with dating. See Zimmerli, "Das 'Gnadenjahr des Herrn'," in *Archäologie und Altes Testament: Zum 70. Geburtstag Kurt Galling*, ed. Arnulf Kuschke (Tübingen: Mohr/Siebeck, 1970) 321–32; reprinted in Zimmerli, *Studien zur alttestamentlichen Theologie und Prophetie*, ThBü 51 (Munich: Kaiser, 1974) 222–34.

23. Cited according to Martin Buber, *On Zion: The History of an Idea*, trans. Stanley Godman (New York: Schocken, 1973) 118.

4. Visionary Experience in Jeremiah

1. Sigmund Mowinckel, *Zur Komposition des Buches Jeremia*, Videnskapsselskapets skrifter: II, Hist.-filos. Klasse (Kristiania: Jacob Dybwad, 1914); Winfried Thiel, *Die deuteronomistische Redaktion von Jeremia 1–25*, WMANT 41 (Neukirchen-Vluyn: Neukirchener, 1973); Hans Wildberger, *Jahwewort und prophetische Rede bei Jeremia* (Zurich: Zwingli, 1942). [Ed.] See William L. Holladay, "A Fresh Look at 'Source B' and 'Source C' in Jeremiah," *VT* 25 (1975) 392–96, 402–12.

2. On this formula, see Zimmerli, *Ezekiel* 1, trans. Ronald E. Clements, Hermeneia (Philadelphia: Fortress Press, 1979) 144–45; on its occurrence in Jeremiah, compare Peter K. D. Neumann, "Das Wort, das geschehen ist . . . Zum Problem der Wortempfangstheologie in Jer. I–XXV," *VT* 23 (1973) 171–217; and Theodor Seidl, "Die Wortereignisformel in Jeremia," *BZ* 23 (1979) 20–47.

3. Gunther Wanke, *Untersuchungen zur sogenannten Baruchschrift*, BZAW 122 (Berlin: de Gruyter, 1971).

4. Heinz Kremers, "Leidensgemeinschaft mit Gott: Eine Untersuchung der 'biographischen' Berichte im Jeremiabuch," *EvTh* 13 (1953) 122–40; and Wanke, *Untersuchungen*.

5. Compare Thiel, *Die deuteronomistische Redaktion*.

6. Walter Baumgartner, *Jeremiah's Poems of Lament*, HTIBS 7 (Sheffield: Almond, 1988; German ed. 1917); Gerhard von Rad, "Die Konfessionen Jeremias," *EvTh* 3 (1936) 265–76; differently Antonius H. J. Gunneweg, "Konfession oder Interpretation im Jeremiabuch," *ZTK* (1970) 395–416; Peter Welten, "Leiden und Leidenerfahrung im Buch Jeremia," *ZTK* 74 (1977) 123–50.

7. Against Claus Rietzschel, *Das Problem der Urrolle: Ein Beitrag zur Redaktionsgeschichte des Jeremiabuches* (Gütersloh: Gütersloher, 1966) 131ff.

8. Thiel, *Die deuteronomistische Redaktion*, 62–72.

9. Thiel, *Die deuteronomistische Redaktion*, 64.

10. Ivar P. Seierstad, *Die Offenbarungserlebnisse der propheten Amos, Jesaja und Jeremia* (Oslo: Universitetsforlaget, 1965) 67.

11. Compare Zimmerli, *Ezekiel 1*, 117–18 on Ezek 1:3; and also p. 42.

12. The formulas "I saw" or "Yahweh showed me," which are characteristic of the fully developed vision, are lacking here; only the "call to attention" (*hinnēh*) is used. See KBL, 238.

13. On the phenomenon of prophetic visions, compare Gustav Hölscher, *Die Profeten: Untersuchungen zur Religionsgeschichte Israels* (Leipzig: Hinrichs, 1914); Johannes Lindblom, "Die Gesichte der Propheten," in *Studia Theologica* (Festschrift for Immanuel Benzinger) 1 (1935) 7–28; idem, *Prophecy in Ancient Israel* (Philadelphia: Fortress Press, 1963); and Friedrich Horst, "Die Visionsschilderungen der alttestamentlichen Propheten," *EvTh* 20 (1960) 193–205. [Ed.] See also Gerhard von Rad, *Old Testament Theology*, vol. 2: *The Theology of Israel's Prophetic Traditions*, trans. D. M. G. Stalker (New York: Harper & Row, 1965); Thomas W. Overholt, *Channels of Prophecy: The Social Dynamics of Prophetic Activity* (Minneapolis: Fortress Press, 1989); and John J. Pilch, "Visions in Revelation and Alternate Consciousness: A Perspective from Cultural Anthropology," *Listening: Journal of Religion and Culture* 28 (1993) 231–44.

14. For the statistics, compare Oskar Grether, *Name und Wort Gottes im Alten Testament*, BZAW 64 (Giessen: Töpelmann, 1934) 67–68.

15. The formula in Ezek 1:3a is a heading that has been added at a secondary stage. In 11:14-21 an independent oracle has been secondarily inserted into the vision cycle.

16. Thiel, *Die deuteronomistische Redaktion*, 98 n.66.

17. Wolfram Herrmann, "Philologica Hebraica," *Theologische Versuche* 8 (1977) 35–44.

18. Michael Fishbane, "Jeremiah 4:23-26 and Job 3:3-13: A Recovered Use of the Creation Pattern," *VT* 21 (1971) 151–67.

19. Friedrich Giesebrecht, *Das Buch Jeremia*, HKAT 3/2 (Göttingen: Vandenhoeck & Ruprecht, 1907) 28.

20. Paul Volz, *Der Prophet Jeremia*, KAT 10 (Leipzig: Deichert, 1928) 50.

21. Bernhard Duhm, *Das Buch Jeremia*, KHAT 11 (Tübingen: Mohr/Siebeck, 1901) 54.

22. Wilhelm Rudolph argues this, *Jeremia*, HAT 1/12 (Tübingen: Mohr/Siebeck, 1968) 102–3. Thiel argues to the contrary, *Die deuteronomistische Redaktion*, 190–91.

23. Zimmerli, *Ezekiel 1*, 120.

24. Contrast the views of Henning Graf Reventlow, *Liturgie und prophetisches Ich bei Jeremia* (Gütersloh: Gütersloher, 1963); and John Berridge, "Jeremia und die Prophetie des Amos," *TZ* 35 (1979) 321–41.

25. Duhm, *Das Buch Jeremia*.

26. Ronald E. Clements, *Prophecy and Tradition* (Atlanta: John Knox, 1975); and Zimmerli in chapter 1 of this volume.

27. Siegfried Herrmann, "Die Bewältigung der Krise Israels: Bermerkungen zur Interpretation des Buches Jeremia," in *Beiträge zur Alttestamentlichen Theologie: Festschrift für Walther Zimmerli*, ed. Herbert Donner et al. (Göttingen: Vandenhoeck & Ruprecht, 1977) 164–78.

28. So with Seidl, "Die Wortereignisformel in Jeremia"; and against Neumann, "Das Wort, 183–84.

29. Reventlow, *Liturgie*.

30. Friedrich Horst, "Die Visionsschilderungen der alttestamentlichen Propheten," *EvTh* 20 (1960) 193–205.

31. Compare Berridge, "Jeremia und die Prophetie des Amos."

32. Horst, "Die Visionsschilderungen," 205.

33. Karl Gross, "Die literarische Verwandschaft Jeremias mit Hosea" (Ph.D. diss., Leipzig Univ., 1930); and idem, "Hoseas Einfluss auf Jeremias Anschauungen [2 parts]," *NKZ* 42 (1931) 241–56, 327–43.

34. Hans Schmidt, *Die grossen Propheten*, 2d ed., SAT 2/2 (Göttingen: Vandenhoeck & Ruprecht, 1923) 206–7.

35. Compare Zimmerli, *Ezekiel 1*, 493–501.

36. A critical assessment in Wanke, *Untersuchungen*, 59ff.

37. Against Karl-Friedrich Pohlmann, *Studien zum Jeremiabuch*, FRLANT 118 (Göttingen: Vandenhoeck & Ruprecht, 1978).

38. Thiel, *Die deuteronomistische Redaktion*.

39. Pohlmann, *Studien zum Jeremiabuch*, 20–31.

40. Siegfried Herrmann, *Die prophetischen Heilserwartungen im Alten Testament: Ursprung und Gestaltwandel*, BWANT 85 (Stuttgart: Kohlhammer, 1965) 165–66; and Thiel, *Die deuteronomistische Redaktion*, 253–61.

41. B. A. Pareira, "The Call to Conversion in Ezekiel" (Ph.D. diss., Pontificia Universitas Gregoriana, 1975); and Thomas M. Raitt, "The Prophetic Summons to Repentance," *ZAW* 83 (1971) 30–49.

42. Rudolf Smend, *Die Bundesformel*, ThSt 68 (Zurich: EVZ, 1963).

43. Zimmerli, "Knowledge of God according to the Book of Ezekiel," in *I Am Yahweh*, edited by Walter Brueggemann, trans. Douglas W. Stott (Atlanta: John Knox Press, 1982) 29–98; idem, *Ezekiel 1*, 36–38.

44. Peter R. Ackroyd, *Exile and Restoration*, OTL (Philadelphia: Westminster, 1968) 55–56.

45. On Ezekiel 15, compare also Zimmerli, *Ezekiel 1*.

46. On the issue of "visions of their own minds," compare Gottfried Quell, *Wahre und falsche Propheten*, BFCT (Gütersloh: Bertelsmann, 1952) 161ff.; and E. L. Ehrlich, *Der Traum im Alten Testament*, BZAW 73 (Berlin: Töpelmann, 1953). The root *ḥzh* occurs in the Book of Jeremiah only here and in 14:14; in both passages the noun form *ḥazôn* ("vision") is used in a polemical way.

47. On this see Walter Baumgartner, *Jeremiah's Poems of Lament*, trans. David E. Orton, HTIBS 7 (Sheffield: Almond, 1988; German ed. 1917); and Gerhard von Rad, "Die Konfessionen Jeremias," *EvTh* 3 (1936) 265–76; in a different sense, see Antonius H. J. Gunneweg, "Konfession oder Interpretation im Jeremiabuch," *ZTK* 67 (1970) 395–416; and Peter Welten, "Leiden und Leidenserfahrung in Buch Jeremia," *ZTK* 74 (1977) 123–50.

48. Emending the Hebrew text to a plural; see BHS.

49. John Wolf Miller, *Das Verhältnis Jeremias und Hesekiels sprachlich und theologisch untersucht* (Assen: Van Gorcum, 1955).

50. Hartmut Gese, "Anfang und Ende der Apokalyptik, dargestellt am Sacharjabuch," 70 (1973) 20–49; and Christian Jeremias, *Die Nachtgesichte des Sacharja: Untersuchungen zu ihrer Stellung im Zusammenhang der Visionsberichte in Alten Testament und zu ihrem Bildmaterial*, FRLANT 117 (Göttingen: Vandenhoeck & Ruprecht, 1977).

5. THE MESSAGE OF THE PROPHET OF EZEKIEL

1. Gustav Hölscher, *Hesekiel, der Dichter und das Buch: Eine literarkritische Unter-suchung*, BZAW 39 (Giessen: Töpelmann, 1924); C. C. Torrey, *Pseudo-Ezekiel and the Original Prophecy*, YOS 18 (New Haven: Yale Univ. Press, 1930).

2. Volkmar Herntrich, *Ezechielprobleme*, BZAW 61 (Giessen: Töpelmann, 1933).

3. Thus, for example, Alfred Bertholet in *Das Buch Hesekiel*, KHAT 12 (Tübingen: Mohr/Siebeck, 1936).

4. R. H. Pfeiffer, *Introduction to the Old Testament* (New York: Harper, 1941).

5. Compare, for example, the commentaries of Georg Fohrer, *Ezekiel*, HAT 13 (Tübin-gen: Mohr, 1955); Joseph Ziegler, *Ezechiel*, EB (Würzburg: Echter, 1948); Walter Eichrodt, *Ezekiel: A Commentary*, trans. Cosslett Quin, OTL (Philadelphia: Westminster, 1970).

6. D. J. Wiseman, *Chronicles of the Chaldean Kings (626–556 B.C.) in the British Museum* (London: Trustees of the British Museum, 1961).

7. Richard A. Parker and Waldo H. Dubberstein, *Babylonian Chronology 626 B.C. to A.D. 75*, BUS 19 (Providence: Brown Univ. Press, 1956).

8. Code of Hammurabi, rev. 27, line 79 (see *ANET*, 179a).

9. Rudolf Smend, *Der Prophet Ezechiel*, KeH (Leipzig: Hirzel, 1880) xvi, xxi.

10. For details, I must refer to Zimmerli, *Ezekiel 1*, trans. Ronald E. Clements, Hermeneia (Philadelphia: Fortress Press, 1979); and *Ezekiel 2*, trans. James D. Martin, Hermeneia (Philadelphia: Fortress Press, 1983), especially the Introduction. Compare further the individual studies in Zimmerli, *Gottes Offenbarung: Gesammelte Aufsätze zum Alten Testament*, ThBü 19 (Munich: Kaiser, 1963).

11. One might ask whether Ezek 3:24 should be added here. Or do we hear something there of a special prophetic examination?

[12.] On the following, compare also chapter 6 in this collection.

13. The "hand of Yahweh" also occurs occasionally in Isaiah and Jeremiah. In Isa 8:11 there seems to be a hint of something like a harsh seizing of the hand. There it is a mat-ter of communication of a word. Jeremiah 15:17 also means the burden of the receipt of the word. The word with its content of judgment isolates the prophet from the circle of the happy. But nothing is said here of the experience of being enraptured.

14. Compare also the presentation on the form of the proof-saying (*Erweiswort*) on pp. 87–89 below.

15. See esp. John Wolf Miller, *Das Verhältnis Jeremias und Hesekiels sprachlich und theologisch untersucht* (Assen: Van Gorcum, 1955).

16. W. F. Albright, "The Seal of Eliakim and the Latest Preexilic History of Judah, with Some Observations on Ezekiel," *JBL* 51 (1932) 77–106. In addition, Martin Noth, "The Jerusalem Catastrophe of 587 B.C. and Its Significance for Israel," in *The Laws in the Pen-tateuch and Other Essays*, trans. D. R. Ap-Thomas (Philadelphia: Fortress Press, 1966) 260–80.

17. The fifth day of the fourth month in the fifth year after King Jehoiachin was taken away, which Ezek 1:1-2 points to, is to be dated as July 31, 593, according to Parker and Dubberstein, *Babylonian Chronology*.

18. The vocabulary and thought patterns of Ezekiel speak clearly against making Ezekiel into simply a representative of deuteronomic theology. On the other hand, it is quite clear that for him Jerusalem is the only legitimate place of worship, and, as such, is the place of Yahweh's presence. Only on this basis can the import of the pronounce-

ment of judgment in Ezek 11:23 be fully measured (the departure of Yahweh's glory from Jerusalem). In opposition, see Ezek 43:1-12.

19. One cannot overlook the clear division of the book into words of doom (Ezekiel 1–24), sayings about foreign countries (25–32), and actual words of deliverance (33–48).

20. Georg Fohrer, *Die symbolischen Handlungen der Propheten*, ATANT 25 (Zurich: Zwingli, 1953); Adrianus van den Born, "De Symbolische Handelingen der Oud-Testamentische Profeten" (Ph.D. diss., Nijmegen, 1935); idem, *Profetie Metterdad: Een Studie over de Symbolische Handelingen der Profeten* (Roermond-Masseik: Romen, 1947). [Ed.] See also Gerhard von Rad, *Old Testament Theology*, vol. 2: *The Theology of Israel's Prophetic Traditions*, trans. D. M. G. Stalker (New York: Harper & Row, 1965) 95–98, 232–33; Johannes Lindblom, *Prophecy in Ancient Israel* (Philadelphia: Fortress Press, 1973) 165–73; and David Stacey, *Prophetic Drama in the Old Testament* (London: Epworth, 1990).

21. Compare Zimmerli, "Zur Vorgeschichte von Jes LIII," in *Congress Volume: Rome*, VTSup 17 (Leiden: Brill, 1969) 236–44.

22. For the baggage, compare the image in James B. Pritchard, *Ancient Near Eastern Pictures relating to the Old Testament*, 2d ed. (Princeton: Princeton Univ. Press, 1959) #366.

23. The symbolic actions of quaking during eating in Ezek 12:17-20 and the "sighing" in 21:6 [MT 21: 11] may not be interpreted as active "mimicry" of these attitudes. Rather, they reflect a passive experience that becomes a sign for the message. So also Ezek 4:4-8.

24. The idea recognizable here of a remnant of the "sighing" spared in Jerusalem disappears completely in what follows. The "escapes" in Ezek 6:8-10 and 14:22-23 seem to have quite a different character.

25. Compare, for example, Albrecht Alt, "Jerusalems Aufstieg," in *Kleine Schriften zur Geschichte des Volkes Israel* (Munich: Beck, 1959) 3.243–57; and Martin Noth, "Jerusalem and the Israelite Tradition," in *The Laws in the Pentateuch and Other Studies*, 132–44.

26. To this "tradition of finding," compare Robert Bach, "Die Erwählung Israels in der Wüste" (Ph.D. diss., Bonn, 1951).

27. The reference to Jer 3:6-11 makes the search for mythical backgrounds of the story unnecessary; see Johannes Hempel, *Die althebräische Literatur und ihr hellenistisch-jüdisches nachleben* (Wildpark-Potsdam: Athenaion, 1930) 168.

28. For the term "creed," see Gerhard von Rad, "The Form-Critical Problem of the Hexateuch," in *The Problem of the Hexateuch and Other Essays*, trans. E. W. Trueman Dicken (New York: McGraw-Hill, 1966) 1–78.

29. Hosea 5:13; 7:11-12; 8:9-10; 12:1 [MT v. 2]; Isaiah 30:1-7; 31:1-2.

30. See von Rad, "The Form-Critical Problem."

31. The express statement of election occurs in Ezekiel only in 20:5.

32. Thus Ezekiel can call the "house of Israel" precisely the "rebellious house." See Ezek 2:5-6; 3:9, 26-27; 12:2-3, 9, 25; 17:12; 24:3 (also 2:7; 44:6).

33. Exodus 32:34 may contain a hidden reference to the catastrophe of Northern Israel.

34. Exodus 13:2; 22:27b; 34:19-20. The earlier period clearly viewed redeeming through an animal sacrifice—as Exod 34:20 expressly decrees—as an obvious regulation.

35. The positive use of the image among the people can be supposed in Ps 80:8-13 [MT 9-14], as well as behind Hos 10:1; Jer 2:21. See also Isa 5:1-7 and John 15:1-2.

36. See Zimmerli, "The Word of Divine Self-Manifestation (Proof-Saying): A Prophetic Genre," in *I Am Yahweh*, ed. Walter Brueggemann, trans. Douglas W. Stott (Atlanta: John Knox, 1982) 99–110.

37. When Fohrer finds it necessary to reject the form of the "proof-saying" because 1 Kgs 20:13, 28 is a secondary insertion in 1 Kings 20, he overlooks the wide distribution of related forms in preliterary prophecy; Georg Fohrer, *Introduction to the Old Testament,* trans. David E. Green (Nashville: Abingdon, 1968).

38. See Zimmerli, "Knowledge of God according to the Book of Ezekiel," in *I Am Yahweh,* 29–98.

39. See Zimmerli, "I Am Yahweh," in *I Am Yahweh,* 1–28. Also Karl Elliger, "I bin der Herr—euer Gott," in *Theologie als Glaubenswagnis: Festschrift für Karl Heim zum* 80. *Geburtstag* (Hamburg: Furche, 1954) 9–34.

40. That it must be translated this way, and not "I, Yahweh, am your God," is clearest in the quotation from the Decalog in Ps 50:7, when one goes back through its Elohistic editing.

[41.] See Sigmund Mowinckel, "The Spirit and the Word in the Prophets," in *The Spirit and the Word: Prophecy and Tradition in Ancient Israel,* ed. K. C. Hanson, FCBS (Minneapolis: Fortress Press, 2002) 83–99.

42. See especially K. von Rabenau, "Die Entstehung des Buches Ezechiel in formgeschichtlicher Sicht," *WZMLU* 5 (1955–56) 659–94.

43. Thus, for example, Ezek 12:9; 21:3 [MT 21:8]; 37:18.

44. The dating may have originally stipulated the eleventh year; see Zimmerli, *Ezekiel 2,* 191–94.

[45.] On Ezekiel's inability to speak, see Robert R. Wilson, "An Interpretation of Ezekiel's Dumbness," *VT* 22 (1972) 91–104.

46. The date in Ezek 3:16a was originally connected with 3:22-23, as demonstrated by the present difficult sequence of 16a and 16b.

47. The dating of the Egyptian sayings in Ezekiel 29–31 could also be mentioned here.

48. Other language used in the Book of Ezekiel suggests that the "escapee" was not an individual refugee who had fled to Babylon in a mysterious way, but one company of those deported in 587. [Ed.] See Zimmerli, *Ezekiel 2,* 192.

49. In the final editing of the book, Ezek 33:1-20 was included before 33:21-22 because of the theme of 33:1-10.

50. This can be seen from the similar (editorial) concluding word in Ezek 26:21; 27:36b; and 28:19b.

51. The origin of the undated passage Ezek 30:1-19 is also questionable on the basis of its content. And 29:17-21 represents, as the date shows, a late addition that is no reason to deny it to the prophet.

52. In Ezek 29:17-20 a statement about Tyre is combined with one about Egypt in a quite unique way.

53. This motif is found in Ezek 26:20 (see also 28:10, 12) in the ending of a word on Tyre, in 31:14, 15-18, and especially in the impressive description of 32:17-32.

54. The magnificent lamentation on the luxury ship Tyre and its demise is included in a prosaic commercial list in Ezek 27:12-25. See Hans Peter Rüger, "Das Tyrusorakel Ez. 27" (Ph.D. diss., Univ. of Tübingen, 1961).

55. One may not interpret the announcement of the invasion and the destruction of Gog and Magog in Ezekiel 38–39 as an abbreviated threat against the Babylonian power. Ezekiel's original words, the intention of which is the completion of Isaiah's proclamation of Yahweh's final victory over his enemies in the land of the Israel and Jeremiah's announcement of the "enemy of the north," were later overlaid with apocalyptic features.

56. The scene was early misconstrued as the general resurrection of the dead, as paintings in the Dura-Europas synagogue show. Compare, for example, Rachel Wischnitzer-Bernstein, "The Conception of the Resurrection in the Ezekiel Panel of the Dura Synagogue," *JBL* 60 (1941) 43–55.

57. See Zimmerli, "Der 'neue Exodus' in der Verkündigung der beiden Exilspropheten," in *Gottes Offenbarung*, 192–204.

58. Compare Rudolf Smend, *Die Bundesformel*, ThSt 68 (Zurich: EVZ, 1963).

59. This is proved in detail in Zimmerli, "Plans for Rebuilding after the Catastrophe of 587," in *I Am Yahweh*, 111–33.

60. This terminology is from Gerhard von Rad, "Faith Reckoned as Righteousness," in *The Problem of the Hexateuch*, 125–30. See also Rolf Rendtorff, *Die Gesetze in der Priesterschrift*, FRLANT 44 (Göttingen: Vandenhoeck & Ruprecht, 1954) 74–76. [Ed.] See also Rodney R. Hutton, "Declaratory Formulae: Forms of Authoritative Pronouncement in Ancient Israel" (Ph.D. diss., Claremont Graduate School, 1983).

61. Gerhard von Rad, " 'Righteousness' and 'Life' in the Cultic Language in the Psalms," in *The Problem of the Hexateuch*, 243–66.

6. The Word of God
in the Book of Ezekiel

1. Gustav Hölscher, *Hesekiel: Der Dichter und das Buch*, BZAW 39 (Giessen: Töpelmann, 1924).

2. Compare, for example, Volkmar Herntrich, *Ezekielprobleme*, BZAW 61 (Giessen: Töpelmann, 1932); and the commentary by Alfred Bertholet and Kurt Galling, *Hesekiel*, HAT 13 (Tübingen: Mohr/Siebeck, 1936).

3. Charles Cutler Torrey, *Pseudo-Ezekiel and the Original Prophecy*, YOSR 18 (New Haven: Yale Univ. Press, 1930); Nils Messel, *Ezechielfragen*, SNVAO (Oslo: Dybwad, 1945); and others.

4. Karl Jaspers, "Der Prophet Ezechiel: Eine pathologische Studie," in *Arbeiten zur Psychiatric, Neurologie und ihren Grenzgebieten: Festschrift für Kurt Schneider*, ed. Heinrich Kranz (Willsbach: Scherer, 1947) 1–9.

5. Jeremiah 2:2 should be interpreted in the light of Hosea; compare also 3:6-14.

6. The fall—Jer 9:11 [MT v. 10]; 13:5-6; the new betrothal—2:21-22 (2:19-20).

7. Amarna Letters 285–290. [Ed.] For an English translation of the Amarna letters, see William L. Moran, *The Amarna Letters* (Baltimore: Johns Hopkins Univ. Press, 1992).

8. Even though one may assign Ezek 16:36ff. to Ezekiel or to the redactor (Hölscher), in any case 16:44 is still in keeping with the sense of 16:3.

9. Gerhard von Rad, "The Form-Critical Problem of the Hexateuch," in *The Problem of the Hexateuch and Other Essays*, trans. E. W. Trueman Dicken (New York: Macmillan, 1966) 1–78.

10. The failure of purely formal criteria of analysis is particularly obvious in this chapter, in which Hölscher sees a weak fantasy of the editor (20:25 is "really the only original thought in the whole chapter"). From the point of view of tradition history, Ezekiel 20 takes the central position and in no case is it to be separated from Ezekiel 16 and 23.

11. Jeremiah (7:31-34; 19:5-9) and Deuteronomy (12:31; 18:19-20) can see in the offering of the first-born only Canaanite ungodliness. The daring of Ezekiel's thought is attempted nowhere else in the Old Testament.

12. Verses 27-29, which still deal with the sin of the high places in the land, are formally out of keeping with the strict order of material in the chapter, and, furthermore, they anticipate in an awkward way the new beginning in v. 30; thus they are clearly to be regarded as a later expansion (Hölscher, 109 n.1). But they plainly show that at an early stage there was objection to the fact that the history of Israel in the land was not mentioned, and so in these verses an attempt was made to add at least a fragment of the history of sin in the land.

13. Do we have some light here on the thesis of Martin Noth that the Priestly code ended with the story of Moses' death, and that there was no conquest tradition in P? Noth, *Überlieferungsgeschichtliche Studien: Die Sammelnden und bearbeitenden Geschichtswerke im Alten Testament* (Tübingen: Niemeyer, 1967) 180–216; idem, *A History of Pentateuchal Traditions*, trans. Bernhard W. Anderson (Englewood Cliffs, N.J.: Prentice-Hall, 1972) 10.

14. Perhaps a predecessor of Ezekiel's thought can be found in Exodus 32:34, although there the exile (only in northern Israel, which worshiped images?) is conceived as punishment for the sin with the golden calf. But even if this understanding is correct, the formulation in Exodus does not approach the harshness of Ezekiel's expression.

15. In this connection the harshest formulation is to be found in Hos 12:1-5 [MT vv. 2-6], where the sinful character of Israel is already found in the patriarch Jacob.

16. See other uses in Ezek 20:12, 19, 20 (26). The development of this theme in the sense of the commands of the Holiness Code (Leviticus 17–26) is clearly to be seen in passages such as 18:5-13; 22:6-12.

17. Lev 18:2, 4, 30; 19:(2), 3, 4, 10, etc. In the shortened form "I am Yahweh": 18:5, 6; 19:12, 14; etc. On this formula, see further, Zimmerli, "I Am Yahweh," in *I Am Yahweh*, ed. Walter Brueggemann, trans. Douglas W. Stott (Atlanta: John Knox, 1982) 1–28.

18. The question could well be raised whether or not there is a structural connection between this comprehensive account of sin and the comprehensive account of righteousness, such as that noted by Gerhard von Rad in the Psalms: "'Righteousness' and 'Life' in the Cultic Language of the Psalms," in *The Problem of the Hexateuch and Other Essays*, 243–66.

19. The expression "We and our fathers have sinned" belongs to the style of the lament and confession of the people on fast days (Jer 3:25; 14:20; similarly in the confession of the individual, Ps 51:3-5 [MT vv. 5-7]). Ezekiel, an Old Testament theologian of original sin, speaks in chapter 20 only of the sins of the fathers, and thus radicalizes the whole idea.

20. Why is the preliminary statement "He is godless" missing here? On this type of declaratory formula, compare Gerhard von Rad, "Faith Reckoned as Righteousness," in *The Problem of the Hexateuch and Other Essays*, 125–30.

21. Or should we translate, "We are like the nations"?

22. A. Menes, "Tempel und Synagoge," *ZAW* 50 (1932) 272–73.

23. The attempt to date this complex of ideas as late as the post-exilic period and to posit a strong influence from Deutero-Isaiah in the direction of new cultic forms (such as by Kraus) must be regarded as extremely doubtful; Hans-Joachim Kraus, *Die Königsherrschaft Gottes im Alten Testament* (Tübingen: Mohr/Siebeck, 1951). [Ed.] See

also Kraus, *Worship in Israel: A Cultic History of the Old Testament,* trans. Geoffrey Buswell (Richmond: John Knox, 1966) 7–25.

24. Deut 4:34; 5:15; 26:8; 2 Kgs 17:36; Jer 32:21; Ps 136:11 [12]; compare also Exod 6:6; Deut 7:19; 9:29; 11:2; 1 Kgs 8:42; 2 Chron 6:32. In Jer 27:5 and 32:17 there is a unique use of the formula in the framework of creation theology. On the place of creation ideas in the salvation history, compare Gerhard von Rad, "The Theological Problem of the Old Testament Doctrine of Creation," in *The Problem of the Hexateuch and Other Essays,* 131–43. Although the formula cited in these passages appears mostly in deuteronomic or deuteronomistic texts, it must represent an older complex, since it is consciously used in an opposite sense in the refrain of judgment passages such as Isa 5:25; 9:12, 17, 21 [MT vv. 11, 16, 20]; 10:4; or in a passage derived from this usage, Isaiah's word concerning the final victory over Assyria, Isa 14:26-27.

25. A similar combination of formulas can be observed in Jer 21:5. But this is clearly a judgment passage, and therefore it lacks the conscious double use of the formula that we find in Ezek 20:33, 34.

26. The expression "wilderness of the peoples" is quite unique and is intended to characterize an indefinite place outside of the foreign lands in which the refuges and exiles are currently living. It is clearly an artificial construction analogous to the following "wilderness of Egypt." On the figure of the shepherd who separates different kinds of sheep with his staff, compare Matt 25:32, where there is a separation of sheep and goats (see Lev 27:32).

27. On the text, see the critical apparatus in BHS. [Ed.] See also Zimmerli, *Ezekiel 2,* trans. J. D. Martin, Hermeneia (Philadelphia: Fortress Press, 1983) 253–55.

28. Ezekiel 6:7, 10, 13, 14; 7:4, 27; etc. We need a thoroughgoing examination of the connection of this formula with the analogous formula of the salvation oracle, which appears in the passages such as Isa 41:20; 45:3, 6 7; 49:23, 26. On this see Joachim Begrich, *Studien zu Deuterojesaja,* BWANT 25 (Stuttgart: Kohlhammer, 1938) 10–11.

7. Form and Tradition
in the Book of Ezekiel

1. K. von Rabenau, "Die Entstehung des Buches Ezechiel in formgeschichtlicher Sicht," *WZMLU* 5 (1955–56) 569–683.

2. See Zimmerli, *Ezekiel 1,* trans. Ronald E. Clements, Hermeneia (Philadelphia: Fortress Press, 1979) 393, 396.

3. Compare Oskar Grether, *Name und Wort Gottes im Alten Testament,* BZAW 64 (1934) 67ff.

4. Siegfried Herrmann, "The Royal Novella in Egypt and in Israel: A Contribution to the History of Genre in the Historical Books of the Old Testament," in *Reconsidering Israel and Judah: Recent Studies on the Deuteronomistic History,* ed. Gary N. Knoppers and J. Gordon McConville, SBTS 8 (Winona Lake, Ind.: Eisenbrauns, 2000) 493–515 (original German article 1953–54).

5. Johannes Lindblom, *Prophecy in Ancient Israel* (Philadelphia: Fortress Press, 1962).

6. Gerhard von Rad, "Faith Reckoned as Righteousness," in *The Problem of the Hexateuch and Other Essays,* trans. E. W. Trueman Dicken (New York: McGraw Hill, 1966)

125–30; and Rolf Rendtorff, *Die Gesetze in der Priesterschrift*, FRLANT 62 (Göttingen: Vandenhoeck & Ruprecht, 1954) 74–76; 2d ed. 1963. [Ed.] See also Gerhard von Rad, *Old Testament Theology*, vol. 1: *The Theology of Israel's Historical Traditions*, trans. D. M. G. Stalker (New York: Harper & Row, 1962) 370–83; and Rodney R. Hutton, "Declaratory Formulae: Forms of Authoritative Pronouncement in Ancient Israel" (Ph.D. diss., Claremont Graduate School, 1983).

7. Gerhard von Rad, "'Righteousness' and 'Life' in the Cultic Language of the Psalms," in *The Problem of the Hexateuch and Other Essays*, 243–66; and Zimmerli, "'Leben' und 'Tod' im Buche des Propheten Ezechiel," *TZ* 13 (1957) 494–508.

8. Compare, for example, Edzard Rohland, "Die Bedeutung der Erwählungstraditionen Israels für die Eschatologie der alttestamentlichen Propheten" (Ph.D. diss., Univ. of Heidelberg, 1956).

9. Robert Bach, "Die Erwählung Israels in der Wüste" (Ph.D. diss., Univ. of Bonn, 1951).

10. John Wolf Miller, *Das Verhältnis Jeremias und Hesekiels sprachlich und theologisch untersucht* (Assen: Van Gorcum, 1955).

11. Compare Zimmerli, "The Word of God in the Book of Ezekiel," chap. 5 in this volume.

12. Compare Werner Kessler, "Aus welchen Gründen wird die Bezeichnung 'Jahwe Zebaoth' in der späteren Zeit gemieden?" *WZMLU* 7 (1958) 767–72.

13. Zimmerli, "The Word of Divine Self-Manifestation (Proof-Saying): A Prophetic Genre," in *I Am Yahweh*, ed. Walter Brueggemann, trans. Douglas W. Stott (Atlanta: John Knox, 1982) 99–110.

14. Zimmerli, "I Am Yahweh," in *I Am Yahweh*, 1–28.

15. Zimmerli, "Knowledge of God according to the Book of Ezekiel," in *I Am Yahweh*, 29–98.

8. BIBLICAL THEOLOGY

1. This essay understands by the term "biblical theology," following Ebeling's definition of terms, "the theology contained in the Bible" and not "the theology that accords with the Bible," which is developed in doctrinal theology. Gerhard Ebeling, "The Meaning of 'Biblical Theology,'" in idem, *Word and Faith*, trans. James W. Leitch (Philadelphia: Fortress Press, 1963) 79 [79–97]. I wish to insist on the necessity to present a biblical theology, contrary to Schmid, who poses the question whether a self-contained biblical theology is still possible at all or whether it would not rather have to be dissolved in doctrinal theology. Hans H. Schmid, "Unterwegs zu einer Neuen Biblischen Theologie?" in *Biblische Theologie Heute: Einführung, Beispiele, Kontroversen*, ed. Klaus Haaker, BTS 1 (Neukirchen-Vluyn: Neukirchener, 1977) 77–95.

2. Friedrich Nietzsche, *The Complete Works of Friedrich Nietzsche*, ed. Oscar Levy (New York: Russell & Russell, 1964) vol. 9, 85.

3. Compare the presentations of the more recent developments in the history of research in the articles on biblical theology in: Zimmerli, "Biblische Theologie I. Altes Testament," in *TRE* 6:426–55; and Otto Merk, "Biblische Theologie II. Neues Testament," in *TRE* 6:455–69). [Ed.] See Brevard S. Childs, *Biblical Theology of the Old and New Testaments: Theological Reflection on the Christian Bible* (Philadelphia: Fortress Press,

1993); James Barr, *The Concept of Biblical Theology: An Old Testament Perspective* (Minneapolis: Fortress Press, 1999); Dan O. Via, *What Is New Testament Theology?* GBS (Minneapolis: Fortress Press, 2002).

4. It is a fact that the Old Testament has devoted conscious reflection only relatively late to the self-expression of God in his word under the proper name Yahweh (Exod 3:14 and 6:2-8). But this does not deny the insight that the Old Testament witness of Yahweh knows him as one again and again disclosing himself in event and word, not as the one ever "appropriated" by Israel. The assumption concerning the history of Israel's religion (although likely in my opinion) that a God by the name of Yahweh was worshiped already before Israel's time at Sinai (Siegfried Herrmann, *A History of Israel in Old Testament Times* [Philadelphia: Fortress Press, 1975] 75–77) should not obscure the theological insight in the impossibility of controlling Yahweh according to Israel's faith. I think, therefore, that, in contrast to a history of Israelite religion, a presentation of the theology of the Old Testament should begin with the idea expressed in the phrase "I am Yahweh," although it is evidenced at a relatively late period. [Ed.] Note how Zimmerli developed this in *Old Testament Theology in Outline*, trans. David E. Green (Atlanta: John Knox, 1978).

5. So John 19:19; "This is Jesus the King of the Jews" (Matt 27:37); "This is the King of the Jews" (Luke 23:38); more terse yet, "The King of the Jews" (Mark 15:26).

6. In what follows in this essay, I recognize the necessity to coordinate the statements about the one God and his giving of himself in his word, in contrast to a purely diachronically operating juxtaposition that isolates the statements. I do this with the full knowledge of the original independence of the statements (compare above all in the section "Canon within the Canon"). This involves unquestionably a theological coordination in thought, but that does not necessarily lead to a dissolution of biblical into doctrinal theology (see note 1 above).

7. Compare Zimmerli, "Die Schuld am Kreuz," in idem, *Israel und die Christen: Hören und Fragen*, 2d ed. (Neukirchen-Vluyn: Neukirchener, 1980) 17–30.

8. Christian faith without the message of Easter is without evidence in the New Testament. It may be that research in the history of religion can lead one to surmise "that there are lines of tradition that do not start from the confession of the resurrection (Schmid, "Unterwegs," 81). Nevertheless, no New Testament evidence exists that is not informed by God's affirmation of the crucified—that is, by his "life," regardless of how this is to be defined.

9. Ecclesiastes speaks of "the creator" in addressing young people (Eccl 12:1); but he does not risk, in what follows, going beyond the statement about "God's gift" that is only to be accepted in each concrete situation. He does not speak of God's "addressing" us. The human answer in prayer is admonished to be extremely sparse in words (5:2). But it should not be overlooked that prayer is not abandoned or rendered impossible. Confronted by fate, prayer is meaningless. [Ed.] See Norbert Lohfink, *Qoheleth*, trans. Sean McEvenue, CC (Minneapolis: Fortress Press, 2003); and Thomas Krüger, *Qoheleth*, trans. O. C. Dean Jr., Hermeneia (Minneapolis: Fortress Press, forthcoming).

10. Compare the request of the man on the cross (Luke 23:42).

11. On the consequences of the formulation in Lev 26:42, compare the observations in Zimmerli, "'Heiligkeit' nach dem sogenannten Heiligkeitsgesetz," *VT* 30 (1980) 509–10 [493–512].

12. Rolf Rendtorff, "Die Erwählung Israels als Thema der deuteronomischen Theologie," in *Die Botschaft und die Boten: Festschrift für Hans Walter Wolff zum 70. Geburtstag,* ed. Jörg Jeremias and Lothar Perlitt (Neukirchen-Vluyn: Neukirchener, 1981) 75–86.

13. Norbert Lohfink, *Das Hauptgebot: Eine Untersuchung literarischer Einleitungsfragen zu Dtn 5-11,* AnBib 20 (Rome: Pontifical Biblical Institute Press, 1963); Werner H. Schmidt, *Das erste Gebot: Seine Bedeutung für das Alte Testament,* THE 165 (Munich: Kaiser, 1970).

14. Lauha summarizes the passage in Eccl 7:15-22 belittlingly as "the golden mean." Aarra Lauha, *Koheleth,* BK 19 (Neukirchen-Vlyun: Neukirchener, 1978) 131.

15. Rudolf Smend, "Das Ende ist gekommen," in *Die Botschaft und die Boten,* 67–72.

16. We do not need to enter into the extensive discussion concerning the time when this phrase was penned. Dietrich's daring thesis, that Isa 6:9-10 is a secondary interpolation from the end of Isaiah's activity (705–701 B.C.E.) placed into an older report of the call (in 6:19a, 12, 13, 11) by a transposition of v. 11 to its present position, will hardly stand further scrutiny; Walter Dietrich, *Jesaja und die Politik,* BEvT 74 (Munich: Kaiser, 1976) 175–80.

17. Adolf von Harnack, *Marcion: The Gospel of the Alien God,* trans. John E. Steeley and Lyle D. Bierma (Durham, N.C.: Labyrinth, 1990), 134. "The thesis that is to be argued in the following may be stated thus: the rejection of the Old Testament in the second century was a mistake which the great church rightly avoided; to maintain it in the sixteenth century was a fate from which the Reformation was not yet able to escape; but still to preserve it in Protestantism as a canonical document since the nineteenth century is the consequence of a religious and ecclesiastical crippling."

18. Emmanuel Hirsch, *Das Alte Testament und die Predigt des Evangeliums* (Tübingen: Mohr/Siebeck, 1936).

19. Rudolf Bultmann, "The Significance of the Old Testament for the Christian Faith," in *The Old Testament and Christian Faith,* ed. Bernhard W. Anderson (New York: Harper & Row, 1963) 8–35; even more clearly in Bultmann, "Promise and Fulfillment," in *Essays on Old Testament Hermeneutics,* ed. Claus Westermann and James Luther Mays (Richmond: John Knox, 1960) 50–75.

20. Friedrich Baumgärtel, *Verheissung: Zur Frage des evangelischen Verständnisses des Alten Testaments* (Gütersloh: Bertelsmann, 1952).

21. Antonius H. J. Gunneweg, *Understanding the Old Testament,* OTL (Philadelphia: Westminister, 1978). For a discussion with Gunneweg, see Zimmerli, "Von der Gültigkeit der 'Schrift' Alten Testaments in der christlichen Predigt," in *Textgemäss: Aufsätze und Beiträge zur Hermeneutik des Alten Testaments: Festschrift für Ernst Würthwein zum 70. Geburtstag,* ed. A. H. J. Gunneweg and Otto Kaiser (Göttingen: Vandenhoeck & Ruprecht, 1979) 184–202, esp. 195–98. Gunneweg oscillates between the rejection of Baumgärtel's calling the religion of the Old Testament an "alien religion" (184) and the rejection of the identity of God in both testaments. He says of the God of the Old Testament: "This God has many names and such varied characteristics that any talk of *the* God of the Old Testament runs the risk of becoming an empty formula" (221–22). Could one not state analogously about the New Testament that the Christ in the arc of tension between Mark and John may become "an empty formula"? Compare to this point the section on "Canon within the Canon" in this chapter.

22. Compare also Franz Hesse, *Abschied von der Heilsgeschichte,* ThSt 108 (Zurich: Theologischer, 1971).

23. The discussion was revived by Ernst Käsemann, "The Problem of the Historical Jesus," in *Essays on New Testament Themes*, trans. W. J. Montague, SBT 1/41 (Naperville, Ill.: Allenson, 1964) 15–47.

24. Bultmann is forced, for the sake of consistency, to eliminate this sentence (John 4:22) as a gloss; Rudolf Bultmann, *The Gospel of John: A Commentary*, trans. G. R. Beasley-Murray et al. (Philadelphia: Westminster, 1971) 189 n. 6. But has it, for that reason, become insignificant for a biblical theology?

25. Although it is developed purely diachronically, compare the presentation by Rudolf Smend and Ulrich Luz, *Gesetz*, BibKon (Stuttgart: Kohlhammer, 1981).

26. With Bultmann, *The Presence of Eternity: History and Eschatology*, Gifford Lectures 1955 (New York: Harper, 1957); and Baumgärtel, *Verheissung*.

27. Hans Walter Wolff, "Das thema 'Umkehr' in der alttestamentlichen Prophetie," *ZTK* 48 (1951) 148a [129–48]; reprinted in Wolff, *Gesammelte Studien zum Alten Testament*, ThBü 22 (Munich: Kaiser, 1964) 149 [130–50].

28. Hans H. Schmid, *Gerechtigkeit als Weltordnung: Hintergrund und Geschichte der alttestamentlichen Gerechtigkeitsbegriffes*, BHT 40 (Tübingen: Mohr/Siebeck, 1968); idem, "Rechtfertigung als Schöpfungsgeschehen," in *Rechtfertigung: Festschrift für Ernst Käsemann zum 70. Geburtstag*, ed. J. Friedrich et al. (Tübingen: Mohr/Siebeck, 1976) 403–14. It is hardly coincidental that Schmid's "Unterwegs" questions the possibility of a biblical theology altogether. The starting point in concepts which are, from the point of view of the history of religions, largely rooted in (historically determined) traditions from Israel's neighbors, cannot genuinely grasp the distinctive element of the biblical witness that is, after all, contingent on history. See Schmid, *Altorientalische Welt in der alttestamentlichen Theologie: 6 Aufsätze* (Zurich: Theologischer, 1974).

29. Hartmut Gese, "Erwägungen zur Einheit der biblischen theologie," *ZTK* 67 (1970) 417–36; idem, *Essays on Biblical Theology*, trans. Keith Crim (Minneapolis: Augsburg, 1981); Peter Stuhlmacher, *Reconciliation, Law, and Righteousness: Essays in Biblical Theology*, trans. Everett R. Kalin (Philadelphia: Fortress Press, 1986).

30. For a discussion of the traditio-historical view of Gerhard von Rad, see Zimmerli, "Alttestamentliche Traditionsgeschichte und Theologie," in *Probleme biblischer Theologie: Gerhard von Rad zum 70. Geburtstag*, ed. Hans Walter Wolff (Munich: Kaiser, 1971) 632–47. For a discussion of Gese's view, see my contribution in the volume mentioned above, *Textgemäss*, 190–94.

31. Samuel Terrien, *The Elusive Presence: Toward a New Biblical Theology* (San Francisco: Harper & Row, 1978).

32. Otto Betz, "The Problem of Variety and Unity in the New Testament," *HBT* 2 (1980) 3–14.

33. On this problem, compare Ernst Käsemann, *Das Neue testament als Kanon: Dokumentation und kritische Analyse zur gegenwärtigen Diskussion* (Göttingen: Vandenhoeck & Ruprecht, 1970). [Ed.] See also Brevard S. Childs, *The New Testament as Canon: An Introduction* (Philadelphia: Fortress Press, 1984).

34. A valuable survey on the attempts in that direction that have already been made in New Testament research is provided by Otto Merk in "Biblische Theologie II. Neues Testament," esp. 469–74. The article also contains extensive references (474–77).

35. Zimmerli, "Zum Problem der 'Mitte des Alten Testaments'," *EvTh* 35 (1975) 97–118; and idem, "Biblische Theologie I. Altes Testament," esp. 445–54.

36. The intention that is stated here has been pursued, in somewhat different form, by Brevard S. Childs, *Introduction to the Old Testament as Scripture* (Philadelphia: Fortress Press, 1979). On the questions pertaining to Childs's book, see my review in *VT* 31 (1981) 235–44; see also the multiple reviews in *HBT* 2 (1980) 113–97, by Bruce C. Birch, Douglas A. Knight, James Luther Mays, David P. Polk, and James A. Sanders.

37. Zimmerli, *Israel und die Christen.*

Bibliography

WALTHER ZIMMERLI'S WORKS IN ENGLISH

Books

1957   With Joachim Jeremias. *The Servant of God.* Translated by Harold Knight et al. SBT 1/20. London: SCM. Original German article 1952.

1965   *The Law and the Prophets: A Study of the Meaning of the Old Testament.* Translated by Ronald E. Clements. New York: Harper & Row. German ed. 1963.

1971   *Man and His Hope in the Old Testament.* Translated by Gilbert W. Bowen. SBT 2/20. Naperville, Ill.: Allenson. German ed. 1968.

1978   *Old Testament Theology in Outline.* Translated by David E. Green. Atlanta: John Knox. 2d German ed. 1975.

1979   *Ezekiel 1.* Translated by Ronald E. Clements. Hermeneia. Philadelphia: Fortress Press. German ed. 1969.

1983   *Ezekiel 2.* Translated by James D. Martin. Hermeneia. Philadelphia: Fortress Press. German ed. 1969.

1982   *I Am Yahweh.* Edited by Walter Brueggemann. Translated by Douglas W. Stott. Atlanta: John Knox.

Articles

1963   "The Place and Limit of Wisdom in the Framework of Old Testament Theology." *SJT* 17:146–58. Reprinted in *Studies in Ancient Israelite Wisdom,* edited by James L. Crenshaw, 314–26. New York: Ktav, 1976. Original German article 1963.

1963   "Promise and Fulfillment." In *Essays on Old Testament Hermeneutics,* edited by Claus Westermann, 89–122. Atlanta: John Knox. Translated by James Wharton. Original German article 1952.

1965   "The Special Form- and Traditio-Historical Character of Ezekiel's Prophecy." *VT* 15:515–27.

1967   "The Word of God in the Book of Ezekiel." *JTC* 4:1–13. Translated by James F. Ross. Original German article 1951.

1969   "The Message of the Prophet Ezekiel." *Int* 23:131–57. Translated by Mrs. Lewis Wilkins and James D. Martin. Later German article 1974.

1976   "Concerning the Structure of Old Testament Wisdom." In *Studies in Ancient Israelite Wisdom,* edited by James L. Crenshaw, 175–99. New York: Ktav, 1976. Original German article 1933.

1976   "Ezekiel." In *IDBS,* 314–17. Edited by Keith Crim. Nashville: Abingdon.

1976   "Hope in the OT." In *IDBS,* 417–19.

1976   "Slavery in the OT." In *IDBS,* 829–30.

1977   "Prophetic Proclamation and Reinterpretation." In *Tradition and Theology in the Old Testament,* edited by Douglas A. Knight, 69–100. Philadelphia: Fortress Press. Translated by Douglas A. Knight. German edition 1978.

1979   "The History of Israelite Religion." In *Tradition and Interpretation: Essays by Members of the Society for Old Testament Study,* edited by G. W. Anderson, 351–84. Oxford: Oxford Univ. Press.

1982   "Biblical Theology." *HBT* 4:95–130. Translated by Ulrich Mauser. Later, expanded German article 1984.

1982   "I Am Yahweh." In *I Am Yahweh,* 1–28. Original German article 1953.

1982   "Knowledge of God according to the Book of Ezekiel." In *I Am Yahweh,* 29–98. Original German article 1954.

1982   "Plans for Rebuilding after the Catastrophe of 587." In *I Am Yahweh,* 111–33. Original German article 1968.

1982   "Visionary Experience in Jeremiah." In *Israel's Prophetic Tradition: Essays in Honour of Peter R. Ackroyd,* edited by Richard Coggins et al., 95–118. Cambridge: Cambridge Univ. Press, 1982.

1982   "The Word of Divine Self-manifestation (Proof-Saying): A Prophetic Genre." In *I Am Yahweh,* 99–110. Original German article 1957.

1984   "The Fruit of the Tribulation of the Prophet." In A Prophet to the Nations: Essays in Jeremiah Studies, edited by Leo G. Perdue and Brian W. Kovacs, 349–65. Winona Lake, Ind.: Eisenbrauns. Translated by Leo G. Perdue. Original German article 1981.

1985   "The 'Land' in the Pre-Exilic and Early Post-Exilic Prophets." In *Understanding the Word: Essays in Honour of Bernhard W. Anderson,* edited by James T. Butler et al., 247–62. JSOTSup 37. Sheffield: JSOT Press, 1985.

1995   "From Prophetic Word to Prophetic Book." In *The Place Is Too Small for Us: The Israelite Prophets in Recent Scholarship,* edited by Robert P. Gordon, 419–42. SBTS 5. Winona Lake, Ind.: Eisenbrauns, 1995. Translated by Andreas Köstenberger. Original German article 1979.

ASSESSMENTS OF ZIMMERLI'S WORK

Bardtke, Hans. "Der Prophet Ezechiel in der modernen Forschung: Zum Ezechiel-Kommentar von Walther Zimmerli." *TLZ* 96 (1971) 721–34.

Brueggemann, Walter. "Foreword." In Walther Zimmerli, *I Am Yahweh.* Edited by Walter Brueggemann. Translated by Douglas W. Stott. Atlanta: John Knox, 1982.

Fensham, F. C. "Walther Zimmerli, 1907–1983." *Journal of Northwest Semitic Languages* 12 (1984) 25–26.

Johnstone, William. "They Set Us on New Paths. Part 5: Six Commentaries on the Hebrew Bible." *Expository Times* 100 (1989) 164–69.

Kloeden, Wolfdietrich von. "Zimmerli, Walther." In *Biographisch-Bibliographisches Kirchenlexikon* 14:478–86. Herzberg: Bautz, 1998.

Levenson, Jon D. "Ezekiel in the Perspective of Two Commentators." *Int* 38 (1984) 210–17.

Martin-Achard, Robert. "Hommage." *Revue de Theologie et de Philosophie* 116 (1984) 273–74.

Motte, Jochen. *Biblische Theologie nach Walther Zimmerli: Darstellung und Würdigung der alttestamentlichen Theologie Walther Zimmerlis und der sich aus ihr ergebenden Perspektive zum Neuen Testament in systematisch-theologischer Sicht.* Europäische Hochschulschriften, Theologie 521. Frankfurt: Lang, 1995.

Perlitt, Lothar. "Walther Zimmerli." *ZAW* 96 (1984) 1–2.

Schmid, Johannes H. *Biblische Theologie in der Sicht heutiger Alttestamentler: Hartmut Gese, Claus Westermann, Walther Zimmerli, Antonius Gunneweg.* Monographien und Studienbücher 326. Giessen: Brunnen, 1986.

Scullion, John J. "Recent Old Testament Theology: Three Contributions." *Australian Bible Review* 24 (1976) 6–17.

Smend, Rudolf. "Walther Zimmerli." In idem, *Deutsche alttestamentler in Drei Jahrhunderten*, 276–98. Göttingen: Vandenhoeck & Ruprecht, 1989.

Willi, Thomas. "Zimmerli, Walther." In *DBI* 2:673–74.

FESTSCHRIFTEN IN HONOR OF ZIMMERLI

Coats, George W., and Burke O. Long, editors. *Canon and Authority: Essays in Old Testament Religion and Theology.* Philadelphia: Fortress Press, 1977.

Donner, Herbert, Robert Hanhart, and Rudolf Smend, editors. *Beiträge zur alttestamentlichen Theologie: Festschrift für Walther Zimmerli zum 70. Geburtstag.* Göttingen: Vandenhoeck & Ruprecht, 1977. [Zimmerli's bibliography, 559–80]

Smend, Rudolf, et al. *In Memoriam Walther Zimmerli: Gedenkfeier am 12. Mai 1984 in der Aula der Georg-August-Universität Göttingen.* Göttinger Universitätsreden 73. Göttingen: Vandenhoeck & Ruprecht, 1984.

SELECT BIBLIOGRAPHY ON PROPHECY

Balentine, Samuel E. "The Prophet as Intercessor: A Reassessment." *JBL* 103 (1984) 161–73.

Baltzer, Klaus. "Considerations regarding the Office and Calling of the Prophet." *HTR* 61 (1968) 567–81.

———. *Deutero-Isaiah: A Commentary on Isaiah 40–55.* Translated by Margaret Kohl. Hermeneia. Minneapolis: Fortress Press, 2001.

Ben Zvi, Ehud, and Michael H. Floyd, editors. *Writings and Speech in Israelite and Ancient Near Eastern Prophecy.* SBLSymSer 10. Atlanta: Scholars, 2000.

Blenkinsopp, Joseph. *A History of Prophecy in Israel.* Rev. ed. Louisville: Westminster John Knox, 1996.

Brenneman, James E. *Canons in Conflict: Negotiating Texts in True and False Prophecy.* New York: Oxford Univ. Press, 1997.

Bright, John. *Covenant and Promise: The Prophetic Understanding of the Future in Pre-exilic Israel.* Philadelphia: Westminster, 1976.

Brueggemann, Walter. *Hopeful Imagination: Prophetic Voices in Exile.* Philadelphia: Fortress Press, 1986.

———. *The Prophetic Imagination.* 2d ed. Minneapolis: Fortress Press, 2001.

———. *Texts That Linger, Words that Explode: Listening to Prophetic Voices.* Edited by Patrick D. Miller. Minneapolis: Fortress Press, 2000.

Carroll, Robert P. "Prophecy and Society." In *The World of Ancient Israel*, edited by R. E. Clements, 203–25. Cambridge: Cambridge Univ. Press, 1989.

Chaney, Marvin L. "Bitter Bounty: The Dynamics of Political Economy Critiqued by the Eighth-Century Prophets." In *Reformed Faith and Economics*, edited by Robert L. Stivers, 15–30. Lanham, Md.: University Press of America, 1989.

Clements, Ronald E. "Patterns in the Prophetic Canon." In *Canon and Authority: Essays in Old Testament Religion and Theology*, edited by George W. Coats and Burke O. Long, 42–55. Philadelphia: Fortress Press, 1977.

Coggins, Richard, Anthony Phillips, and Michael Knibb, editors. *Israel's Prophetic Traditions: Essays in Honour of Peter Ackroyd.* Cambridge: Cambridge Univ. Press, 1982.

Culley, Robert C., and Thomas W. Overholt, editors. *Semeia* 21: *Anthropological Perspectives on Old Testament Prophecy*, 1982.

Darr, Katheryn Pfisterer. "Literary Perspectives on Prophetic Literature." In *Old Testament Interpretation: Past, Present, and Future. Essays in Honor of Gene M. Tucker*, edited by James Luther Mays et al., 127–43. Nashville: Abingdon, 1995.

Dempsey, Carol J. *The Prophets: A Liberation-Critical Reading.* Minneapolis: Fortress Press, 2000.

Floyd, Michael H. *Minor Prophets: Part* 2. FOTL 22. Grand Rapids: Eerdmans, 2000.

Gitay, Yehoshua, editor. *Prophecy and Prophets: The Diversity of Contemporary Issues in Scholarship.* SBLSS. Atlanta: Scholars, 1997.

———. "The Individual versus the Institution: The Prophet versus His Book." In *Religion and the Reconstruction of Civil Society: Papers from the Founding Congress of the South African Academy of Religion, January 1994*, edited by J. W. de Gruchy and S. Matrin. Miscellania Congregalia 51. Pretoria: Univ. of South Africa, 1995.

Gordon, Robert P., editor. *The Place is Too Small for Us: The Israelite Prophets in Recent Scholarship.* SBTS 5. Winona Lake, Ind.: Eisenbrauns, 1995.

Gottwald, Norman K. "The Biblical Prophetic Critique of Political Economy: Its Ground and Import." In *The Hebrew Bible in Its Social World and in Ours*, 349–64. SBLSS. Atlanta: Scholars, 1993.

———. "Were the 'Radical' Prophets also 'Cultic' Prophets?" In *The Hebrew Bible in Its Social World and in Ours*, 111–17.

Grabbe, Lester L. *Priests, Prophets, Diviners, Sages: A Socio-Historical Study of Religious Specialists in Ancient Israel.* Valley Forge, Pa.: Trinity, 1995.

Gunkel, Hermann. "The Israelite Prophecy from the Time of Amos." In *Twentieth Century Theology in the Making*, edited by Jaroslav Pelikan, translated by R. A. Wilson, 48–75. New York: Harper & Row, 1969.

———. "The Prophets: Oral and Written." In *Water for a Thirsty Land: Israelite Literature and Religion*, edited by K. C. Hanson, 85–133. FCBS. Minneapolis: Fortress Press, 2001.

Hanson, Paul D. *The Dawn of Apocalyptic: The Historical and Sociological Roots of Jewish Apocalyptic Eschatology*. Rev. ed. Philadelphia: Fortress Press, 1979.

Hutton, Rodney R. *Charisma and Authority in Israelite Society*. Minneapolis: Fortress Press, 1994.

———. "Magic or Street-Theater? The Power of the Prophetic Word." *ZAW* 107 (1996) 247–60.

Koch, Klaus. *The Prophets*. Translated by Margaret Kohl. 2 vols. Philadelphia: Fortress Press, 1983–84.

Lang, Bernhard. *Monotheism and the Prophetic Minority: An Essay in Biblical History and Sociology*. SWBA 1. Sheffield: Almond, 1983.

Lindblom, Johannes. *Prophecy in Ancient Israel*. Philadelphia: Fortress Press, 1973.

Long, Burke O. "Prophetic Authority as Social Reality." In *Canon and Authority: Essays in Old Testament Religion and Theology*, edited by George W. Coats and Burke O. Long, 3–20. Philadelphia: Fortress Press, 1977.

March, W. Eugene. "Prophecy." In *Old Testament Form Criticism*, edited by John H. Hayes, 141–77. TUMSR 2. San Antonio: Trinity Univ. Press, 1974.

Miller, Patrick D. "The World and Message of the Prophets: Biblical Prophecy in Its Context." In *Old Testament Interpretation: Past, Present, and Future. Essays in Honor of Gene M. Tucker*, edited by James Luther Mays et al., 97–112. Nashville: Abingdon, 1995.

Moor, Johannes C. de, editor. *The Elusive Prophet: The Prophet as a Historical Person, Literary Character and Anonymous Artist*. OtSt 45. Leiden: Brill, 2001.

Nogalski, James D. *Literary Precursors to the Book of the Twelve*. BZAW 217. Berlin: de Gruyter, 1993.

———. *Redactional Processes in the Book of the Twelve*. BZAW 218. Berlin: de Gruyter, 1993.

———, and Marvin A. Sweeney, editors. *Reading and Hearing the Book of the Twelve*. SBLSymSer. Atlanta: Society of Biblical Literature, 2000.

Overholt, Thomas W. *Channels of Prophecy: The Social Dynamics of Prophetic Activity*. Minneapolis: Fortress Press, 1989.

———. *Prophecy in Cross-Cultural Perspective*. SBLSBS 17. Atlanta: Scholars, 1986.

Parker, Simon B. "Possession Trance and Prophecy in Pre-exilic Israel." *VT* 28 (1978) 271–85.

Peckham, Brian. *History and Prophecy: The Development of Late Judean Literary Tradition*. ABRL. New York: Doubleday, 1993.

Peterson, David L., editor. *Prophecy in Israel: Search for an Identity*. IRT 10. Philadelphia: Fortress Press, 1987.

———. *The Roles of Israel's Prophets*. JSOTSup 17. Sheffield: JSOT Press, 1981.

Rad, Gerhard von. *Old Testament Theology*. Vol. 2: *The Theology of Israel's Prophetic Traditions*. Translated by David M. G. Stalker. Edinburgh: Oliver & Boyd, 1965. Reprinted OTL. Louisville: Westminster John Knox, 2001.

Stansell, Gary. *Micah and Isaiah: A Form and Tradition Historical Comparison*. SBLDS 85. Atlanta: Scholars, 1988.

Steck, Odil Hannes. *The Prophetic Books and Their Theological Witness*. Translated by James D. Nogalski. St. Louis: Chalice, 2000.

Sweeney, Marvin A. "Formation and Form in Prophetic Literature." In *Old Testament Interpretation: Past, Present, and Future. Essays in Honor of Gene M. Tucker*, edited by James Luther Mays et al., 113–26. Nashville: Abingdon, 1995.

——. *Isaiah 1–39; with an Introduction to Prophetic Literature.* FOTL 16. Grand Rapids: Eerdmans, 1996.

——. *Twelve Prophets.* 2 vols. BerO. Collegeville, Minn.: Liturgical, 2000.

Tucker, Gene M. "Prophecy and Prophetic Literature." In *The Hebrew Bible and Its Modern Interpreters,* edited by Douglas A. Knight and Gene M. Tucker, 325–68. Philadelphia: Fortress Press, 1985.

Westermann, Claus. *Basic Forms of Prophetic Speech.* Translated by Hugh Clayton White. Philadelphia: Westminster, 1967.

Wilson, Robert R. "Prophecy and Ecstasy: A Re-examination." *JBL* 98 (1979) 321–37.

——. *Prophecy and Society in Ancient Israel.* Philadelphia: Fortress Press, 1980.

Wolff, Hans Walter. *Amos the Prophet: The Man and His Background.* Translated by Foster R. McCurley. Philadelphia: Fortress Press, 1973.

——. *Micah the Prophet.* Translated by Ralph D. Gehrke. Philadelphia: Fortress Press, 1981.

SELECT BIBLIOGRAPHY ON JEREMIAH

Auld, A. Graeme. "Prophets and Prophecy in Jeremiah and Kings." *ZAW* 96 (1984) 66–82.

Baumgartner, Walter. *Jeremiah's Poems of Lament.* Translated by David E. Orton. HTIBS 7. Sheffield: Sheffield Academic, 1987. German ed. 1917.

Brueggemann, Walter. *A Commentary on Jeremiah: Exile and Homecoming.* Grand Rapids: Eerdmans, 1998.

——. "Jeremiah's Use of Rhetorical Questions." *JBL* 92 (1973) 358–74.

Carroll, Robert P. *From Chaos to Covenant: Prophecy in the Book of Jeremiah.* New York: Crossroad, 1981.

——. *Jeremiah: A Commentary.* OTL. Philadelphia: Westminster, 1986.

Clements, Ronald E. *Jeremiah.* IBC. Atlanta: John Knox, 1988.

Craigie, Peter C., et al. *Jeremiah 1–25.* WBC 26. Dallas: Word, 1990.

Diamond, A. R. *The Confessions of Jeremiah in Context: Scenes of Prophetic Drama.* JSOTSup 45. Sheffield: JSOT Press, 1987.

——, Kathleen M. O'Connor, and Louis Stulman, editors. *Troubling Jeremiah.* JSOTSup 260. Sheffield: Sheffield Academic, 1999.

Fretheim, Terence E. *Jeremiah.* SHBC. Macon, Ga.: Smith & Helwys, 2002.

Gerstenberger, Erhard S. "Jeremiah's Complaints: Observations on Jer 15:10-21." *JBL* 82 (1963) 393–408.

Holladay, William L. *Jeremiah 1.* Hermeneia. Philadelphia: Fortress Press, 1986.

——. *Jeremiah 2.* Hermeneia. Minneapolis: Fortress Press, 1989.

——. *Jeremiah: A Fresh Reading.* New York: Pilgrim, 1990.

——. *Jeremiah: Spokesman Out of Time.* Philadelphia: United Church Press, 1974.

Keown, Gerald L., Pamela J. Scalise, and Thomas G. Smothers. *Jeremiah 26–52.* WBC 27. Waco: Word, 1996.

Lundbom, Jack R. *Jeremiah 1–20.* AB 21A. New York: Doubleday, 1999.

——. *Jeremiah: A Study in Ancient Hebrew Rhetoric.* SBLDS 18. Missoula, Mont.: Scholars, 1975.

——. "Jeremiah, Book of." In *ABD* 3:706–21.

McKane, William. *Jeremiah.* 2 vols. ICC. Edinburgh: T. & T. Clark, 1986–96.

Miller, Patrick D. "Jeremiah." In *The New Interpreter's Bible*. Vol. 6. Nashville: Abingdon, 2001.

Overholt, Thomas W. *The Threat of Falsehood: A Study in the Theology of the Book of Jeremiah*. SBT 2/15. Naperville, Ill.: Allenson, 1970.

Perdue, Leo G., and Brian Kovacs, editors. *A Prophet to the Nations: Essays in Jeremiah Studies*. Winona Lake, Ind.: Eisenbrauns, 1984.

Raitt, Thomas M. *A Theology of Exile: Judgment/Deliverance in Jeremiah and Ezekiel*. Philadelphia: Fortress Press, 1977.

Thompson, J. A. *The Book of Jeremiah*. NICOT. Grand Rapids: Eerdmans, 1980.

Select Bibliography on Ezekiel

Allen, Leslie C. *Ezekiel 20–48*. WBC 29. Dallas: Word, 1990.

Berquist, Jon L. *Surprises by the River: The Prophecy of Ezekiel*. St. Louis: Chalice, 1993.

Blenkinsopp, Joseph. *Ezekiel*. IBC. Louisville: Westminster John Knox, 1990.

Block, Daniel Isaac. *Ezekiel*. 2 vols. NICOT. Grand Rapids: Eerdmans, 1997.

Brownlee, William H. *Ezekiel 1–19*. WBC 28. Waco: Word, 1986.

Darr, Katheryn Pfisterer. "Ezekiel." In *The New Interpreter's Bible*. Vol. 6. Nashville: Abingdon, 2001.

Galambush, Julie. *Jerusalem in the Book of Ezekiel: The City as Yahweh's Wife*. SBLDS 130. Atlanta: Scholars, 1992.

Greenberg, Moshe. Ezekiel. 2 Vols. AB 22, 22A. Garden City, N.Y.: Doubleday, 1983.

Hals, Ronald M. *Ezekiel*. FOTL 19. Grand Rapids: Eerdmans, 1989.

Lapsley, Jacqueline E. *Can These Bones Live? The Problem of the Moral Self in the Book of Ezekiel*. BZAW 301. New York: de Gruyter, 2000.

Lust, J., editor. *Ezekiel and His Book: Textual and Literary Criticism and Their Interrelation*. BETL 74. Leuven: Leuven Univ. Press, 1986.

Mein, Andrew. *Ezekiel and the Ethics of Exile*. OTM. Oxford: Oxford Univ. Press, 2001.

Odell, Margaret S., and John T. Strong, editors. *The Book of Ezekiel: Theological and Anthropological Perspectives*. SBLSymSer 9. Atlanta: Society of Biblical Literature, 2000.

Zimmerli, Walther. *Ezekiel 1*. Translated by Ronald E. Clements. Hermeneia. Philadelphia: Fortress Press, 1979.

———. *Ezekiel 2*. Translated by James D. Martin. Hermeneia. Philadelphia: Fortress Press, 1983.

———. *I Am Yahweh*. Edited by Walter Brueggemann. Translated by Douglas W. Stott. Atlanta: John Knox, 1982.

Select Bibliography on Old Testament Theology and the History of Israelite Religion

Albertz, Rainer. *A History of Israelite Religion in the Old Testament Period*. 2 vols. Translated by John Bowden. OTL. Louisville: Westminster John Knox, 1994.

Anderson, Bernhard W. *The Contours of Old Testament Theology*. Minneapolis: Fortress Press, 1999.

Barr, James. *The Concept of Biblical Theology: An Old Testament Perspective.* Minneapolis: Fortress Press, 1999.

Bellis, Alice Ogden, and Joel S. Kaminsky, editors. *Jews, Christians, and the Theology of the Hebrew Bible.* SBLSymSer. Atlanta: Society of Biblical Literature, 2000.

Brueggemann, Walter. *Old Testament Theology: Essays on Structure, Theme, and Text.* Edited by Patrick D. Miller. Minneapolis: Fortress Press, 1992.

———. *Theology of the Old Testament: Testimony, Dispute, Advocacy.* Minneapolis: Fortress Press, 1997.

Childs, Brevard S. *Biblical Theology of the Old and New Testaments: Theological Reflection on the Christian Bible.* Minneapolis: Fortress Press, 1993.

———. *Introduction to the Old Testament as Scripture.* Philadelphia: Fortress Press, 1979.

———. *Old Testament Theology in a Canonical Context.* Philadelphia: Fortress, 1986.

Cross, Frank Moore. *Canaanite Myth and Hebrew Epic: Essays in the History of the Religion of Israel.* Cambridge: Harvard Univ. Press, 1973.

Gerstenberger, Erhard S. *Yahweh the Patriarch: Ancient Images of God and Feminist Theology.* Translated by Frederick J. Gaiser. Minneapolis: Fortress Press, 1996.

———. *Theologies in the Old Testament.* Translated by John Bowden. Minneapolis: Fortress Press, 2002.

Hanson, Paul D. *The People Called: The Growth of Community in the Bible, with a New Introduction.* Louisville: Westminster John Knox, 2001.

Hasel, Gerhard F. *Old Testament Theology: Basic Issues in the Current Debate.* 4th ed. Grand Rapids: Eerdmans, 1991.

Kaiser, Otto. *Der Gott des Alten Testaments: Theologie des Alten Testaments.* 2 vols. UTB. Göttingen: Vandenhoeck & Ruprecht, 1993–98.

Keel, Othmar, and Christoph Uehlinger. *Gods, Goddesses, and Images of God in Ancient Israel.* Translated by Thomas H. Trapp. Minneapolis: Fortress Press, 1997.

Knierim, Rolf P. *The Task of Old Testament Theology: Substance, Methods, and Cases.* Grand Rapids: Eerdmans, 1995.

Levenson, Jon D. *Sinai and Zion: An Entry into the Jewish Bible.* Minneapolis: Winston, 1985.

Linafelt, Tod, and Timothy K. Beal, editors. *God in the Fray: A Tribute to Walter Brueggemann.* Minneapolis: Fortress Press, 1998.

Miller, Patrick D. *Israelite Religion and Biblical Theology: Collected Essays.* JSOTSup 267. Sheffield: Sheffield Academic, 2000.

———. *The Religion of Ancient Israel.* LAI. Louisville: Westminster John Knox, 2000.

———, Paul D. Hanson, and S. Dean McBride, editors. *Ancient Israelite Religion: Essays in Honor of Frank Moore Cross.* Philadelphia: Fortress Press, 1987.

Perdue, Leo G. *The Collapse of History: Reconstructing Old Testament Theology.* OBT. Minneapolis: Fortress Press, 1994.

Preuss, Horst Dietrich. *Old Testament Theology.* OTL. Louisville: Westminster John Knox, 1995–96.

Rad, Gerhard von. *Old Testament Theology.* Translated by D. M. G. Stalker. 2 vols. New York: Harper & Row, 1962–65. Reprinted in OTL. Louisville: Westminster John Knox, 2001.

Rendtorff, Rolf. *Canon and Theology: Overtures to an Old Testament Theology.* Translated by Margaret Kohl. OBT. Minneapolis: Fortress Press, 1993.

———. *Theology of the Old Testament.* Translated by David E. Orton. Leiden: Deo, 2004.

Schmidt, Werner H. *The Faith of the Old Testament: A History.* Philadelphia: Westminster, 1983. (5th German ed. 1987.)

Smith, Mark S. *The Early History of God: Yahweh and the Other Deities in Ancient Israel.* 2d ed. Grand Rapids: Eerdmans, 2002.

———. *The Origins of Biblical Monotheism: Israel's Polytheistic Background and the Ugaritic Texts.* New York: Oxford Univ. Press, 2001.

Smith-Christopher, Daniel L. *A Biblical Theology of Exile.* OBT. Minneapolis: Fortress, 2002.

Tigay, Jeffrey H. *You Shall Have No Other Gods: Israelite Religion in the Light of Hebrew Inscriptions.* HSS 31. Atlanta: Scholars, 1986.

Toorn, Karel van der. *Family Religion in Babylonia, Syria and Israel: Continuity and Changes in the Forms of Religious Life.* SHCANE 7. Leiden: Brill, 1996.

———, Bob Becking, and Pieter W. van der Horst, editors. *Dictionary of Deities and Demons in the Bible.* 2d ed. Leiden: Brill, 1999.

Zevit, Ziony. *The Religions of Ancient Israel: A Synthesis of Parallactic Approaches.* New York: Continuum, 2001.

Index of Authors

Editor's note: Dates (when available) have been supplied for authors of earlier generations in order to provide historical context.

Index of Ancient Sources

FORTRESS CLASSICS
—— *in* ——
BIBLICAL STUDIES

EDITED BY K. C. HANSON

The Quest of the Historical Jesus
First Complete Edition
Albert Schweitzer

Water for a Thirsty Land
Israelite Literature and Religion
Hermann Gunkel

Jesus and the Message of the New Testament
Joachim Jeremias

The Spirit and the Word
Prophecy and Tradition in Ancient Israel
Sigmund Mowinckel

Parable and Gospel
Norman Perrin

The Fiery Throne
The Prophets and Old Testament Theology
Walther Zimmerli